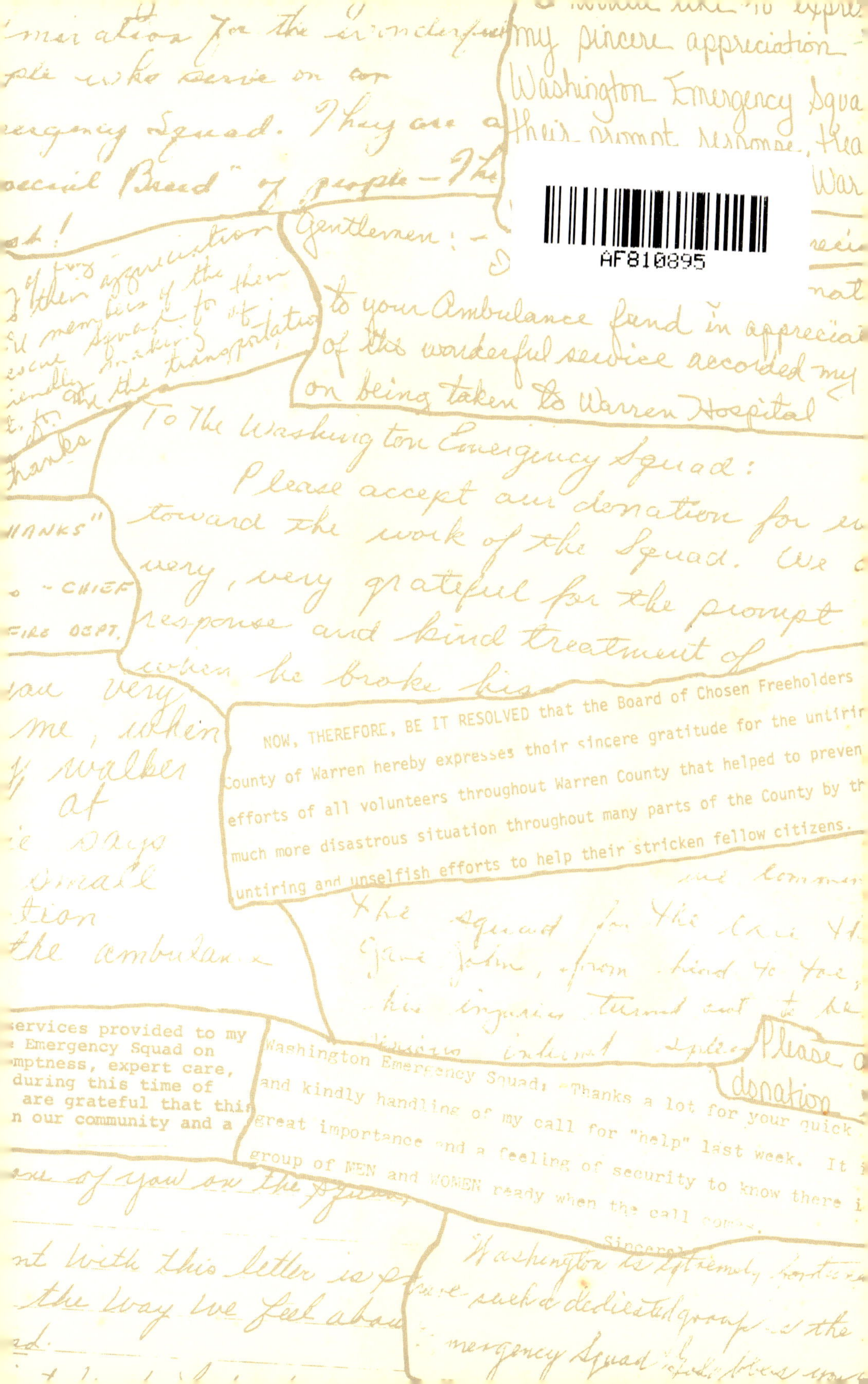
my sincere appreciation
Washington Emergency Squa
Gentlemen:
to your Ambulance fund in apprecia
of the wonderful service accorded my
on being taken to Warren Hospital
To The Washington Emergency Squad:
Please accept our donation for
toward the work of the Squad. We
very, very grateful for the prompt
response and kind treatment of
when he broke his
NOW, THEREFORE, BE IT RESOLVED that the Board of Chosen Freeholders
County of Warren hereby expresses their sincere gratitude for the untirin
efforts of all volunteers throughout Warren County that helped to preven
much more disastrous situation throughout many parts of the County by th
untiring and unselfish efforts to help their stricken fellow citizens.
THANKS"
- CHIEF
FIRE DEPT.
the ambulance
ervices provided to my
Emergency Squad on
mptness, expert care,
during this time of
are grateful that this
n our community and a
Washington Emergency Squad: Thanks a lot for your quick
and kindly handling of my call for "help" last week. It
great importance and a feeling of security to know there i
group of MEN and WOMEN ready when the call comes.
Please
donation
of you on the Squad
nt with this letter is
the way we feel abou
Washington is extremely fortunate
have such a dedicated group as the
Emergency Squad

YOUR FABULOUS VOLUNTEERS

For Edith Valuntitelli
one of my best friends
Russell E. Harpster
May 1990

Your Fabulous Volunteers

Richard E. Harpster

A History of the Washington Emergency Squad
and Emergency Services in Warren County
with a foreword by
James Daniel, Reader's Digest Roving Editor
and an appendix by
Dr. Harold S. Sloan, Fairleigh Dickinson
University Trustee Emeritus

Published by
WASHINGTON EMERGENCY SQUAD
Washington, New Jersey

Printed by
HARMONY PRESS
Phillipsburg, New Jersey

The Washington Emergency Squad extends sincere thanks to Richard E. Harpster who donated his services in conducting the research and preparing the manuscript for this book, to James Daniel for contributing the foreword, to Dr. Harold S. Sloan for contributing the appendix, and to the Institute for Instructional Improvement for funding the publication. The entire receipts from the sale of this book will benefit the squad.

50th YEAR EDITION

Manufactured in the United States of America

International Standard Book Number 0-9604020-1-2

Library of Congress Catalog Card Number 80-80473

Contents

Dedication

This book is dedicated to the memory of Vernon C. "Bab" Oakes (1895-1939), a fabulous volunteer. For over two decades his life was devoted to saving the lives of others. He attained the status of an authority on first aid. He inspired others to involve themselves as volunteers, taught them high standards of performance, and insisted they be given the finest equipment available with which to exercise the skills they learned. In high office his integrity, industry and leadership commanded the respect of the community he served. His devotion to the cause he loved won the hearts of all those whose lives he touched.

Acknowledgements

This edition of *Your Fabulous Volunteers* marks the 50th year of the Washington Emergency Squad. It contains additional material and reflects many changes that have occurred since the first edition was published five years ago.

This story of your fabulous volunteers is told in two versions: one in words, the other in pictures. To mention all the names of those who have contributed to one or the other of these versions would almost require a directory of who's who in Warren County. Many of these names are mentioned in the following pages.

I have received communications from knowledgeable people pointing out some errors in the original edition. Their interest has contributed to making this account a more accurate one and is greatly appreciated.

The surviving members of the original emergency and ambulance squads, along with the other old-timers who are quoted in these pages, deserve special thanks for their patience in permitting the author to pick their brains for early experiences and interesting anecdotes.

The author is particularly indebted to Alvin Sloan who laboriously assembled the author's voluminous research notes in time sequence and then cast them in the form of a coherent story. It was he who collected the illustrations appearing in this volume. They record not only the origin and development of the Washington Emergency Squad, but add a valuable pictorial chapter to one facet in the history of the Borough of Washington and Warren County.

Sincere thanks are due also to the professional photographers, Marilyn Cressman, Robert W. Kerr of Royal Photographics, Howard Niper, Reinhold Radke, Arthur Steinmann of Minassian Studio, and Richard W. York, whose skill and personal interest in the success of the project made this version of the book possible.

The manuscript was edited by Larry K. Smith, Director of Speech and Forensics at West Morris Central High School. The author is grateful to him for ferreting out solecisms that plague many authors. The book is a better one because of his efforts.

Whatever credit remains belongs to the author, and it is he alone who is responsible for any sins of omission or commission that may be found in these pages.

Washington, New Jersey RICHARD E. HARPSTER
November 1, 1985

Richard W. York photo

WRITER VISITS SQUAD GALLERY — *James Daniel, left, Reader's Digest Roving Editor, examines disaster photos with member James Pence during meeting of Washington Emergency Squad in March 1979.*

Foreword

by James Daniel, Reader's Digest Roving Editor

Your Fabulous Volunteers is a gem of a book, the type of local history, replete with names and anecdotes, of which our country has never and can never have enough. For persons living in Washington, New Jersey, and surrounding Warren County, it records half a century of courage, self-sacrifice, and achievement in creating an excellent system of first aid and ambulance service to the ill and injured. It does this for the Borough and Township of Washington and also for Phillipsburg, Lopatcong, Belvidere, Stewartsville, Hackettstown, Blairstown, Franklin, Oxford, Allamuchy-Green, Independence and Mansfield, whose place names are a litany in themselves. The history is written not a moment too soon. A wait of a year or two could have diminished the number of survivors whose recollections are so vital to this book.

But this is more than another excellent local history. It covers and illumines a vital aspect of the American character and experience. John W. Gardner, former United States Secretary of Health, Education and Welfare, while chairman of the citizens' group Common Cause, wrote that the 17th century and early 18th century colonial governors were constantly amazed by the way Americans voluntarily got together and solved their problems without resort to government. The richness and diversity of the nonprofit, voluntary sector of our society is still a source of wonder and, perhaps, the chief support undergirding our nation. Occasionally (even in New Jersey) there are those who want government to regulate this sector because of fancied shortcomings and abuses. But, says Gardner, it is already regulated by the public in the giving, or withholding, of their financial support. That, he says, is as it should be and how Americans want it to be.

John Gardner also says that the voluntary movement has been "the birthplace of every significant social movement of the past 100 years." He could have said a thousand as well. Ours is for the most part a voluntary hospital system, and in this century the first aid and ambulance services that bridge the gap between the suddenly injured and ill and the hospital with its network of specialized services came about because of volunteers like those described in this book. Washington—the New Jersey Washington, not the D. C. one—is one of the important places where future historians will look to see how the movement began. At the time the heroes of this book were organizing and assuming responsibility, most ambulance service in the United States, outside of a very few big city hospitals, was part of the proprietary undertaking business. So-called ambulance drivers were hearse drivers, more interested in snatching bodies than on saving lives. "Who's dead or dying" was more on their minds than "Who here can be saved?"

Certain it is that from the pioneering efforts here described emerged a steadily improving system of emergency medical service in which volunteers remain the first line of defense and the nation's chief resource. Not only are they closer to where the needs arise, they demonstrably care more. And their general level of training and skill is steadily rising. Considering their numbers, they equal or surpass the salaried and sometimes privately owned profit services that in places seek to oust the volunteers. For financial and for logistical reasons the voluntary approach is likely to predominate in providing injured and sick Americans with a constantly improving service.

This foreword would not be complete without a reference to Alvin Sloan and his father, both of whom have given so much to make this book possible. Volunteer firemen and emergency squad persons can never be grateful enough to the Sloans, a family whose history is entwined with that of Washington and also with much that is truest and best in our national life.

To any individual lucky enough to buy or be given a copy of this book, I say, take good care of it. If you have delved into the economics of used books, you have discovered that in any collection of used books the valuable ones—as documents and also often in a financial sense as well—are seldom the pretty ones with pictures and fancy covers. Usually they are modestly printed pamphlets and books that record authentic local and regional events, or are associated with the lives of persons locally and regionally famous, or exemplify how life was at a particular time. This book belongs to that lode certain to be mined in the future. It will be esteemed long after the current novel or the ballyhooed cocktail table picture book has been thrown out with the trash.

Weston, Connecticut JAMES DANIEL
January 3, 1980
(Reprinted from first edition.)

Preface

The Random House Dictionary of the English Language defines the word FABULOUS as follows:

> almost unbelievable; incredible;
> marvelous; superb; exceptionally
> good or unusual.

The members of the Washington Emergency Squad are all of these things. Only 34 in number, they devoted 5,402 person-hours responding to 1,368 calls for help during 1984.

They give their own time to become highly trained before they become active in rescue work, to continue training during their years of service, and to attend the many meetings and events of the squad. They raise the money to provide the equipment with which they work.

These, and the many more who served before them, are truly fabulous volunteers. This book is concerned with your fabulous volunteers, their history, their training, their work and their problems.

1

A Call for Help

It is an ordinary evening. James and Jeanne Jones are watching their favorite television show in the living room of their Washington home. Suddenly James complains of severe chest pains. His frightened wife comforts him; then, realizing there might be serious trouble, runs to the telephone and calls the number of the Washington dispatcher, 689-2111.

The dispatcher responds immediately, ascertains that Mr. Jones is having chest pains and difficulty breathing, notes the Jones address, and requests that Mrs. Jones turn on the porch light and await the arrival of squad personnel.

Then the dispatcher activates the emergency alarms—twelve blasts of the fire whistle and a verbal message over the police radio system that is also heard in the homes of all emergency squad members. The dispatcher notes on the log that the time is 10:25 P.M.

The next three or four minutes seem like an eternity to Jeanne, and she calls the emergency number again. She is informed that help is on the way.

At 10:31, six minutes from the time of Jeanne's first call, an ambulance arrives at the Jones residence with life-sustaining equipment, and squad members carry a stretcher into the house.

A decision is made that hospital treatment is required. Minutes later James is on the way to Warren Hospital with Jeanne at his side. Radio communication is established with the hospital emergency room, and treatment is given under the direction of a physician.

The trip is speeded by police escorts arranged by the dispatcher. At the hospital James is carried into the emergency room where the doctor attends him.

One of the nearly 1,400 missions which are carried out by the Washington Emergency Squad every year has been completed. A life has been saved.

Many people follow the activities of the emergency squad, fire department and police department on short wave radios or scanners.

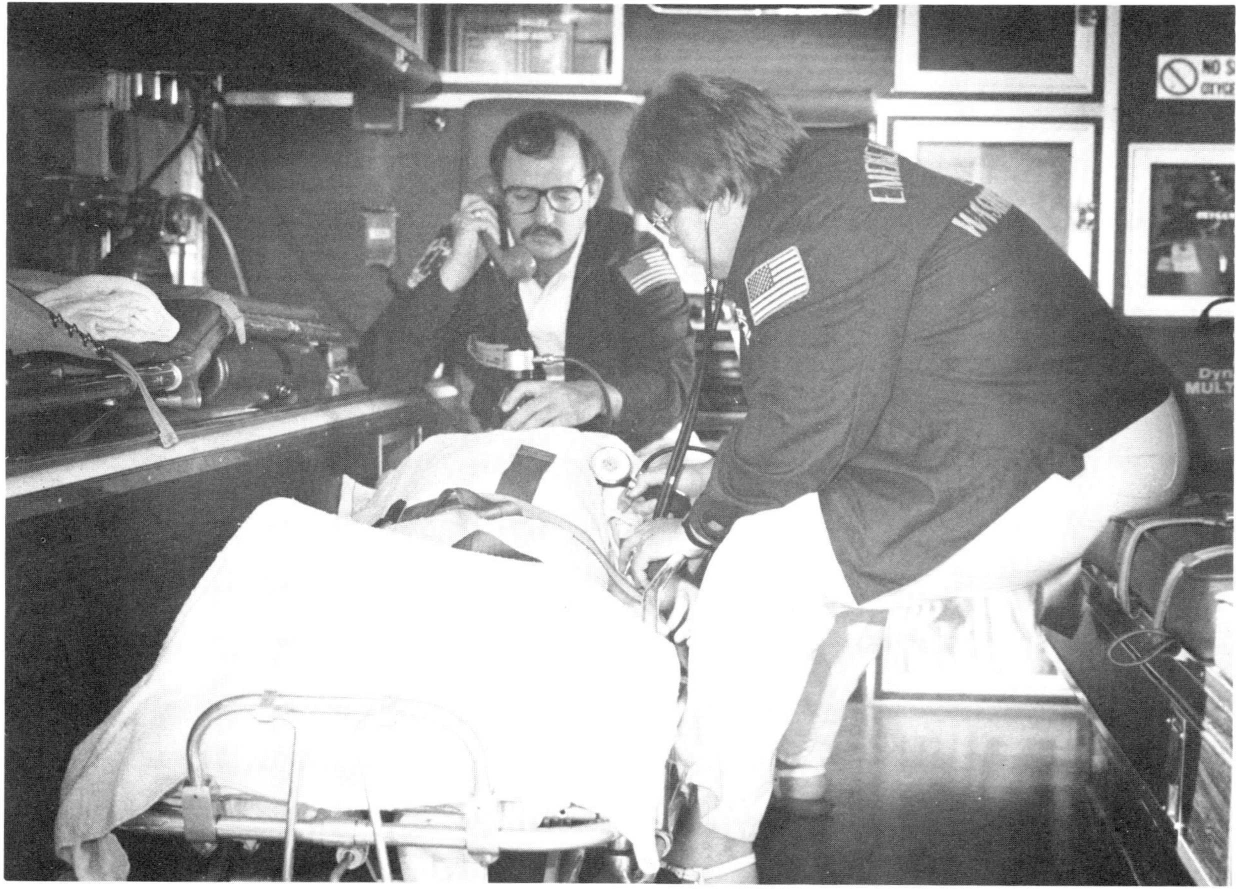

Royal Photographics photo

ON THE ROAD — *Diana Dunlap, R.N., checks patient's vital signs while Larry Collins relays information to Warren Hospital emergency room physician via radio.*

Any multiple-wave-length radio with police bands will do, but a scanner, available at radio and department stores, is programmed to the wave lengths of dispatching agencies of your choice.

The crisp notices, instructions and directions that would have been heard during the Jones emergency are recorded below with explanations of the code words used.

ACTUAL MESSAGE	**EXPLANATION**
Beep beep beep . . . Station 83 Rescue alert for an emergency call 204 Grand Avenue. Time out 22:25 hours. KDB 389. (Beep signal and message repeated.)	*A distinctive beep signal indicates Washington Emergency Squad. The number 83 indicates Washington Borough in the Warren County station code. 22:25 hours is 25 minutes after the 22nd hour of the day, or 10:25 P.M.*[1] *KDB-389 is the call signal of the Washington Borough dispatching service.*
83-12 from Washington.	*Numbers from 10 to 20 indicate police patrol cars in the Warren County vehicle code.*[2] *The dispatcher is calling borough patrol car number 12.*
83-12. Go ahead Washington.	*Police car answers.*
83-12 from Washington. Station 83 rescue will be responding to 204 Grand Avenue for a possible heart attack—the Jones' residence.	*Police car is informed of call.*
83-12. Received. Enroute to call.	*Police car answers call to assist.*
Washington from 83-12. On call at 204 Grand Avenue.	*Police car has arrived at the Jones residence.*
	It is now 10:28 P.M. Dispatcher

[1]Some Washington dispatchers would give the time as 10:25 P.M.

[2]Prior to 1979 vehicles dispatched by Washington had numbers assigned by the borough. In 1980 a new system was inaugurated in which code words preceded the numbers: "bravo" for borough, "tango" for township, "echo" for emergency, etc. The present countywide system was introduced in 1984.

	receives call on hotline from squad building from the first squad member to arrive and gives member all information about call.
Washington from 83-51. On the air.	*Numbers from 51 through 54 indicate ambulances. 83-51 is Washington Emergency Squad ambulance number 51.*
83-51 from Washington. 10-4.	*10-4 is acknowledgement of message received. Communication between dispatcher and ambulance has been established.*
Washington from 83-51. Enroute to call.	*Ambulance has full crew and is leaving squad building.*
83-51 from Washington. 10-4.	
Washington from 83-51. On call.	*Ambulance has arrived at Jones residence. (It is now 10:31 P.M.)*
83-51 from Washington. 10-4.	
Washington from 83-51. Enroute to Warren Hospital. Could you give us a 32 to hospital?	*32 is code word for escort. Borough patrol car escorts ambulance to Brass Castle Road.*
83-51 from 76-11. I read that and will pick you up at Brass Castle Road and take you to Morrie's.	*76 is Washington Township code number. 76-11 is township patrol car number 11. Patrol heard request for escort.*
83-51. Received, 76-11.	
83-51 from Washington. 74 car will pick you up at Morrie's and take you to the hospital.	*74 is Lopatcong Township code number. Lopatcong police car will be waiting across from Morrie's Acres Restaurant.*
83-51. Received, Washington	
Washington from 83-12. 23.	*23 means call is completed.*

Borough police car has escorted ambulance to Brass Castle Road and is now available for a future call.

83-12 from Washington. 10-4. 22:56 hours.

Washington from 83-51. Off the air at Warren.

Ambulance crew is at the hospital and can be reached by telephone.

83-51 from Washington. 10-4.

Washington from 76-11. Clear from 32. Back in Township.

Township police car is available for future calls.

76-11 from Washington. 10-4. 23:15 hours.

Washington from 83-51, Clear from Warren. Returning to borough.

83-51 from Washington. 10-4.

Dispatcher knows ambulance is returning. If another ambulance call comes in, dispatcher may dispatch this ambulance rather than summon a second crew to take out another ambulance.

Washington from 83-51. We'll be out at the pumps.

Crew is filling ambulance gasoline tank at borough garage.

83-51 from Washington. 10-4.

Washington from 83-51. Clear from the pumps and back at the building.

83-51 from Washington. 10-4. Time out 22:25 hours. Your time in is 23:40 hours.

Call came in at 10:25 P.M. and it is now 11:40 P.M.

Washington from 83-51. Received. Off the air.

Ambulance duty crew chief enters time and particulars of call in squad record.

Photo courtesy of Albert Einstein Medical Center

BEFORE THE DAYS OF EMERGENCY SQUADS — *Early in this century hospitals sent their own ambulances to transport the sick and injured. This photo was taken about 1900.*

2

Before the Days of Emergency Squads

The fabulous volunteers of the Washington Emergency Squad arrived at the Jones residence six minutes after Jeanne called for help. But not so many years ago this service was not available. During the early years of this century, very few skilled first-aid or ambulance services existed, except for paid personnel in a few large cities.

In her book *The Ambulance*, published in 1978 by Exposition Press, Katherine Traver Barkley presents a history on the means of getting sick and injured people to hospitals. In words and pictures she shows ambulances in the forms of horse drawn wagons, trolley cars, trains and early motor vehicles. Such motorized ambulances as did exist were usually operated by hospitals or undertakers, and they were required to make long trips from their bases in order to reach emergency scenes. That fact, together with the poor roads of the era, resulted in very slow responses to calls.

Many of the means described in that book were used in Warren County before the first emergency and ambulance squads were established. The first squads were widely separated and were handicapped because of the large areas which they were called upon to serve. As more squads were established and more sophisticated equipment became available, services greatly improved.

A Warren County man who is very much aware of the difficulties faced when an emergency occurred before the days of emergency squads is Frederick R. "Buss" Johnson. He owns Johnson's Farm, one of the last old-time country boarding houses and picnic grounds in this part of the state, on Summerfield Road in White Townsip. With his own hands, from what was originally a tumbled-down farmhouse, barn and farm land, he has built an extensive parkland, complete with swimming pool, quaint stone guest houses, recreational facilities and picnic sites.

Johnson is 74 years old and came to the farm when he was a small boy. His father was an artist and worked mostly in the West, so he was away from home most of the time. "Buss" lived on the farm with his mother and two brothers.

One day in 1914, when he was climbing a ladder at the barn, he slipped and fell a distance of ten feet, landing on the hub of an old wagon wheel. "I tried to walk, but I remember my leg wouldn't hold me up," he recalls.

His mother carried him into the house, then ran to a neighbor's home for help. The time was early in February, and there was a considerable amount of snow on the ground. The neighbor, having no telephone, mounted his horse and began the journey to Belvidere, some six miles away, to summon the doctor who administered to the needs of the people in that area.

Late that evening the neighbor returned. Both he and his horse were exhausted from the long and cold journey. "He told my mother the doctor was too busy and couldn't make it but said the doctor promised he would get out to the farm on the following day," Johnson says.

The doctor instructed the neighbor to tie a board to the boy's leg and make sure he remained in bed until he arrived. The next day, around noon, the doctor, having travelled over uncleared, snow-filled roads in his horse-drawn buggy, pulled up to the Johnson farmhouse.

"Sure enough, it's a broken leg," Johnson quotes the doctor as saying, "but it must be set in a hospital because I can't set it here." The doctor left instructions with Johnson's mother and then left to make arrangements.

"We had an old iron bed, and they took it apart to get it out of the house. Then they put it together on a wagon. They put me in the bed and covered me with lots of blankets. So there I was, in bed, on the back of a horse-drawn wagon, on my way to Belvidere. I hollered all the way as the bumps sent pain shooting into my leg," Johnson says.

The wagon made its way to the Belvidere railroad station where Johnson was required to wait in the baggage room—still in bed and still covered with lots of blankets—because the bed would not fit through the waiting-room doors.

Some 20 minutes later a southbound steam-powered train pulled into the station. "They carried the bed, with me in it, to the baggage car. They helped my mother aboard, and the train headed for Phillipsburg. When we arrived, the doctor had made arrangements for a horse-drawn ambulance to be waiting. They loaded me into the ambulance and took me and my mother to Easton Hospital. The bed was returned to Belvidere by train, and I guess we got it back home somehow or other, but they didn't charge us for the trip," Johnson recalls.

"My mother visited me at the hospital twice a week during the several

Richard W. York photo

***UNPLEASANT MEMORY** — Frederick R. "Buss" Johnson climbs ladder in barn where he was injured 71 years ago.*

weeks I was there. She had to walk from our farm to the railroad station at Foul Rift. In those days the roads weren't plowed, and she had to walk through the snow. It was about four miles to the station and another mile from Phillipsburg to the hospital. I'll never forget that ordeal as long as I live,'' he concludes.

But the broken leg he suffered as a young boy, and the experience of being transported to the hospital in a bed on a horse-drawn buckboard over snow-covered dirt roads, makes him even more appreciative of today's volunteer rescue squads than most people.

Fred Bodenstein, who passed away while this book was being prepared, and Martin Young, both retired state troopers who became

***MOUNTED PATROL** — State trooper Fred Bodenstein on his mount, Jiggs, ready to gallop off to any emergency in the early 1930's.*

Washington residents, were assigned to the Washington barracks in 1931. Young recalls that passing motorists were often called upon to take injured people to hospitals. He says state police were not usually the first to arrive at the scene of a disaster because there were no radios in those days, and sometimes it would be hours before the troopers were even notified of an accident.

Bodenstein patrolled the Warren County countryside on horseback. He recalled that his barracks arranged with farmers who had telephones to relay police messages. The only way that he heard of an emergency was when he saw a flag hanging from a farmhouse window. This meant that he was to stop and telephone his headquarters. The barracks, having received word of an emergency, had telephoned the farmers with whom it had arrangements on Bodenstein's route.

Later, when patrol cars came into use, it was not uncommon for the troopers to bundle one or more victims into the patrol car and hasten to the nearest hospital.

Even in homes, where most emergencies occur, the wait for a doctor was often a torturous heart-rending and time-consuming experience. Young recalls that it was not unusual for a physician to be called to the scene of an emergency and then find it necessary to transport victims to the hospital in his own car.

The Warren Hospital, then located in a former schoolhouse on Wilbur Avenue in Phillipsburg, owned an ambulance, but it was frequently out of order, and no particular person was assigned to drive it. The watchman filled that post when calls were received at night. When the ambulance did get off with a doctor and a nurse aboard, first aid was on the way, but the scene was often so distant that the aid was too late in arriving anyway.

Early in 1950 the hospital administrator, Raymond Stem,[1] recommended that the hospital discontinue its ambulance service. He carried the day, but only over the protests of some hospital trustees who felt, as one expressed it, "A hospital without an ambulance is like an apple tree without apples."

There are other people in Warren County who remember the old Warren Hospital ambulance. They include Kenneth Gaylord, who came to the Washington barracks as a young state trooper in 1937 and after his retirement served as sheriff of Warren County for nearly 20 years. He also remembers hauling the sick and injured to the hospital in his troop car on occasion. "There was nobody any happier to see the creation of the Washington Emergency Squad than I was," Gaylord

[1]Raymond Stem later became a Warren County freeholder.

***WARREN HOSPITAL AMBULANCE** — Driver and ambulance ready for calls in the 1920's. Hospital was located in former school building on Wilbur Avenue, Phillipsburg.*

says.

The hazards of life without emergency squads were vividly exemplified in the Rockport train disaster of 1925, considered at that time to be one of the worst tragedies in railroading history. More than 40 people died at the scene or shortly after reaching hospitals.

A Lackawanna Railroad train, carrying German immigrants from the midwest on the first leg of a trip to visit their homeland, was derailed at a point some two miles west of the Hackettstown station. A violent thunderstorm had caused a landslide, and a huge pile of debris had been deposited on the railroad tracks. The engine overturned, and the cars telescoped in a massive heap of wreckage. Dead, dying and injured human beings littered the scene.

That fateful night a student nurse, Lilly Sutton,[1] was summoned from her Hackettstown home at 3 A.M. to join other rescuers at the site of the tragedy.

"There were no rescue squads then. When I arrived, there were doc-

[1]Lilly Sutton became Mrs. Amos Smith and now resides in Washington Township.

ROCKPORT WRECK — *Lackawanna Railroad coaches lie across derailed locomotive. Escaping steam killed and injured many passengers.*

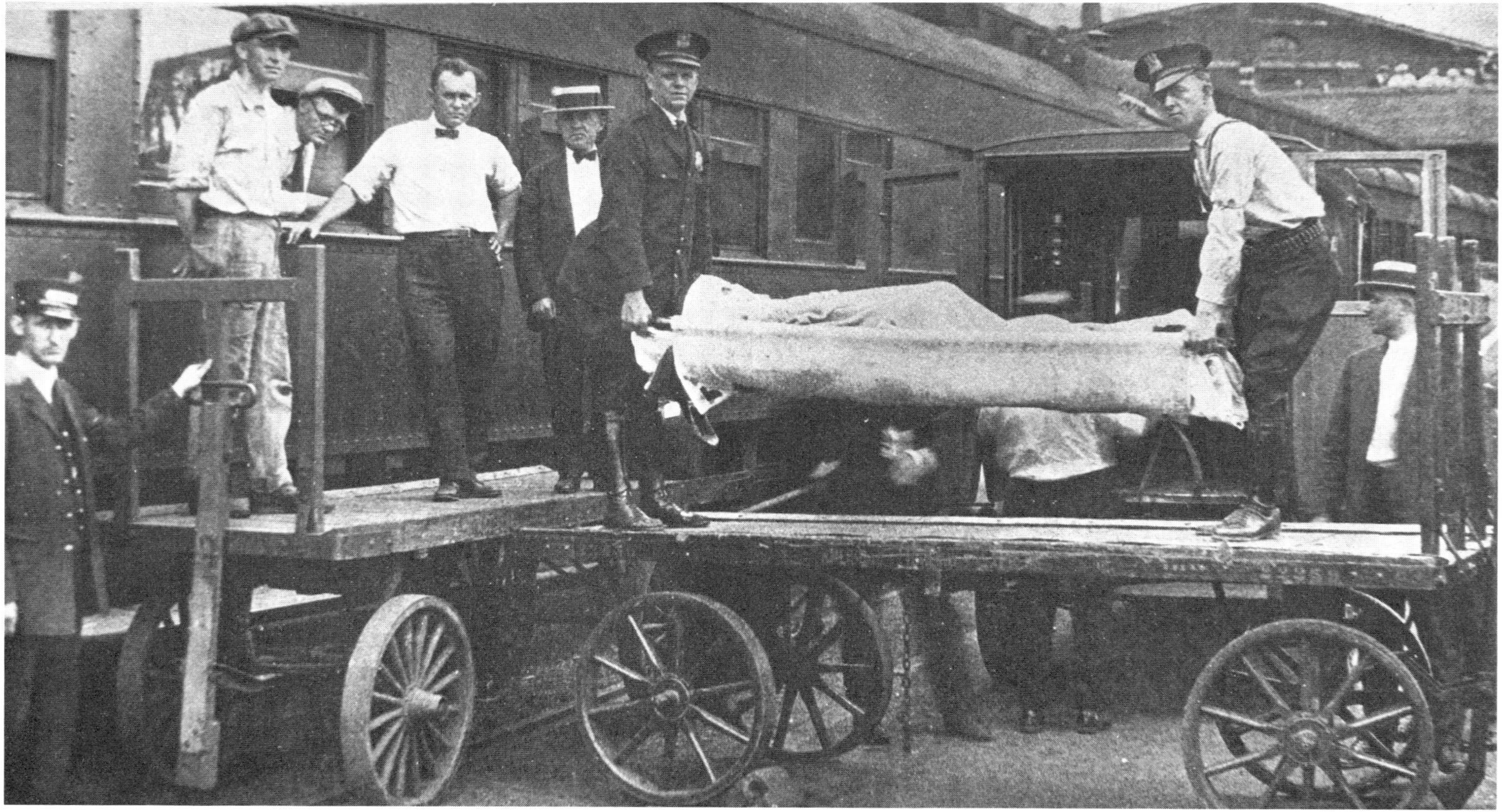

MAKESHIFT TRANSPORTATION — *Victim of Rockport Lackawanna Railroad wreck being transferred from special train to hospital ambulance at Phillipsburg in June 1925.*

tors and nurses all over the place. Scores of people were at the scene helping where they could. Wrecked coaches had landed on top of the overturned steam engine. Many of the merchants in Hackettstown sent gallons of olive oil to treat the burned and scalded victims,'' Mrs. Smith recalls.

The most frustrating problem was the interminable delay in getting the injured to hospitals.

Earlier that evening, during the same storm that caused the railroad disaster, a lightening bolt struck a lumberyard in Hackettstown. The Hackettstown volunteer firemen called neighboring communities for help in fighting the stubborn fire which resulted. One of the assisting fire companies was from Washington. The Washington firemen heard about the railroad wreck and rerouted their return trip in order to visit Rockport and see if they could be of assistance. Washington residents were startled a short time later when they saw their fire truck speeding through the town taking victims to the hospital in Phillipsburg, according to the late Washington Township resident Charles Jensen, who lived on East Washington Avenue at the time.

As slow as they were, however, trains offered the best means of transportation. One was sent from Washington and another from Dover. By the time the rescuers had completed their work, it was daylight. It had taken almost six hours for the trains to be loaded with the injured and start their trips to Phillipsburg, Dover and Morristown, where the casualties were transferred to ambulances which had been sent to the railroad stations by nearby hosptials.

Most of the helpers and the curious who had come from Hackettstown walked home, down the railroad tracks to the station, where members of the press had gathered and set up a communication center to send news of the great rail disaster to the far corners of the world.

What the lack of prompt and skilled first aid cost in death and suffering at Rockport can only be imagined, but luckily for us today, the training of skilled first-aiders had already begun in Washington through the foresight and effort of one man.

Richard W. York photo of painting

***EMERGENCY SQUAD PIONEER** — Vernon C. "Bab" Oakes, founder and first captain of the Washington Emergency Squad.*

3

Vernon C. Oakes, Emergency Squad Pioneer

Vernon C. "Bab" Oakes was born in Washington, the son of the proprietor of a local barber shop. He aspired to become a doctor, but the lack of sufficient family finances, and the wish of his father that he follow the family tradition of operating the barber shop, prevented his pursuit of that goal. He was an avid reader of medical books and acquired a very respectable knowledge of first-aid procedures.

He joined the volunteer fire department in 1918 at the age of 23, and his quality of leadership was quickly recognized. He was elected assistant foreman of Washington Steamer Company No. 1 later that year.

First-aid service in Washington had its beginning within the fire department, and it was "Bab" Oakes who saw the need, interested his superior officers, and assumed the responsibilities involved. He appealed to Chief Delbert Major for permission to buy a supply of first-aid materials in order to treat firemen and others who received injuries at fire scenes. The request was granted, and Oakes began his career as a fabulous volunteer, destined to spend most of his working life advancing the cause of first aid.

The next two decades marked a period of rapid growth for Washington and its fire department. More fire-fighting equipment was needed for a growing community, and more first-aid supplies were required to satisfy the increasing concern for human injuries. In 1921 a new Seagrave fire truck was purchased, and later a new American LaFrance fire truck was added, while liberal amounts of first-aid supplies were donated by the local drug stores, Jenkins and Meeker Warren County Drug Store and Stover's Pharmacy. With each expansive surge Oakes' stature grew, and his responsibilities increased.

In 1925, in order to apportion manpower better within the fire department, Washington Truck Company No. 2 was organized and the personnel divided into two companies. Twenty of the older men, in point of service, remained in Washington Steamer Company No. 1

YOUNG FIRE CHIEF — *Vernon C. "Bab" Oakes, 31-year-old member of Washington Truck Company No. 2, was elected chief of the Washington Fire Department. The first to command the department after it was divided into two companies, he served in that capacity in 1926 and 1927.*

while the 20 younger men were assigned to the new Washington Truck Company No. 2.

A significant tribute was paid to the company of younger men. "Bab" Oakes was elected as the first chief to command the expanded fire department. He held the post for the customary two years.

In 1934 added recognition was given to the first-aid program under Chief Frank Hassemer. He authorized Oakes to appoint seven firemen to perform first-aid duties and made him the head of the eight-man unit.

Oakes made many visits to the Newark Fire Department, which he believed to be one of the finest at the time. He studied its equipment and methods of operation and brought back ideas to be used in improving the Washington Fire Department.

Alvin Sloan, who was a borough councilman in 1935, recalls a trip he took with Oakes that year. " 'Bab' was cutting my hair," Sloan relates, "and told me he was going to close the barber shop the next day and make one of his visits to the Newark Fire Department. He asked me to go with him, which I agreed to do.

"We took a Lackawanna train to Newark and then a long walk to the firehouse. When we arrived, all of the personnel knew 'Bab' and gave him a great welcome. He introduced me to them, and I believe they thought he was kidding when he said I was a councilman, because I

BACKED THE SQUAD IDEA — *Three fire chiefs backed Vernon Oakes in the creation of first-aid service. From left: Delbert Major, Frank Hassemer and Walter Castner.*

looked like a kid at the time. Anyway, they proudly showed us their equipment and explained to 'Bab' some new items they had acquired since his last visit.

"We spent a lot of time looking at the emergency equipment. Some of the firemen were assigned to the rescue unit.

"On the return train trip 'Bab' told me I had seen the very finest fire and rescue organizations. He said that Washington had an excellent volunteer fire department and suggested that we could create and operate a good volunteer rescue unit as well.

"He asked me to talk to the mayor and the other councilmen. I liked the idea and spread the word. It was near the end of the year. I became mayor the following year, and his dream became a reality. Ken Cregar was a fireman and the council member in charge of police and fire matters. He had a lot to do with getting the project off the ground and causing the other council members to support the creation of a volunteer rescue squad. He became a charter member of the squad and worked closely with 'Bab' Oakes."

In 1936 Chief Walter Castner reappointed Oakes head of the eight-man first-aid group of firemen, and Oakes was given permission to raise money for the purchase of an inhalator, leg splints, stretcher, blankets, floodlights, and additional medical and first-aid supplies. The money was obtained and the equipment purchased in an unbelievably short time.

At a firemen's meeting on June 24, 1936, the squad membership was increased to 12, six from each fire company. With a well manned and equipped rescue organization a reality, a milestone announcement was made. The Washington Fire Department First Aid and Rescue Squad, as it was then named, would no longer be restricted to fire calls. It was available to the public for all kinds of emergency services.

The roster included Walter Castner, George Hay, John King, Lewis Lanning, Pierre "Pat" Mullin and Samuel Vannatta from Washington Steamer Company No. 1, and Frank Castner, Kenneth Cregar, Charles "Buss" Eagan, Randal Kries, Oakes and Wilbur Willis from Washington Truck Company No. 2. Oakes served as captain.

The inhalator arrived two days later, and squad members were instructed in its use on June 30 by Dr. William H. Varney and Dr. Junius M. Lemmon. The machine, which cost $200, was a sophisticated piece of equipment at the time and later played a part in some remarkable rescues.

Nothing Oakes ever did was more indicative of a man ahead of his time than one of his first acts as head of the 12-man squad. He induced each member to have his blood typed and to volunteer as a donor. This was long before the days of the Red Cross bloodmobiles, but a call to the squad, stating the type of blood needed, would bring a suitable member to the hospital on short notice. The squad was now offering the public not only its services, but its blood. Its members were donors 29 times during the first six years of the program.

On July 4, 1936, at 4 P.M., the squad received its first emergency call. A bather found a nine-year-old girl from Little Ferry, New Jersey, who had been missing for twenty minutes while swimming in the Musconetcong River in Hackettstown. Some New Jersey Power and Light Company employees were summoned because they were working nearby and were the only apparent source of help available to desperate onlookers. Since electrical shock is a constant threat to linemen, their truck carried oxygen which they administered to the child for an hour until the supply was exhausted. The Washington squad was called. Captain Oakes, Frank Castner and Charles Eagan used the inhalator and artificial respiration. Unfortunately, their efforts did not save the life of the child.

By the end of 1936 the squad had answered five calls.

All first-aid materials and equipment were kept in a cabinet, built by the squad members for the purpose, and installed on the long running board of the fire department's ladder truck. On all calls other than fires, squad members would transfer equipment from the ladder truck to whatever private automobile was available.

A key item of equipment was lacking. An emergency vehicle that would carry all first-aid materials and emergency equipment, and would be used exclusively by the squad, was needed.

Permission of the borough council to solicit funds for the purchase of such a vehicle was requested and granted. Some questions had arisen when the idea of an emergency truck was first mentioned, but Mayor Alvin Sloan[1] and Councilman Kenneth Cregar endorsed the project with enthusiasm and assured the council and the public that all costs would be raised by voluntary contributions of cash and labor.

Residents were generous, as usual, but the cost was formidable and the squad members decided to stretch the funds by donating their own labor to build the body of the truck. The plan was given a boost when Cregar, treasurer of the fund drive, announced that Lester Bunn, proprietor of Shirley Auto Sales, would provide a new Dodge truck chassis at his cost price.

The work of building the truck body was assigned to the squad members, each assuming the portion for which his mechanical or elec-

---

[1]Alvin Sloan, elected justice of the peace at the age of 22, borough councilman at 23, and mayor at 24, was reputed to be the youngest mayor in the United States at the time.

Minassian photo

ORIGINAL WASHINGTON FIRE DEPARTMENT FIRST AID AND RESCUE SQUAD IN 1936 — *Equipment was stored in homemade cabinet installed on running board of ladder truck. Front row, from left: Frank Castner, Randal Kries, Kenneth Cregar, George Hay, Samuel Vannatta, John King and Walter Castner. Back row: Charles Eagan, Lewis Lanning, Captain Vernon Oakes, Pierre Mullin and Wilbur Willis.*

Minassian photo

***ACTIVE IN SQUAD CREATION** — These three men were important figures in the creation of the Washington Emergency Squad. From left: Vernon C. "Bab" Oakes, founder and first captain; Mayor Alvin Sloan, elected at age of 24 and reputed to have been the youngest mayor in the United States at the time; and Councilman Kenneth Cregar, fireman and squad member who was also police and fire commissioner.*

trical skills were suited. When completed, this may have been the only emergency truck in the world with a fire bell up front. Some fireman along the way suggested that a time-worn bell, taken off one of the old fire trucks, should be refurbished and become part of the new rig. The squadmen accepted the idea.

Normally, old fire engine bells were rung by hand. A cord, stretched from the bell to the front seat of the vehicle, was yanked by whoever sat on the passenger side, and the engine would respond to calls with the bell ringing loud and clear. But the late Otto Eger, a master mechanic employed by the local Ford dealer, decided that the bell should be electrified.

According to old-timer Charles "Buss" Eagan, "He worked on that idea for weeks. He tried all kinds of gadgets and they were all of his own invention. Finally he rigged some kind of device which permitted anyone in the cab of the truck to throw a switch and the bell would ring as long as desired. We had a siren, of course, but the bell rang along with it."

The bell was transferred to the second emergency truck, but later trucks were equipped with winches where the bell would have been located, making its installation impractical. In 1983 the firemen found the bell among some old and obsolete equipment and gave it to the emergency squad as a keepsake. In 1985 it was installed in front of the Vernon Oakes Building as a memorial to Otto's brother, Joseph, a deceased squad member with an outstanding record of service.

The following account of the building of the truck appears in a history Oakes wrote about the early days of the squad:

"Chief Walter Castner had charge of the cabinet work and helped in every possible way, day after day, and had many fine ideas which were used in the construction of the truck. Edward Feldman, Randal Kries, Charles Rupell, Russell Beam, Alden Marlatt, Fletcher Wright, John King, Frank Castner and all other members helped at one time or another. Charles Eagan had charge of the electrical work. It would be impossible to give the names of all the people who helped, whether in a financial or material way, but suffice it to say that we were glad to live in a town where the fire department was backed up one hundred percent by the people as well as by the mayor and common council."

Actually, Oakes was praising the governing bodies of two successive years. The 1936 officials were Mayor Alvin Sloan and Councilmen Paul Black, Levi Cressman, H. Wilmot Eckel, Dr. William F. Skinner, Charles E. Smith and John P. Winters. Cressman and Winters did not seek reelection and were replaced on the 1937 council by Clarence Ackerson and Kenneth Cregar, a fireman and squad member who served as fire and police commissioner.

Oakes wanted the squad to be a recognized part of the borough government, so he requested the mayor and council to adopt an amendment to the fire-department ordinance recognizing the squad operation. He asked that the membership be increased and the name be changed to

***FIRST EMERGENCY TRUCK** — 1937 Dodge with body handmade by firemen. Rescue equipment was stored under benches.*

Washington Emergency Squad.

The council, recognizing the impressive accomplishments and potential of the squad, responded at its meeting of December 8, 1937, by adopting an ordinance to create, regulate and control an emergency squad of 16 men, eight to be appointed from each of the two fire companies, with the fire chief to serve as an ex officio member. The fire chief at the time was Walter Castner. He and several chiefs who succeeded him were already squad members, so the membership remained at 16 for many years.

Of the 12 charter members only nine remained to be reappointed. George Hay, who had experienced a layoff from his railroad job because of the depressed economy at the time, was called back to that employment and was obliged to give up his position as patrolman in the borough police department and his membership in the fire department and rescue squad. Lewis Lanning had received a leave of absence from the squad.[1] Samuel Vannatta was the victim of a tragic automobile accident.

The three, all members of Washington Steamer Company No. 1, had been replaced by Oakes with Russell Beam, Edward Feldman and William Sheats.

Four more members were needed to bring the squad up to its newly authorized membership of 16. In addition to reappointing the 12 active members with Oakes as captain, Mayor Sloan appointed Alden Marlatt and Harold Sheats from Washington Steamer Company No. 1, and Charles Rupell and A. Fletcher Wright from Washington Truck Company No. 2.

The appointments were unanimously confirmed by the council and the entire membership was sworn in by Borough Attorney Clark C. Bowers.

On December 10, 1937, the people of Washington received a magnificent present when the Washington Emergency Squad presented the new truck to the borough as a Christmas gift. The occasion was a celebration program sponsored by the Washington Booster Club. It took place on Belvidere Avenue where the C.W.Y.A. Community Center building now stands. The vehicle was wrapped in cellophane with a huge red ribbon tied around it. Its glistening white paint made an impressive sight sparkling under the street lights.

The gift was accepted for the people of Washington by Mayor Sloan, who expressed appreciation and gratitude on the part of the residents of

[1]Lewis Lanning became active in the squad again in 1940 and served until he lost his life a year later in an electrical accident which occurred on his job as a power and light company lineman. The squad was summoned to the scene of that accident, but efforts to save Lanning's life were unsuccessful.

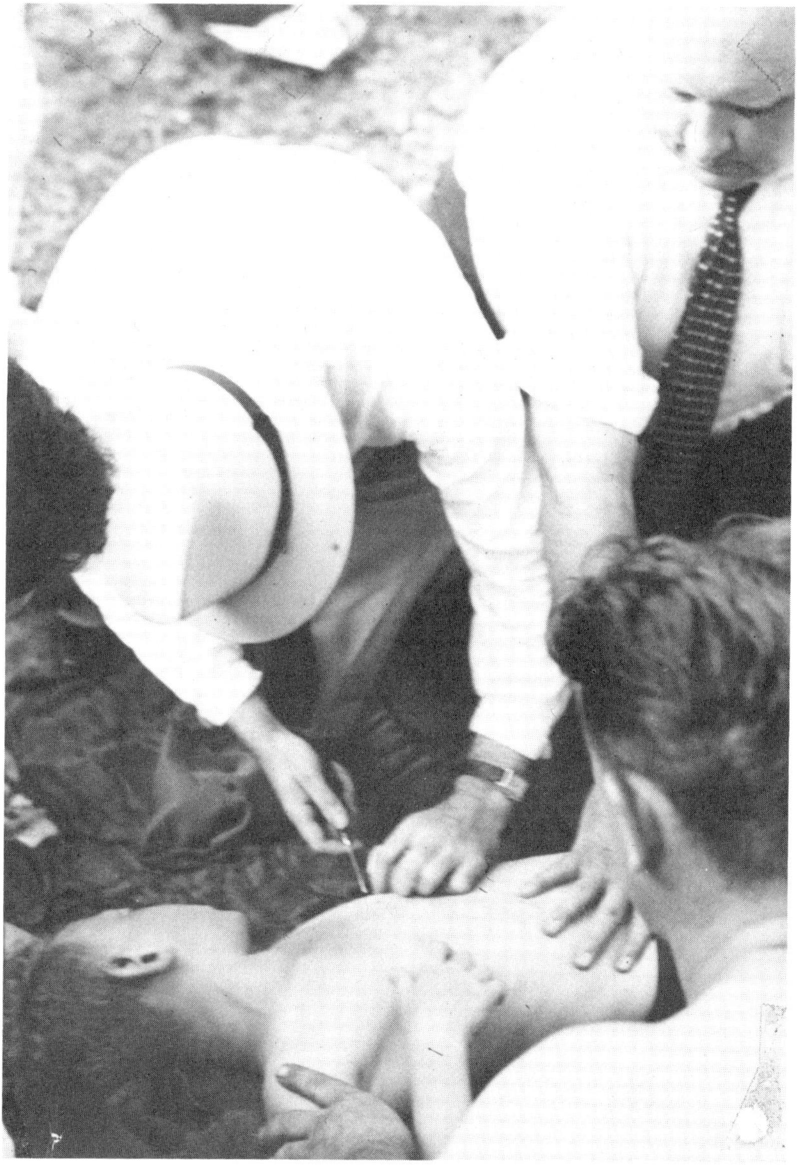

DOCTOR HELPS — *Squad is assisted by Dr. William H. Varney on a call in 1938. Captain Vernon Oakes observes. In those days Dr. Varney answered many calls to offer assistance to the squad.*

the Washington area. He also paid a stirring tribute to the firemen, squad members and to all who worked to make the magnificent gift possible.

The placing of the new truck in service marked the end of a two-year period during which the squad had removed its equipment from the ladder truck to private vehicles 43 times in order to respond to as many emergency calls, had treated 88 injured people, and had used the inhalator for a total of nine and a half hours.

The truck had been placed in service a few days before the public ceremony, and a life was saved on its first call. The call came from Belvidere at 12:55 A.M. on December 6. A man had been overcome by carbon-monoxide gas while repairing a car in a closed garage.

Captain Oakes, Frank Castner, Walter Castner, Charles Eagan, Edward Feldman, John King, Randal Kries, Alden Marlatt, Harold Sheats and Wilbur Willis responded to the call. When the call came in, the inhalator was on display in the window of the Ford furniture store in Washington as part of the publicity for the truck dedication ceremony which was to take place four days later. Eagan, Feldman and King, the first members to respond, sped to the store in King's car and

Borough First Aid Squad Has Emergency Record

New records were made by the first aid squad of the Washington Fire Department when it answered an emergency call at Belvidere Monday afternoon.

The call was received at 12.55 P. M., and 15 minutes later the squad was at the county seat and using the inhalator on Alonzo Paul, 40, who had been overcome by carbon monoxide gas. The squad succeeded in resuscitating Paul after a half-hour's work. He had previously been given up by a Belvidere physician.

Washington Star, December 9, 1937

retrieved the inhalator.

When the squad arrived at the scene at 1:10 P.M., Alonzo Paul had been given up for dead by an attending physician. Undaunted, and with great pride and confidence in their ability and equipment, the squadmen decided to work on the victim anyway. Using the inhalator for 30 minutes, they successfuly revived the 40-year-old man.

Paul and his wife Laura lived on Water Street. He was an employee of the Celenese plant at the time. He lived until 1961 when he died of a heart attack at the age of 64.

One of his sons, Earl Paul, Sr., still resides in Belvidere. He remembers the incident well. He says his father had been working on the family car when someone found him overcome by carbon monoxide. He was carried into his home, and a doctor was summoned. "I remember the doctor being there, and I remember we called the Washington Emergency Squad," Paul recalls. "He was gasping, and I recall that the squad used artificial respiration and that he recovered."

A few days after that incident, Oakes received a personal letter from Dr. N. C. Marlett in which he wrote, "I want to thank you and the squad for your promptness in response to our call. There is no doubt that Mr. Paul owes his life to your heroic work.

"I have never seen a better trained and more efficient squad than

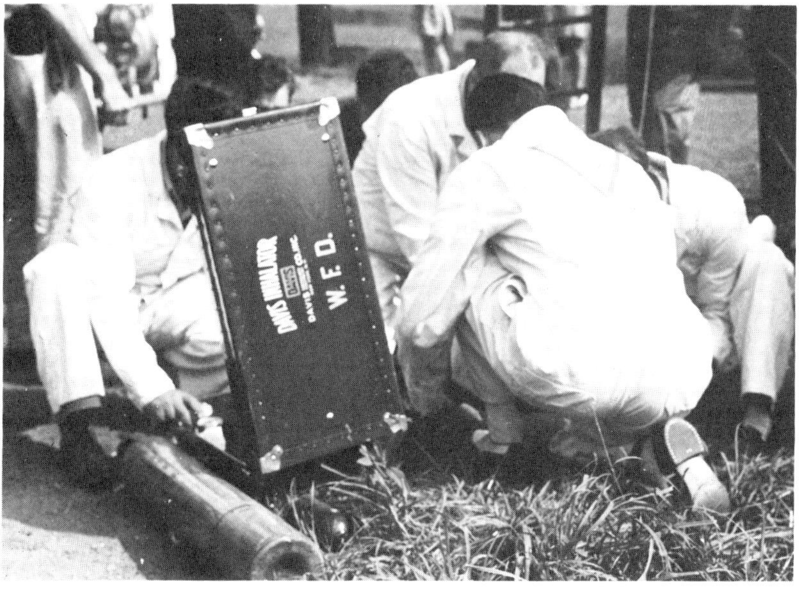

REVIVING PATIENT — *Early Squad members using their first piece of major equipment, the Davis Inhalator.*

yours. The teamwork and efficiency are outstanding.''

A second letter came to the squad from Mr. and Mrs. Alonzo Paul and their sons, who wrote, ''We wish to express our sincere thanks for the aid given us last week in saving the life of Mr. Paul. We appreciate the fact that you risked your lives in making a record run over here.''

Vernon ''Bab'' Oakes' foresight and labor had brought his dream to reality at last, but he did not live long to enjoy his success. During most of his working life he had lavished his time and strength saving the lives of others, but he was unable to save his own from the ravages of economic insecurity.

Oakes was conducting the barbershop business, but most of his time and energy were expended on the emergency squad. Declining business had caused him to move his shop from its street-level location to the front room of his upstairs apartment, in order to reduce operating expense. Many times the patrons entering his shop were told to have a seat while Mrs. Oakes, his son or his daughter, ran to the firehouse, a block

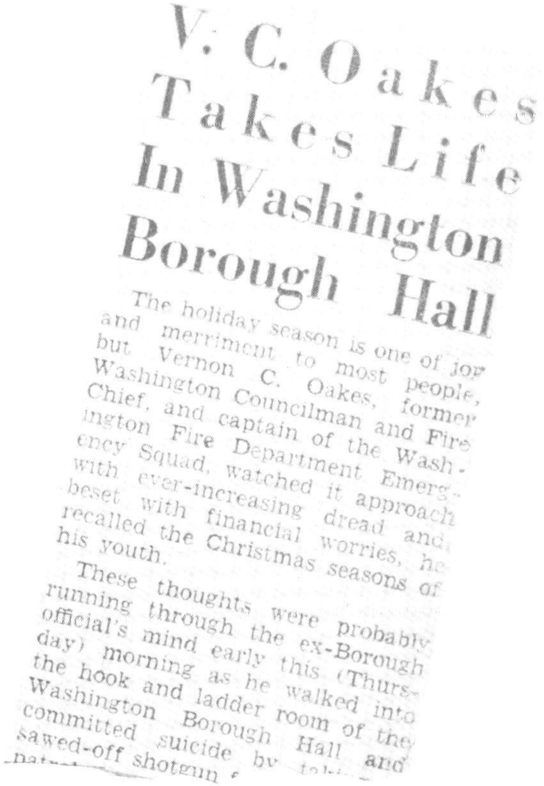

V. C. Oakes Takes Life In Washington Borough Hall

The holiday season is one of joy and merriment to most people, but Vernon C. Oakes, former Washington Councilman and Fire Chief, and captain of the Washington Fire Department Emergency Squad, watched it approach with ever-increasing dread and beset with financial worries, he recalled the Christmas seasons of his youth.

These thoughts were probably running through the ex-Borough official's mind early this (Thursday) morning as he walked into the hook and ladder room of the Washington Borough Hall and committed suicide by taking sawed-off shotgun

Washington Star,
December 21, 1939

and a half away, to inform him that a customer was waiting in the shop. He would then return to the shop, only to leave again when the barbering was completed. If there was a fire or an emergency call, customers were told that it was not known when the barber would return.

The years during which Oakes devoted most of his time and strength to the fire department and the emergency squad were the years of the Great Depression, and Oakes was close to the poverty level. His friends recall that nearly everybody was having financial difficulties, and their own troubles probably blinded them to the fact that "Bab" was having even worse ones. His family was suffering, but he was too proud to ask for help. If there was a truck body to be built, new squad members to train, money to be raised, or blood to be given—all took preference over earning a livelihood.

He was last seen alive four days before Christmas of 1939 by Harry Apgar, patrolman on duty at the square. It was in the early hours of the morning, and he was walking in the direction of the Borough Hall, which housed his beloved emergency truck. This was not unusual for Oakes, even at that hour, and Apgar thought nothing of it. But this time "Bab" entered the hook and ladder truck room and there, where so much of his heart was, ended his own life with a shotgun.

The emergency squad truck, to which he had devoted so much of his time and talent, bore his casket in the funeral procession. The truck was escorted by Washington's volunteer firemen, marching in full uniform. The firemen stood at attention as the body of the founder and first captain of the Washington Emergency Squad was lowered into its grave.

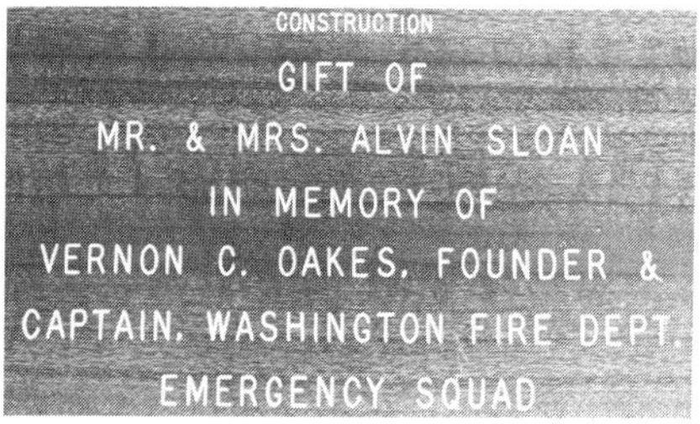

Richard W. York photos

MEMORIAL PLAQUES — *Plaque, top, was placed on emergency truck after the death of Captain Vernon Oakes and has been transferred to each succeeding truck. Oakes' memory is also honored by plaque, bottom, that was placed on the door of the Warren Hospital pharmacy room when the first new building was opened in 1958.*

Minassian photo

***LEST WE FORGET** — Oil painting of Vernon C. "Bab" Oakes presented to the Washington Fire Department at the fire chief's dinner in January 1980. Artist Manuela Slesina Quick, of Hackettstown, was commissioned by former Mayor and Mrs. Alvin Sloan to create the portrait. In photo are, standing, from left: James Burk, of Hackettstown; June Oakes Burk, daughter and only surviving relative of Captain Oakes; and Alvin Sloan, master of ceremonies. Seated: Mrs. Charles Wright and Fire Chief Charles Wright. Portrait, which had just been unveiled, is on wall. It will keep alive the memory of an outstanding example of your fabulous volunteers.*

***AMBULANCE CORPS PIONEER** — Carl E. Gardner, founder and head of the American Legion Ambulance Corps.*

4

Carl E. Gardner, Ambulance Corps Pioneer

The efforts of the emergency squad in performing first aid were paralleled and complemented by a separate ambulance corps which transported patients to the hospital during the early days of rescue services in Washington. Here, too, was a central figure. Carl E. Gardner, born and raised in Washington Township, organized a group of World War I veterans for the purpose in the early 1930's as a project of the local American Legion post. What Vernon C. Oakes was to the emergency squad, Carl E. Gardner was to the ambulance corps.

Gardner served overseas during World War I. He was an ambulance driver in the medical corps and had always been interested in first-aid work even before he went into the army.

Harvey Mowder, late Washington Township clerk and well-known local historian, was one of Gardner's close friends. He recalled many facts about Gardner's war service and his interest in the local ambulance service when he returned from the conflict.

Mowder related that Gardner was awarded the Distinguished Service Cross for his work in France but was reluctant to make the fact known or to talk about it. According to Mowder, Gardner was transporting a wounded colonel back from the front lines in a Model T Ford ambulance when the vehicle was struck by a shell. The explosion disabled the ambulance, but Carl Gardner was not a man to give up easily. With the tool box in hand, he ran to a nearby barbed wire entanglement and cut some of the wire. He repaired the ambulance and drove off, still under fire. He not only saved his own life but that of the colonel as well. It was for this act that he was awarded the medal.

When Gardner returned home, he played an active role in the affairs of the local American Legion post. Since he was a former ambulance driver and had a strong interest in first-aid work, he conceived the idea of providing an ambulance service for the Washington area.

In the middle 1930's Gardner told his fellow Legionnaires they

Minassian photo

AMBULANCE CORPS TRAINER *— Harvey Mowder trained the personnel and handled the finances of the American Legion Ambulance Corps.*

should undertake some project to be of service to the general public. Since his Army experience and personal interest fully qualified him for the work, the idea of an ambulance service appealed to both him and the members of the post. As a result the American Legion Ambulance Corps, Inc., was organized.

The officers were Carl Gardner, president; Charles E. Wright, secretary; and James Ervin, treasurer.

Designated drivers were Carl Gardner, Lester Hann, Philip Huyler, John King, Randal Kries, Ralph Landis, Leroy Schamp, Charles Schuler and Albert Wright.

Other members were Charles Bolz, Archibald Cole, Cummins Dalrymple, Russell Gibson, Maurice Lawyer, Alonzo Lunger, Norman Smith and Charles Tingley.

Harvey Mowder, a member of the American Society of Safety Engineers in charge of first aid at the Edison cement plant in New Village, handled the finances and trained the personnel.

The newly formed ambulance corps got off to a precarious start. The first ambulance to be purchased was a used one and was consigned to the scrap heap after a few weeks of futile repair work. A fresh start was made with the purchase of another used vehicle, a 1927 Cadillac ambulance reputed to have cost $3,600 when new.

The ambulance service became available to the public on May 30, 1936, four weeks before the service of the first aid and rescue squad was inaugurated. The first patient to be transported was Edward Gardner, of Jackson Valley, who was injured in an automobile accident on May 31. Two more calls were received during the first four days of opera-

Minassian photo

AMERICAN LEGION AMBULANCE CORPS IN 1937 — *Sixteen members with 1927 Cadillac. Seated, front row, from left: Ralph Landis, Cummings Dalrymple, Norman Smith, Charles Tingley, Maurice Lawyer and Archibald Cole. Back row: Russell Gibson, Chief of Police Frank Lanning, Captain Carl Gardner, Alonzo Lunger, Charles Bolz and Philip Huyler. Standing: Patrolman Harry Apgar, Harvey Mowder and patrolman Harry Hill. Driver: Lester Hann.*

tion, and eight more were received during the next four weeks.

Earlier in the year, when the firemen and the Legionnaires were ordering equipment and preparing to provide their services, some rivalry developed between them. The borough mayor and council realized the rescue squad would be receiving aid from the municipality because it was part of the fire department and wanted to assist the ambulance corps in the same manner. At the council meeting on May 18, a resolution was passed unanimously which authorized the mayor and borough clerk to execute an agreement with American Legion Post 103. Under its terms the borough would provide space for the ambulance in the Borough Hall; furnish gasoline, oil and grease for the vehicle; maintain liability insurance; and handle ambulance calls through the borough police and fire-dispatching service.

Much to the surprise of borough officials, The Washington Star reported in its issue of June 26 that the offer had been refused by the ambulance corps because its members felt such an agreement would give the borough too much control of the ambulance operation. Persons needing the ambulance were instructed to call the state police barracks. Announcement was also made that the ambulance corps would obtain its own inhalator with the financial assistance of the Red Cross.

Mayor Sloan and Kenneth Cregar, an emergency squad member who became a councilman the following year, talked to Oakes and Gardner in an effort to convince them that the goal of the two organizations should be to provide complementary, rather than competitive, services. The effort succeeded, and the ambulance corps accepted the borough aid and cancelled its order for an inhalator.

The emergency squad and the ambulance corps then worked together, arriving at troubled scenes with the firemen ready to administer first aid and the Legionnaires prepared to provide transportation of the ill or injured victims to the hospital.

The agreement between the borough and the ambulance corps contained a provision for cancellation upon a five-day notice by either party to the other, but it continued in force for nearly 18 years.

In 1943 the old and failing Cadillac ambulance was replaced with a used 1941 model Buick, said to have cost $4,800 when new. By 1950 it, too, was showing signs of wear, and the corps members themselves were succumbing to age. The ambulance service deteriorated with financial troubles hastening its decline.

Gardner was opposed to public fund drives. He wanted the squad to "stand on its own two feet," as he put it. People who were transported in the ambulance were asked for donations. If they donated, it was a help, but if they did not, no demands were made. The corps was always

STEP FORWARD — *This 1941 Buick replaced the old Cadillac in 1943. It became the Community ambulance after the Legion post discontinued service.*

short of funds.

According to the late Reuben Stevens, a longtime Legion member and post commander in the middle 1940's, the post was experiencing hard times, and the ambulance had become so much of a burden that the membership decided to discontinue the venture.

When the post withdrew its support, Gardner reorganized the ambulance service as the "Community Ambulance Squad" and performed satisfactory service for several years. By the early 1950's, however, the service had become less reliable. Emergency squad members would arrive at the scene of an accident, and no ambulance would appear. This meant that the firemen would have to devise means of getting victims to the hospital. As a result friction developed between the two organizations.

On December 1, 1953, the firemen appeared at a borough council meeting and asked permission to raise funds for the purchase of their own ambulance. They reported that the Community Ambulance Squad had repeatedly failed to respond to calls and claimed that it was frequently necessary to transport accident victims to the hospital in the rear of the emergency truck, a vehicle not suited for the purpose. They contended, furthermore, that on occasions when no ambulance driver had responded to calls, qualified firemen had driven the ambulance, only to be told later by Gardner to "leave my property alone," even though the ambulance was kept in a borough building.

Mayor Frederick Suttle, himself a Legionnaire, suggested that a public hearing be held to investigate the matter. The council agreed, and the hearing was held a few nights later with mayor Suttle and Councilmen Clarence H. Ackerson, Robert H. Carlson, Clark C. Cooper, Charles Eagan, Jacob Opdyke and Stuart A. Zimmerman present.

The firemen's position was supported by Elton Wright, the borough dispatcher, who told the council that in one case the ambulance had failed to respond to an emergency call even though it had been summoned by a physician. Councilman Cooper said he also was aware of the lack of cooperation and knew of cases where the ambulance squad had failed to respond to calls.

It was further noted the ambulance, for the first time, was carrying commercial license plates. Councilmen asked why it was no longer entitled to NF (no fee) plates. Gardner replied that there was "too much red tape" involved in obtaining free tags.

After a lengthy and sometimes heated discussion, the council decided to permit the firemen to raise funds and purchase an ambulance in order to provide the needed service. The vote was unanimous.

The firemen immediately purchased a used 1951 model Buick am-

Minassian photos

AMBULANCE OLD-TIMERS *— Two members of the original American Legion Ambulance Corps survive: Lester Hann, left, and Harry Apgar.*

bulance for use until a new Cadillac could be delivered. The Community ambulance was removed from the Borough Hall to Gardner's home. For a while he offered ambulance transportation by appointment. However, this service was soon discontinued.

The firemen placed their ambulance service under the command of the fire chief but left the emergency and rescue service in the charge of the captain and other officers of their emergency squad.

In 1973 the firemen combined the two services, placing the operation of the ambulance in the charge of the emergency squad and its officers. Except for that shift there were no significant organizational changes during the next 25 years.

The firemen provided superb first-aid and ambulance services. Hundreds of thousands of miles were recorded on the odometers of the emergency trucks and ambulances. Aging vehicles were replaced with the finest and most modern ones, and newer and better equipment was constantly being purchased and placed in service.

Nevertheless, despite the troubles of 1953 and the undignified demise of the Community Ambulance Squad, it must be remembered that Carl E. Gardner pioneered the first ambulance service in the Washington area, and that he provided good service for more than 17 years.

At the time Gardner died in 1962 at the age of 67, he was chief of police of Washington Township and truant officer of the township schools. He served the Veterans Administration as service officer in charge of registration of graves. In the volunteer sector, he was a member of the township fire department.

Harvey Mowder remembered him as a very public-spirited citizen who always had the welfare of the community in mind and to which he devoted a liberal share of his time and energy. That opinion is shared by the two surviving members of the original American Legion Ambulance Corps, Harry Apgar and Lester Hann, and others who were active at the time.

Carl E. Gardner was, indeed, a fabulous volunteer.

CARL E. GARDNER

5

The Old-Timers

The author called upon several of the surviving members of the early days of the emergency and ambulance squads to draw upon their memories and recount some of their experiences and observations. Their stories show them to be ordinary people with very full lives and varied interests, but with one added dimension—the compulsion to drop whatever they may be doing in order to help others who are in trouble. This is the quality that brings them together in volunteer fire departments and rescue squads.

Then, as now, calls to major disasters and highway accidents were the most visible to the public and received the newspaper headlines. Actually, however, these calls have always been in the minority. Most calls are to private homes or places of employment and involve household and industrial accidents or major medical problems, such as heart attacks and strokes, which befall individuals. Eighty percent of the calls involve respiratory problems.

Some of the unusual calls to which the firemen responded received national publicity, and many of the volunteers won distinction for long service and selfless devotion to the cause.

Included in the following sketches of the early volunteers are incidents, some amusing, many tragic, as seen by those who were there at the time and played a part in the events. Service in a volunteer rescue unit is arduous, but there are fond memories, cherished friendships, and stories that are told and retold by the old-timers.

As the squad begins its 50th year of service in 1985, two of its charter members survive.

George Hay was one of the original squad members selected from the firemen by "Bab" Oakes in 1936. He came to Washington in 1920 when his family moved from Tobyhanna, Pennsylvania, because of his father's job on the Lackawanna Railroad. George joined the fire department in 1926. He was also a railroader, but he was on furlough in 1936 because of one of the many layoffs of railroad employees caused by the Great Depression. He became a borough patrolman that year.

Minassian photo

OLD-TIMER — *George Hay, charter member of original Washington Fire Department First Aid and Rescue Squad.*

Late in 1937 he left the fire department, the squad and the police department because he had been recalled to his railroad job. He moved to Dover, New Jersey.

Hay is now retired and again a resident of Washington. A great admirer of Oakes, he relates, "I remember 'Bab' Oakes came and talked to us about the first-aid operation. He brought Dr. William Skinner, Dr. Junius Lemmon, and Dr. William H. Varney, who devoted two nights a week teaching us first-aid procedures. The most vivid memory I have of the first-aid squad is 'Bab' Oakes. He was a dedicated man, and what he said was law. He worked to beat hell."

The other survivor of the original 12-man squad is Charles "Buss" Eagan. At the time of his retirement, he held the record for number of years of service in the emergency squad.

A native of Jersey City, Eagan came to Washington at the age of five and has remained until this day. He married Ida Lee, a Washington resident, in 1932 and joined the volunteer fire department the same year.

He was employed by the Borough of Washington in many positions and served as a councilman for seven years from 1947 through 1953. He became superintendent of the borough sewer plant in 1961 and served in that capacity until his retirement in 1980.

He was closely involved with Vernon Oakes in the firemen's first-aid group, which was the nucleus of the emergency squad. He did much work on the construction of the body for the first emergency truck and had a hand in the purchase and equipping of all the emergency trucks since that time.

Eagan retired from active duty in 1976 after serving as a fireman for 44 years and a member of the emergency squad for 40 years. He served as fire chief from 1942 through 1945—an extended term because of the shortage of available men during World War II—and as captain of the squad from 1956 through 1959. His mind is a veritable storehouse of anecdotes and historical information about the emergency squad. He responded to scores of calls to highway accidents, disasters of all descriptions, home accident and medical problems, and assisted police in cleaning up after suicides and murders. He points out, "Many of the unpleasant details are never printed in the newspapers."

Along with his work as a squad member, he frequently served as a dispatcher and as a special policeman. Whether it was fire, police or emergency work, he saw it all.

On March 26, 1942, Eagan answered a call to what was probably the greatest tragedy in which the Washington Emergency Squad has ever assisted. The scene was the Sandt's Eddy plant of the Lehigh Portland Cement Company, across the Delaware River in Pennsylvania. The fact that the Washington, New Jersey, squad was called is an indication of the small number of squads in existence at the time and the great distances between them.

It seems that shortly after workmen had unloaded some twenty tons of dynamite from four trucks, the great explosion occurred. The blast killed 31 workers, but few others were injured since the explosion was confined to the quarry.

The Washington Star reported, "The call for aid was originally made by the Lehigh company to the Edison cement plant at New Village, and at the latter plant Harvey S. Mowder, who is first-aid man there, immediately summoned the borough squad and its well-equipped truck and also the local ambulance. Mowder was picked up at New Village by the ambulance.

"When the squad arrived at the Lehigh quarry, other rescue organizations, including those from Easton and Phillipsburg, had already left the scene and the Washington group was given the task of gathering up the bodies—or parts of bodies—of the men killed in the explosion . . . Only nine of the bodies could be positively identified, while parts of other bodies were scattered over a wide radius. 'We would pick up a head here, an arm there, and then a leg over there' was the way the work was described by one squad member. Photographs of the Washington squad at work gathering up the bodies appeared in many large city dailies."

Eagan recalls, "We got to the scene that morning, and a Pennsylvania trooper stopped us. He told us everyone was dead and that we weren't needed. We decided, since we had been called, we should check into the office anyway. Well, as it turned out, they needed help in recovering bodies. It was a nasty task because all of the victims had been blown to bits. We went along and placed white sheets over bodies and parts of bodies to mark them. Later we saw this same trooper in the area, and he was sick to his stomach. We laughed at him. We worked all day.

"At the end of the day the company sent all of our squad members to the Hotel Easton for dinner. I remember that someone in the kitchen yelled out, 'I know who you guys are and I know where you've been today. All I've got to say is that you must have cast-iron stomachs.' "

The squad members who responded to the Sandt's Eddy call were Douglas Barras, Russell Beam, Walter Castner, Kenneth Cregar, Eagan, Edward Feldman, Vernon Geary, Herman Hassemer, Charles Rupell, Harry Shrope, Wilbur Willis, A. Fletcher Wright and Chief of

Richard W. York photo

HELD RECORD — *Charles "Buss" Eagan served as active squad member for 40 years. When he retired in 1976 he held the record for number of years of active service.*

CAUSE OF EXPLOSION KILLING 31 PUZZLES INVESTIGATORS TODAY

AERIAL VIEW OF DEVASTATED AREA — *Newspaper front page shows Sandt's Eddy explosion scene. Blast shattered windows in Easton and Phillipsburg and rocked buildings as far away as Allentown and Bethlehem, according to news item which accompanied photo in the Easton Morning Free Press on March 27, 1942. White dots on ground are cement sacks used to cover bodies and parts of bodies.*

Police Harry Hill. Recovery operations were directed by Captain Castner and Mowder. Ralph Landis took the American Legion ambulance to the scene but, as there was no use for that vehicle, returned to Washington within an hour in order to be available for the usual local calls.

Newspapers lavished praise on the Washington squadmen for the efficient manner in which they undertook the work, and high compliments were also voiced by officials at the scene. Mayor Joseph Morrison of Easton praised the squad saying, "They did a grand job. I am writing them a letter of praise and congratulations. They pitched in like the well-trained crew they are and handled things in a remarkable manner."

The big problem faced in situations like this is nausea, which can immobilize the most dedicated would-be rescuers. It may be assumed that anyone introduced to the world of the emergency squad would be squeamish at first because the average person does not encounter the repulsive scenes to which squad members are exposed. However, this is only an initial shock, and it ultimately disappears. Otherwise a person would be of little use as a squad member.

Even newspaper reporters, who are normally associated with the coverage of everything from suicides to executions, become immune to the shock of death and gore. But if you talk to anyone involved with law enforcement, rescue work, fire fighting, or news reporting, they will tell you the same story. The initial shock can sometimes be devastating, but death, injury and human suffering can, and must, be assimilated in the long run.

Eagan has many memories of highway accidents involving coal trucks. These tractor-trailer rigs hauled coal from the Scranton, Pennsylvania, area to the cities in those days. Their drivers were known to squadmen and police officers as "coal jockeys," and they seemed to have more than their share of accidents. "We pulled lots of coal trucks apart in those days," Eagan says, "and this was before modern equipment was available to do it. We often had to cut vehicles apart with torches and cover trapped occupants with asbestos blankets while we worked.

"Many of these trucks landed in the yard of Chester and Sadie Creveling on the southwest side of the traffic circle at the intersection of the two state highways in Washington. That was the smallest traffic circle in New Jersey, and it was rather difficult to negotiate. Some trucks coming downgrade couldn't make it at the speed they were going and very often would crash in that yard. The Crevelings had loads of coal, milk, oil, chickens, beer and just about any kind of cargo you can think

UNPLEASANT JOB — *From left: Harry Shrope, unidentified plant worker, Russell Beam, Fletcher Wright, Captain Walter Castner and Wilbur Willis carry body from Sandt's Eddy disaster area.*

of, dumped alongside their residence."

Among the grisly scenes that are etched on Eagan's mind is an accident that occurred just west of Broadway, before the Broadway Rescue Squad was organized. A car hit a bridge abutment and a spoke from the steering wheel broke off and was driven into the driver's chest. "It penetrated his rib cage," Eagen tells. "We had to saw him from the steering wheel, and he talked to us all the while we were doing it."

The man died in the Warren Hospital a few hours later.

Another incident Eagan recalls was an accident on the Brass Castle Road. "Two women in a car were forced to bring their vehicle to a halt. Unfortunately the driver pulled the car to the other side of the road. A second car, travelling in the opposite direction, stopped to assist.

"A third car came down the hill, didn't see the two cars until it was too late, and slammed into the rear of the car that had stopped to assist. One of the women was standing between the first and second cars. When the third car impacted, it shoved the second one into the stalled vehicle. The woman had both of her legs severed.

"On the way to the hospital she asked me for a cigarette and was talking to me like a normal person. A few hours after she was admitted to the hospital, she died of shock."

Although it may seem strange for the Washington Emergency Squad to possess and utilize a motorboat, it has been used extensively through the years, especially before some of the nearby emergency squads were organized, and the Washington squad's territory was much larger and contained more bodies of water.

The boat was used at Mountain Lake to retrieve the body of a drowned fisherman and at the Pequest River in Belvidere to find the body of a young boy who was lost in the depth of the river during a torrent of rain.

Eagan says, "The squad was never particularly successful in reviving drowning victims because if their bodies are not recovered in the first few minutes, efforts are in vain. But we did perform a spectacular water rescue. That was when we retrieved some island dwellers from the Delaware River in the great flood of 1955.

"During that episode the motorboat, operated by Quentin Chambellan, was used to cross the roaring river, somewhere upstream from Belvidere, to reach the island. There were four women there, and they had refused to leave when they had the chance. The river was rising at the rate of three feet each hour, and they became trapped in their homes.

"We reached the island okay, and we loaded the women into the boat. We managed to get across the main part of the river, which was full of trees, limbs and other debris and really moving. Just as we got near the shore, the boat upset and the four women were dumped into about four feet of water.

"Naturally we were embarrassed, but one of them said, 'Don't let that worry you, boys. We've been wet before.' "

Another kind of rescue operation in which the squad is sometimes called upon to participate is the search party. When a person is missing and is thought to be lost in a remote area, police, squad members and other volunteers may join in a thorough search of a wide territory. Sometimes the missing person has been hunting, hiking or involved in some other outdoor activity and has failed to return. Or a child or senile elderly individual may have wandered away.

Such a call was a tragic one in which Eagan participated, and he describes it as follows: "In the early 1950's we received a call from the Mountain Spring Camp on Montana Mountain, near Washington. A small boy was missing. The state police were organizing a search party. We responded with our truck in case the victim was found and needed first aid. We also brought the boat because a child's sock had been found on the bank of a small pond, and there was the possibility that he had drowned. Some of us were assigned the task of dragging the pond, while the police and others began a search of the area with dogs and radios.

"Walter Castner, Donald Sinkway and I were in the boat. We thought we had located the body at the bottom of the pond, but we were unable to recover it. A call was put in for the volunteer firemen from New Village, because they had a very large pumper at the time. They responded and pumped enough water out of the pond so that the level was low enough for us to recover what did turn out to be the body of the boy. It was snared near a platform that was used for swimming by the campers."

The squad members themselves had some close calls. On the way to an accident on Route 31, near the entrance to the Sun Tube Company plant,[1] Eagan recalls: "It was in the middle of the night and foggier'n hell. One car had been rammed in the rear by another. The first caught fire, and one person was killed. We climbed into the truck to answer the call, and when we got to the intersection of the two state highways, which was the old traffic circle, the guy driving our truck took a short-cut across the southbound lane on the northwest side of the circle which, of course, was the wrong way to go.

"Well, there was a coal truck coming down there, and he missed us by about fifteen inches. If that truck would have hit us, we'd have all

[1]The Sun Tube Company became the American Can Company.

SEARCH PARTY — *Volunteers about to begin search for missing boy at the Mountain Spring Camp. Four squad members at extreme right are, from left: Ralph Kinsey, James Count, Elias Johnson and Charles Hubbard.*

been killed in our own accident. How that coal truck driver cleared the rear of our truck, I'll never know.

"The next night we had a meeting, and you can surely guess what happened. The driver, who shall remain nameless, was ousted by a unanimous vote."

An amusing incident occurred one December night. "Squad members participate in local Christmas observances, and we were spraying aluminum paint on some Christmas trees which were to serve as decorations in a forthcoming celebration," Eagan says. "We were doing this outdoors so the paint wouldn't be a problem inside.

"One of our members, Wilbur 'Windy' Willis, came along and saw us spraying the trees. He was all dressed up and didn't want to get involved in the work detail, so he hung back a bit and watched from a distance.

"Well, he didn't notice at the time, and neither did we, that a stiff breeze was carrying the spray paint in his direction. He was wearing a brand new dark suit. When he finally came into the light where he could be seen, his suit was completely covered with a perfect coat of aluminum paint."

One of the three squad members appointed by Captain Oakes to fill vacancies which occurred during the first year of the squad's operation survives. He is Russell P. Beam, who replaced Samuel Vannatta.

Beam recalls that building a body for the first emergency truck was the project of highest priority at the time. For him, as well as other squadmen, it became a very time-consuming job. His wife of 54 years, the former Bernice Bergfels, also remembers it well. She says, "Russ and the other squad members spent all their spare time at the Borough Hall working on the truck."

He served as a squad member for 16 years, from 1937 to 1953, and, like other squadmen of the time, still retains grim memories of the call to the site of the Sandt's Eddy explosion.

A native and longtime resident of Washington, he has always been an active and prominent citizen. An accomplished vocalist, he was a member of the Washington Glee Club, an outstanding male chorus, during its entire existence which covered many years.[1] He worked on the production of the firemen's minstrel shows and was interlocutor of several of them. He was a charter member and longtime secretary of the Washington Rotary Club.

Beam served as the borough civil defense director during World War II. He was elected to a seat on the borough council, on which he served

[1]Vernon Oakes was also a member of the Washington Glee Club.

Richard E. Harpster photo

FORMER MAYOR — *Old-timer Russell P. Beam is one of three squad members who became mayors of Washington.*

from 1958 through 1961. Under the old form of government, each councilman headed one or more departments. During his first year he was in charge of sidewalks and lights, and then for three years he headed the very important finance committee.

During the first year of his second term he was elected mayor, one of three squad members—the others were Edward Strohl and Joseph LaPrino—who have become mayors. Beam served in that position for two terms, from 1962 through 1965.

While an active fireman he was elected lieutenant of the fire department, but when he became in line for the chief's job, he turned it down, "because I felt it had too many responsibilities for me at that time," he explains.

He did not shun additional responsibilities when he became mayor, however, and provided excellent leadership during one of the borough's most trying years. In 1963 a disastrous fire—one of the biggest in the history of Warren County—wiped out the portion of the business section on the south side of East Washington Avenue from Broad Street to the H. A. Cohen's Sons store. The fire started in Murphy's variety store late in the afternoon and burned all night before it was brought under control.

"I was painting the porch of our summer place at Mountain Lake when my mother called and told me it looked like the whole town was burning. I came back to Washington and found she was almost right," Beam recalls.

"Naturally, all kinds of problems developed through the night as the fire burned, and firemen from nearby communities helped in the fight. One section of town was blacked out, so the New Jersey Power & Light Company brought in a transformer on a truck. They were able to provide power to the blacked-out area very quickly. As I recall, the section without power included East Washington Avenue, Youmans Avenue, Broad Street, Vannatta Street and Park Avenue," says the former mayor.

"The firemen were using so much water the supply began to dwindle. Edward Feldman, a fireman who was manager of the Washington Water Company, went up to the reservoir on Montana Mountain and opened the main valve all the way. Normally it was kept half open.

"We had a 3 A.M. meeting of the council while the fire was still burning.

"I remember we supplied all the out-of-town fire trucks with gasoline, and would you believe, I was criticized by some people for that? It had always been our custom to not only provide gasoline to the visitors while pumping, but to provide each out-of-town truck with a full tank

DISASTROUS FIRE — *This fire, one of the biggest in Warren County history, destroyed an important section of Washington's business area in 1963. It also created headaches for Mayor Beam and other borough officials.*

of gasoline when it left,'' Beam says.

Later it was his responsibility to get rid of the rubble, and this included knocking down two buildings which had been destroyed by the fire but had not collapsed during the night. One of them fell a day or two later while its owner was arguing with the mayor for authorization to enter the tottering structure to check his safe. The second building, which stood at the corner of Washington Avenue and Broad Street, had to be razed, but it took several days of negotiating between the owner and Borough Attorney Edward Stover and Mayor Beam.

''Then the FBI came to check on the amount of drugs that had been destroyed in the drug stores and how much had been saved,'' Beam recalls. ''There were insurance men from all over who needed information. The business people wanted to rebuild as soon as they could.

''Congressman William B. Widnall (now deceased), who represented our district at that time, brought personnel from the Small Business Administration for a meeting with local business people.

''It was my idea to reconstruct the entire side of the street with antique and quaint-type store fronts, much like Fliegauf's jewelry store appears today. However, I was overruled, and each businessman decided to rebuild to his own likes,'' Beam says.

For 38 years Beam lived in a home he designed and had built on State Street in Washington. Shortly after his marriage in 1931, he purchased the old E. E. Wyckoff market, which was located where the Belvidere Avenue entrance to the First Fidelity Bank is currently situated. Later he worked for Ingersoll-Rand Company, after which he served as a laboratory technician for Consumers' Research for 18 years. For a time he was with the advertising department of the Washington Star, a prize-winning weekly newspaper. He then became plant manager of Fairfield Linens and retired from that position in 1976 when the company ceased operations.

Beam is now 74 years old, and he and Bernice have been residents of Mansfield Township for the past 17 years. Bernice is a longtime member of the fire department's ladies auxiliary in which she served terms as secretary and treasurer.

Of the four members appointed by Mayor Sloan in December 1937 in order to bring the membership up to its newly authorized strength of 16, two are still living.

Joseph Alden Marlatt was the third man drafted into the armed forces from Washington Borough—the first was William Petty and the second was Raymond ''Bucky'' Major—just prior to the beginning of World War II. Marlatt was already a veteran member of the Washing-

Richard E. Harpster photo

APPOINTED TO SQUAD IN 1937 — *Joseph Alden Marlatt is now with the Hunterdon County Sheriff Department.*

ton Emergency Squad.

Now a 69-year-old resident of the East Amwell Township village of Ringoes, he is an employee of the Hunterdon County Sheriff Department.

"Al" — as he is best known among his acquaintances — is a native of Washington.

Prior to his induction Marlatt was manager of the Washington Grand Union market when it was located across the street from the Ford furniture store.

He entered the Army in February 1941. His first assignment was in Fort Benning, Georgia, where he was an instructor in the officers' training school. He spent five years in the service and participated in seven combat missions with the 82nd Airborne Paratroop Division in Europe. He was honorably discharged as a first sergeant in November 1945.

After returning from the military he went back to his old job, but at a different location. The Grand Union had moved to Belvidere Avenue where the Quick-Chek store is now situated.

He left Grand Union to become a correction officer at the old Annandale Reformatory, now known as the Youth Correctional Institution. He retired from Annandale in 1971 and has been with the Hunterdon County Sheriff Department ever since.

Marlatt joined the Washington Fire Department and the emergency squad in 1937. He remembers fighting the Farrell Arms Plaza Hotel fire that destroyed the structure, located on the southeast corner of West Washington and South Lincoln Avenues.[1]

Marlatt served as a fireman and a squadman for nearly 10 years. His first wife, Gloria Costanzo Marlatt, a native of Bayonne, New Jersey, was a member of the fire department's ladies auxiliary. She died in 1964.

Marlatt was a charter member of the Veterans of Foreign Wars post in Washington and recalls when it was organized shortly after World War II at Mount's Restaurant on what is now Route 57, west of the borough.[2] He is now a member of the Flemington American Legion and VFW posts.

His second wife, Mala Sutphin Marlatt, of Wertsville in Hunterdon County, died in 1977. Marlatt now resides in Ringoes, New Jersey.

---

[1]The building had originally been part of the Cornish piano and organ factory. A Krauszer food store now stands on that lot.

[2]Mount's Restaurant later became Altieri's and was destroyed by fire in the late 1940's.

The other surviving appointee of Mayor Sloan is A. Fletcher Wright. He is an honorary member of the squad and is still answering calls after 48 years of service.

Members of the Wright family have played an important part in the fire and emergency services in Washington. They have a combined service record of more than 175 years. Forty-eight of those years have been contributed by Fletcher who, along with his brother Charles and his nephew Jeffrey, is still active.

Charles served as fire chief in 1980-81 and is now fire marshal of Warren County. He is known throughout the state as a competent instructor at the Warren County Fire Academy. Charles' son, Jeffrey, is a member of Washington Truck Company No. 2. Elton, the late father of Fletcher and Charles, was a fireman and the first full-time dispatcher in the borough. He worked for many years — sometimes 16 hours a day — in the old Borough Hall across the street from the post office on Belvidere Avenue. Fletcher's brother, William, and his uncles, Albert (known as "Abbie") and Harry, were also Washington firemen. "Abbie" was a driver of the American Legion ambulance.

Fletcher joined the fire department in 1937 and immediately became a squad member. Captain Oakes wanted him because he was chairman of the Red Cross first-aid organization and held a certificate as an instructor.

Now 69 years of age, he has been active in the squad longer than any other person, living or dead. In 1977 he broke the 40-year length-of-service record held by Charles Eagan, and he may still be seen running toward the firehouse or squad building when the whistle blows and taking the wheel of the emergency truck or an ambulance as a driver.

Despite his long tenure on the squad, Wright was never an officer because, when the time came for him to assume those duties in 1952, it was also his turn to be fire chief. He served in that position through 1953.

Nevertheless, he has figured prominently in the history of the squad. Near the end of his term as fire chief in 1953, Wright was instrumental in the establishment of the ambulance service in the fire department, and he was in charge of the fund drive which raised the money to purchase the squad's first ambulance. Letters were sent to several neighboring municipalities as well as to borough residents because there were few other squads in those days.

During his years as a fireman and a squad member, Wright has seen many changes and has participated in scores of dramatic fires and rescue situations. He answered the call to Sandt's Eddy, Pennsylvania. He recalls the Matlock accident on Route 31 north of Washington in

Richard W. York photo

SET NEW SERVICE RECORD — *A. Fletcher Wright broke the 40-year service record held by Charles Eagan in 1976. Wright, still active, is serving in 1985 — his 48th year.*

FIREMEN'S TEMPORARY AMBULANCE — *When the Washington Fire Department replaced the Community Ambulance Squad in 1954, this 1951 Buick was purchased to provide service until a new Cadillac could be delivered. The immediate past chief of the department, A. Fletcher Wright, left, is shown with Chief John Riegel in front of old Borough Hall.*

1953 in which 10 people in one car were killed. He has vivid memories of the many big fires he has fought both within and beyond the borough boundaries.

A native of Newark, Wright moved to Washington in 1922 and married the former Emma Keenan in 1936. When he first became a fireman, he was employed by the Washington Porcelain Company, located off South Wandling Avenue along the railroad. This company, like many other employers at the time, permitted its workers who were firemen or squadmen to leave work to answer calls. The company did not dock their pay, thereby—in effect—contributing to the work of the volunteer services.

During World War II Wright served in the U.S. Navy from 1943 to 1946. He taught first aid to recruits at the service school in Farragut, Idaho. Upon his return he took a position in the Washington post office as a clerk-carrier. He was later promoted to superintendent of mails. In 1976 he was transferred to the Budd Lake post office where he was supervisor of postal operations.

Wright's life, replete with voluntary public service, includes membership on the Washington Board of Education for the 19 years from 1951 to 1970. Emma is a longtime member of the fire department's ladies auxiliary and served as one of its financial officers.

The Wrights reside in Washington.

The first squad log book shows that six replacement members were appointed during the next five years. They were Harry Apgar, Douglas Barras, Vernon Geary, Herman Hassemer, Harry Shrope and Barney Sinkway. Apgar and Hassemer survive.

The history of Washington from the 1930's through the 1960's cannot be told without the story of Harry Apgar, who served as police chief, fire chief, and longtime member of the emergency squad.

Apgar, now 79 years of age, was born in Port Colden in 1906 and was raised by his grandfather, the late Whitfield Thomas. He began life as a poor boy, as did many in those early years. While a pupil in the Port Colden school, he was employed sewing brooms in the old Port Colden broom factory. From this humble beginning he progressed to become one of the most respected police chiefs in this area of New Jersey.

His first full-time job was in the old Port Murray brick yard where he worked until becoming a lineman for the former New Jersey Power and Light Company, now the Jersey Central Power and Light Company. After 12 years the Great Depression forced the company to cut back its personnel, and Apgar lost his job.

In 1937, when the late Frank Lanning was police chief, Mayor Alvin

Richard W. York photo

FORMER CHIEF OF POLICE — *Harry Apgar was an early member of the American Legion Ambulance Corps and later served in the fire department and emergency squad from 1941 to 1962.*

Sloan appointed Apgar as a patrolman in the Washington police force.

He was appointed chief of the department on May 2, 1961, during the tenure of Mayor Richard Timke, succeeding the late Harry Hill. Apgar retired June 1, 1964, after 27 years of police service.

"I would say the hit-run killing of Fred Glosser on the old Washington traffic circle was one of the most memorable cases I investigated during my tenure as chief," Apgar recalls.

A careening pickup truck struck young Glosser as he was standing on the circle's sidewalk. Several weeks of intensive police work by Apgar, Robert Sloss, a state trooper who was Warren County Traffic Coordinator, and the late Joseph Skelly, Warren County Detective, led them to Abbington, Pennsylvania, where they arrested a suspect who was found guilty in Warren County and sentenced to a jail term.

In 1943 Apgar took time off from his job as a policeman to join the U.S. Navy during World War II. He served in the Seabees and, for the most part, was stationed on Wallace Island, just off the coast of California. His job was to guard Japanese prisoners of war being transferred to the mainland. He returned home in 1945 and assumed his prior position in the police department.

Following his police career he worked nine years for the Coca-Cola Bottling Company as a maintenance man. For many years he also operated a part-time tree service which specialized in removing trees.

When the American Legion Ambulance Corps was organized in 1936, its founder, Carl E. Gardner, appointed all borough policemen as members, so when Apgar became a patrolman in 1937 he also became a member of the ambulance corps. He joined the fire department the same year and was assigned to Washington Steamer Company No. 1.

Apgar was a close friend of Vernon "Bab" Oakes, emergency squad captain. Like many other firemen, he assisted the squad on calls while awaiting a vacancy from his fire company that would open the way for him to become an active member of the squad. That opportunity came in 1941 when Alden Marlatt entered the army. Apgar served in the fire department and the squad until retiring in 1962.

He served as fire chief in 1946 and 1947 and is a past master of Mansfield Lodge No. 36, F. & A. M., of Washington, where he has been a member for 56 years.

Apgar was married in 1928 to Ruby Castner, of Changewater. Ruby is a member of the fire department's ladies auxiliary and served as its president for the 1940-41 term. The couple reside in Washington.

Herman Hassemer, 82, is a former fireman and emergency squad member who retains rich memories of his volunteer services, although

Richard E. Harpster photo

REMEMBERS WASHINGTON — *Herman Hassemer, now a resident of Milton, Delaware, has memories of service in the fire department and emergency squad.*

he left Washington 35 years ago.

Hassemer was born in Newark, New Jersey, and the family moved to Changewater when he was a boy. He attended the old one-room schoolhouse for two years until his family moved to East Church Street in Washington. His father was a carpenter who was later employed in the Cornish piano and organ factory.

He attended the Washington grammar school but quit in the eighth grade to work in the Johnson hardware store during the week and the Candy Kitchen on weekends. Later he got a job at the Washington Brass Foundry, operated by Richard Cochran on Willow Street, where he worked until 1919. He left that employment to become a knitter in the Pohatcong Hosiery Mill.

In 1927 he married Elsie Pauline Kreth, of Brooklyn, New York.

He joined the Phillipsburg Elks lodge in 1925 and is still a member of the Washington lodge.

In 1930 he joined the Washington Fire Department where he became a member of Washington Truck Company No. 2, which he served as secretary for many years. His brother, Frank, mentioned elsewhere in this book, is the oldest living ex-chief of the Washington Fire Department.

One of Hassemer's fondest memories is of the old horse-drawn American LaFrance steam pumper. The pumper was lost when the borough donated the relic to a scrap drive during World War II, which was a very popular thing to do during that era.

"I remember fighting the Farrell Arms Plaza Hotel fire in 1935. The steamer pumped water from the Shabbecong Creek at the bridge on South Lincoln Avenue to the trucks on West Washington Avenue," Hassemer says. "I think that was the last time the steamer was used."

He has vivid memories of the fire at the First National Bank building at the corner of West Washington and Belvidere Avenues in 1939. "I was up a ladder fighting the fire with a hose when the truck to which the hose was connected started to move down the street. It pulled the ladder sideways along the front of the building. I yelled, but at first nobody heard me. Finally, a couple of firemen on the ground saw what was happening and began yelling for the truck to stop. It was a close call," he says.

Hassemer has a collection of photos of the bank building fire and many of the old steam pumper.

He fought a big fire in Hackettstown to which Washington firemen were called for mutual aid. The blaze was caused by a powder plant explosion during World War II. He was also on hand to fight the fire that destroyed the old mill in Changewater.

Hassemer recalls many occasions during the Great Depression when fire department finances were depleted. In order to keep the department out of the red, he was instrumental in creating an honorary contributing membership. Friends of the fire department could be members by contributing a dollar each year. There were as many as 50 contributing members at one time, and the resulting $50 in revenue was a considerable amount in those days, he recalls.

He was the head of the committee that put on summer carnivals to raise funds. In 1933 "Bab" Oakes suggested that a 50th anniversary minstrel show would help the finances, and Hassemer headed the committee that took charge of that project. Oakes directed the show. Hassemer says, "I still have a copy of the program of that show, and at times I get it out and read over the names of those who took part in it. These are fond memories!"

Hassemer was a fireman when "Bab" Oakes directed the first-aid work which ultimately led to the creation of the Washington Emergency Squad. He was an admirer of Oakes and the rescue squad, and he waited patiently for five years until 1941 to join. In that year the resignation of Randall Kries created a squad vacancy in Washington Truck Company No. 2 and made it possible for Hassemer to become a squad member.

He served in the fire department for nearly 20 years until he and Elsie moved to Delaware in 1950. During his years of service he became secretary of his company, and he became president of the Warren County Firemen's Association during World War II. Elsie was a member of the fire department's ladies auxiliary and served as its president for the 1941-42 and 1942-43 terms.

The Hassemers now live in an attractive country home at the edge of Milton, Delaware, where Elsie works with retarded children as a foster grandparent.

There are other old-timers who compiled long records of service. One of them is Melvin "Mel" Burd. He was born in Harmony and moved to Washington at the age of four. At 21 he joined the fire department, serving for 30 years. He was an emergency squadman for 28 of those years, having joined that group as soon as he was eligible. He retired from the service in 1967. Before the firemen acquired their ambulance, Burd served on the American Legion and Community ambulances along with his duties as a fireman. He was fire chief in 1962 and 1963.[1] He resides in Washington with his wife, the former Madge Kinneyman,

---

[1]Melvin Burd was fire chief when the big fire occurred in Washington's business section in 1963.

whom he married in 1972. Madge has served in the fire department's ladies auxiliary since that time.[1] Among hundreds of calls answered by Burd is the following, which is one of the most vivid in his memory.

It was a balmy Friday evening and the date was March 20, 1953. Washington firemen were backstage at the Taylor Street school auditorium. The time was 7:30 P.M. In a half hour the curtain would rise, and the annual fund-raising home-talent minstrel show would be under way. ''Mel'' was in a skelton standby crew set up by the emergency squad in case a call came in during the show.

The show went on as scheduled but with an abbreviated cast. An urgent message was relayed to the emergency squad by the dispatcher at the Borough Hall, a block away. The squad was about to respond to one of the most tragic highway accidents of all time; one that attracted statewide and national attention.

Unfortunately, squad members were able to offer little, if any, aid to the victims of the car-truck crash which took ten lives on what is now Route 31 in Mansfield Township. The accident, which wiped out an entire Hope Township family, for a time was the worst traffic accident involving a private car in the annals of the National Safety Council. (Some years later a car went off a cliff in West Virginia, killing eleven of its occupants, thereby breaking the tragic record set in Warren County.)

When squad members reached the scene, they were confronted with one of the most grisly prospects they had ever encountered. A tractor-trailer had collided head-on with a car. The car was occupied by ten people, five adults and five children. All but two were dead.

The already dead included Mrs. Elizabeth Matlock, a 75-year-old widow; Clarence Matlock, 32, her son and driver of the car; Mrs. Alma VanCamp Matlock, 29, Clarence's wife; and three of the Matlock children, Esther, 10, Joan, 4, and Clarence, Jr., 1. Also dead were Miss Mary Matlock, 50, and Miss Grace Matlock, 48, daughters of Mrs. Elizabeth Matlock and aunts of the children.

Two other Matlock children, Rosemary, 2, and Raymond, 8, were barely alive. Rosemary died in Burd's arms while being carried to the ambulance. As Raymond was being placed in the ambulance he said, ''Please don't hurt me, mister.'' He died five hours later in the Warren Hospital on his eighth birthday.

The Washington Emergency Squad has never been called to the scene of a more lethal traffic accident. Hopefully it never will be.

The funeral of the ten Matlock family members attracted thousands

---

[1]Melvin Burd's first wife, the former Thelma Maginnis, now Thelma Vincent, was president of the fire department's ladies auxiliary for the 1948-49 term.

Minassian photo

***RECALLS WORST ACCIDENT** — Melvin "Mel" Burd answered call to the Matlock tragedy.*

of people to Washington. They overflowed into the streets from the DeVoe Funeral Home on West Washington Avenue. During the service, conducted by Rev. Kenneth Ballard of the Blairstown Presbyterian Church, people stood and watched from the sidewalks, nearby porches, windows and parked cars. Business came to a standstill as the funeral procession formed along Washington Avenue. Many people lined the highway in their parked cars to catch a glimpse of the long cortege as it wound its way up Route 30 (now Route 31) past the site where the ten were killed. Many followed the seven hearses bearing the ten bodies of the Matlock family to cemeteries at Hope and Blairstown in a pouring rain.

There was national newspaper coverage of the unusual funeral, including a picture of a bewildered dog, the Matlocks' fox terrier, sitting in front of the unoccupied residence waiting for the family that never returned.

Volunteers who give so much of themselves to save lives endangered in accidents are interested in how accidents occur and can be prevented. The Matlock tragedy inflamed public opinion, and none in Washington followed the ensuing proceedings more closely than the volunteers. As frequently happens in collisions of such unequal vehicles, the driver of the northbound truck, John Scarantino, 21, of Scranton, Pennsylvania, and a passenger with him, Lawrence Butler, 30, of Dunmore, Pennsylvania, both escaped injury.

At the scene Butler claimed that a coal truck ahead of them suddenly slowed and pulled to the right shoulder, just as the Matlock car was seen coming from the opposite direction going 60 miles an hour and straddling the center line. Unfortunately for the alibi, the driver of a coal truck Sarantino was passing—Walter E. Burger of East Stroudsburg, Pennsylvania—said Scarantino was in such a hurry that he chose to pass on an upgrade and on a curve as well. According to Burger, the Matlock car was entirely in its own lane.

Any doubt about who was telling the truth appeared to be cleared up when it was disclosed that Scarantino's license to drive a truck had been revoked some time before for failure to appear at a hearing to answer a summons for illegally passing on another curve, on another grade, and in the face of oncoming traffic on Kingstown Mountain, near Netcong, New Jersey.

On April 7 Scarantino was found guilty of two motor vehicle violations in the municipal court. Magistrate Arthur Alexander fined him $600 and ordered a 120-day jail sentence, the maximum under the law, as recommended by Warren County Prosecutor John Pursel. Before the sentence could take effect, Scarantino went on trial for man-

TEN DIED — *Remains of Matlock car after head-on collision with truck.*

slaughter in the Warren County Court in Belvidere. On the second day of the trial he changed his plea to guilty and Superior Court Judge Joseph L. Smith sentenced him to serve two to three years in Bordentown Reformatory. Since no sentence could bring any of the victims back to life, the volunteers could only hope that the notoriety of the trial would encourage safer driving.

One of the Washington Emergency Squad's most dedicated members was Anthony "Tony" Damelio. Tony was interviewed for the first edition of this book and died four years later.

A native of Washington, Tony was born in 1903. He worked in Netcong at the Gallo Sand and Gravel Company for twelve years but returned to Washington in 1939 to work for the Ingersoll-Rand Company and later at the Washington Auto Parts as a machinist.

On a January night in 1940, Tony, who lived near the firehouse, received a call from Elton "Elt" Wright, who was the police dispatcher at the time. The American Legion ambulance lacked a driver. "It was colder'n blue blazes," recalled Tony. "He asked me to help with an ambulance call. I remember that 'Toppy' Castner (Walter Castner) and I took a woman from the old Windsor Hotel. (The hotel was located at the corner of Belvidere Avenue and East Church Street, where the Municipal Building is now situated.) I was more scared than the patient."

That was the beginning of a long ambulance driving career for Tony. There is no doubt that he drove ambulances more and farther than anyone else who has served to date. In some years he answered more than 400 calls, and his total number was well up into the thousands. He transported patients as far as New York City, Philadelphia, Elmira and Boston.

Most people in Washington know that for many years Tony was at the wheels of the ambulances more than any other driver, but not so many of them know about the other volunteer work he did during all of those years or some of the personal sacrifices he made.

"My father told me that if you can't go out of your way to do something for somebody else, then there ain't much use in living," Damelio said.

He lived by that philosophy. For many years when he would leave his job in response to the emergency whistle, his pay was docked for the time he was absent from work. He was well known as an amateur chef, and through the years he prepared food for fund-raising banquets of civic organizations, donating his services.

For many years he was in charge of the emergency squad's program

Richard W. York photo

***HIS FAVORITE VEHICLE** — Anthony "Tony" Damelio drove ambulances in Washington for more than 40 years. He gave them and their passengers tender care.*

to provide hospital equipment, including beds, wheelchairs and crutches, to people who could not afford to buy their own. For more than a decade Tony borrowed and begged parts for this equipment to keep it in proper working order, even though it wasn't always appreciated.

"I remember seeing some people give our wheelchairs to their kids to play with. They used them to ride down hills and that really made me mad," Tony said.

In 1967 the Moose lodge took over this service, and Tony, a brother Moose, continued the program for the lodge.

For several years he served as a school-crossing guard, and many a deprived youngster was taken into a downtown store and given a pair of warm mittens on a cold winter day, or a pair of rubbers to keep his feet warm and dry. Many more were taken to the old Baylor's Restaurant for a glass of milk. Tony, of course, paid for these items out of his own pocket.

Tony drove ambulances in Washington for 38 years. During the last 24 years of that time, he was an auxiliary member of the Washington Emergency Squad. Before the fire department had an ambulance service, he had already compiled a long record of service with Carl Gardner in the American Legion and Community ambulance squads, but he was too old to join the fire department as a regular member. That accounted for his auxiliary status in the fire-department organization.

Tony had many fond memories of his career as an ambulance driver, and a few he'd like to have forgotten too. The day somebody stole the ambulance is one of the latter, and one that he remembered most.

" 'Art' Vega (Arthur Vega, late sergeant of the Washington Police Department) and I took a patient to Warren Hospital. 'Art' went upstairs and I was busy with the patient," Tony recalled. "I took the litter out to the ambulance and it was gone.

"I always played a lot of tricks on the guys, and I thought it was a joke. But finally I called the police. I was really mad. I knew there were a lot of people in Washington depending on that ambulance.

"The police came, and this one cop asked me for the license number. I yelled at him saying, if you can't find a big red ambulance with the name Washington Fire Department painted all over it, how in the hell are you going to find a license plate? He told me to shut up or he'd lock me up. I'll tell you, I was one hot Italian that day!"

The ambulance was soon recovered. It had been stolen by a mental patient who drove it to Washington and was making a return trip to Phillipsburg when caught by the police.

"Not one little dent in it either, thank God," Damelio said.

Not everyone has respect for ambulances. Tony remembered once, when the borough police car was providing him with an escort out of town, a car pulled out of Belvidere Avenue right in front of the ambulance as it was proceeding toward Warren Hospital.

"I got the license number and found out the driver's name," Tony recalled. "I caught up with him one day and told him I didn't appreciate his driving habits. He told me in no uncertain terms that he had the green light and that he intended to use his right-of-way. I told him, kiddingly of course, that someday he might need the ambulance and that we might remember what he did.

"Well, a couple of months later we got a call that a man had collapsed on the main street. When I got there it was him—the guy who had pulled in front of me at the intersection. He looked up and saw me and said he was sorry and asked if we would please take him to the hospital. We did, of course, but I'll bet he'll think twice about cutting off another ambulance."

A somewhat similar incident occurred when Tony was on his way to the hospital with another patient. He got behind a slow moving car which refused to pull aside and permit the ambulance to pass.

"It was a woman, and I had to follow her for about five miles. Finally around New Village she pulled over, and as I passed she thumbed her nose at me. I just laughed," said Tony.

In 1976 one of the biggest banquets ever given at the Firemen's Hall in the Municipal Building was held in Tony's honor. It was a big night for him, and his friends would not have missed it for the world. They were honoring a man who was small in physical stature but with one of the biggest hearts around.

In January of 1978 Tony's hundreds of friends were stunned to learn that he was in an Allentown hospital undergoing serious surgery. For months after that it was touch and go for him. His weight dropped to below 100 pounds, and there was much concern for his survival. It took about a year, but he recovered.

"No, I'm not going to drive the ambulance any more. I've got a perfect safety record and I want to retire with that record behind me," he said. Despite his thousands of hours behind the wheels of the ambulances and the untold number of miles he covered, he had never been involved in an accident.

Tony lived five more years. According to a daughter, Joyce Damelio Lisk, of Washington, he enjoyed the last years of his life and never stopped giving people a helping hand whenever he could. He lived alone, his wife, Bessie Denmark Damelio, having died in 1975.

The dispatchers and the many citizens who listen to police, fire and emergency calls on scanners will never forget the message Tony gave thousands of times upon returning from emergency calls, "Open door one for little Tony, please."

Not so many people could keep up with Joseph A. Eger who, at the age of 74, had been driving the ambulances and other emergency-squad vehicles for 40 years and was also active in business, sports and the Boy Scouts of America.

On the morning of Wednesday, May 1, 1985, Eger drove an ambulance on a transportation call, as he had done thousands of times before, returned the ambulance to the squad building, and went home.

The next call received by the Washington Emergency Squad came late that afternoon. It was from the Eger residence. The squad responded. Upon arrival at the scene the squad members were at once shocked and saddened. Joe Eger had suffered a heart attack and had passed away.

Born in Orange, Eger moved to West Portal when he was two years old. He attended school there and in Pattenburg and then traveled to Hampton High School by train.

"I walked from the top of Jugtown Mountain down to the village of West Portal and caught the east-bound train every morning for school. It was a flag stop, and you had to hang out the flag so the train would stop. I got off at the Hampton station and walked to the high school," Eger said.

He never finished high school, however, because his father died, and he quit school to go to work. His first job was with the signal crews of the Lehigh Valley Railroad. He later moved to Washington, where he lived with his sister, Marie Wildrick, who currently resides on Broad Street. His first job in Washington was in the old silk mill on Railroad Avenue.

In 1933 Eger went to work washing cars for Smith Motor Company. A few years later he become parts manager. He worked there until 1955 and then bought a share of the S.E.A. Automotive Distributers, where he remained until retiring in 1979. By the time he retired he was sole owner of the auto parts business. His son, Jeffrey, now owns and operates the company.

During the 1930's Eger played baseball for the West Portal and Asbury teams as a pitcher. After he moved to Washington he pitched for the Broadway White Sox. He was also an avid bowler in the Bi-State Traveling League. During the height of his bowling career, he bowled 975 consecutive games, missing only three Friday night bowling matches in 31 years.

Richard W. York photo

ANOTHER MEMBER WITH 40 YEARS OF ACTIVE SERVICE — *The late Joseph A. Eger served the community in the fire department, the emergency squad, and the George Washington Council, Boy Scouts of America.*

In 1957, when Jeffrey was seven years old, Eger became interested in the Boy Scouts of America. He was appointed to the transportation committee of the organization. He was very active and received a special award for his work when the scout camp was moved from Pahaquarry Township to Yards Creek. In 1973 he received the Silver Beaver, the highest award given by the organization to an unpaid staff member. In 1978 he became a member of the executive board of the George Washington Council, the organization division that covers this area of New Jersey. In 1983 he became chairman of the "bowlathon" fund-raising activity. At the time of his demise, he was still active in scouting and still a member of the executive board of the council.

Eger joined the Washington Fire Department in May 1945 and became exempt in January 1956. He was a member of the emergency squad during those years and served as president of the squad in 1949. He was also president of Washington Truck Company No. 2 during the same year. In 1954 he became lieutenant of the squad and served in that position for two years.

"I have no idea how many squad or ambulance calls I have answered," said Eger, "but someone once calculated that I have responded to at least 100 ambulance calls per year. That would add up to about 4,000 calls. I still drive the ambulance, but mostly for transportation calls now."

Eger drove squad vehicles for 40 years without an accident. He traveled to Allentown, Baltimore, New York, Philadelphia, the U.S. Veterans Hospital in Orange, and many other destinations on the transportation calls.

He resided in Washington with his wife, the former Dorothy Elizabeth Bowne. They were married in 1936. Dorothy is a longtime member of the fire department's ladies auxiliary and served as its vice-president.

William "Bill" Allen was born in Mountain Lake 68 years ago and was raised in Belvidere. He graduated from Belvidere High School and for a time was employed in a grocery store in that town. He came to Washington in 1938.

In 1941 he entered the United States Army Air Corps and served until February of 1946. He was stationed in Texas, Arizona and California.

For 25 years he was a supervisor in the New Jersey motor vehicle inspection service, from which he retired in 1979. During his tenure he was assigned to inspection stations in Somerville, Plainfield, New Brunswick and Flemington.

He is a life member of the American Legion post in Washington and

Richard W. York photo

LONGTIME SECRETARY — *William "Bill" Allen served in the fire department for 25 years and was secretary of the ambulance service until it was combined with the emergency squad in 1973.*

a member of Mansfield Lodge No. 36, F. & A.M.

Allen joined the Washington Fire Department in 1948 and served actively for 25 years. He was one of the firemen who worked to establish the ambulance service in the fire department. The effort succeeded in December 1953 when the borough council approved the project. He served as secretary of the ambulance service until it was combined with the emergency squad in 1973.

Allen's first wife, the former Marian Slater, died in 1968.[1] In 1970 he married the former Miriam Smith Newton. Miriam is a member of the fire department's ladies auxiliary. The Allens reside in Washington.

Many members of the present Washington Emergency Squad will be remembered in the future for outstanding service extending far beyond the usual call of duty. They uphold the tradition of those described in the preceding pages. They are super volunteers, and one of them is an old-timer, William E. Brewster.

Brewster is a sergeant in the borough police department and has spent much of his leisure time in volunteer work.

Had he listened to some of his relatives, he might be earning his living as a coal miner in West Virginia where many of them were miners. When he was a youngster, Brewster's parents moved numerous times. He recalls attending 13 different schools in 12 years.

In 1945 the family moved to West Virginia, his mother's native state. In 1951 he joined the navy and spent the next four years in the Caribbean theater of operations. When he came home, the coal mines were closing and the railroads were cutting back employment. However, an uncle told Brewster he could get him a job in the mines. He took him to the mines to decide for himself if he wanted the job. "I left after four hours determined that I would rather starve than be a coal miner," Brewster says.

Since his great-grandfather, on his father's side, had settled in Washington many years before and built a home on Route 57 across from the Acme Market, Brewster and his family decided to try their luck in Washington. In 1955 they came north and Brewster had no problem securing employment. His first job was at the old Tung-Sol plant on Park Avenue where he met the girl who was to become his wife, Rosemarie Heater.

He joined the Washington Fire Department in 1963 and later became a member of its emergency squad. When he became an exempt fireman in 1983, he was one of four men who were active members of both the fire department and the squad. (The other three were Steven Alpaugh,

---

[1]Marian Slater Allen was secretary of the fire department's ladies auxiliary.

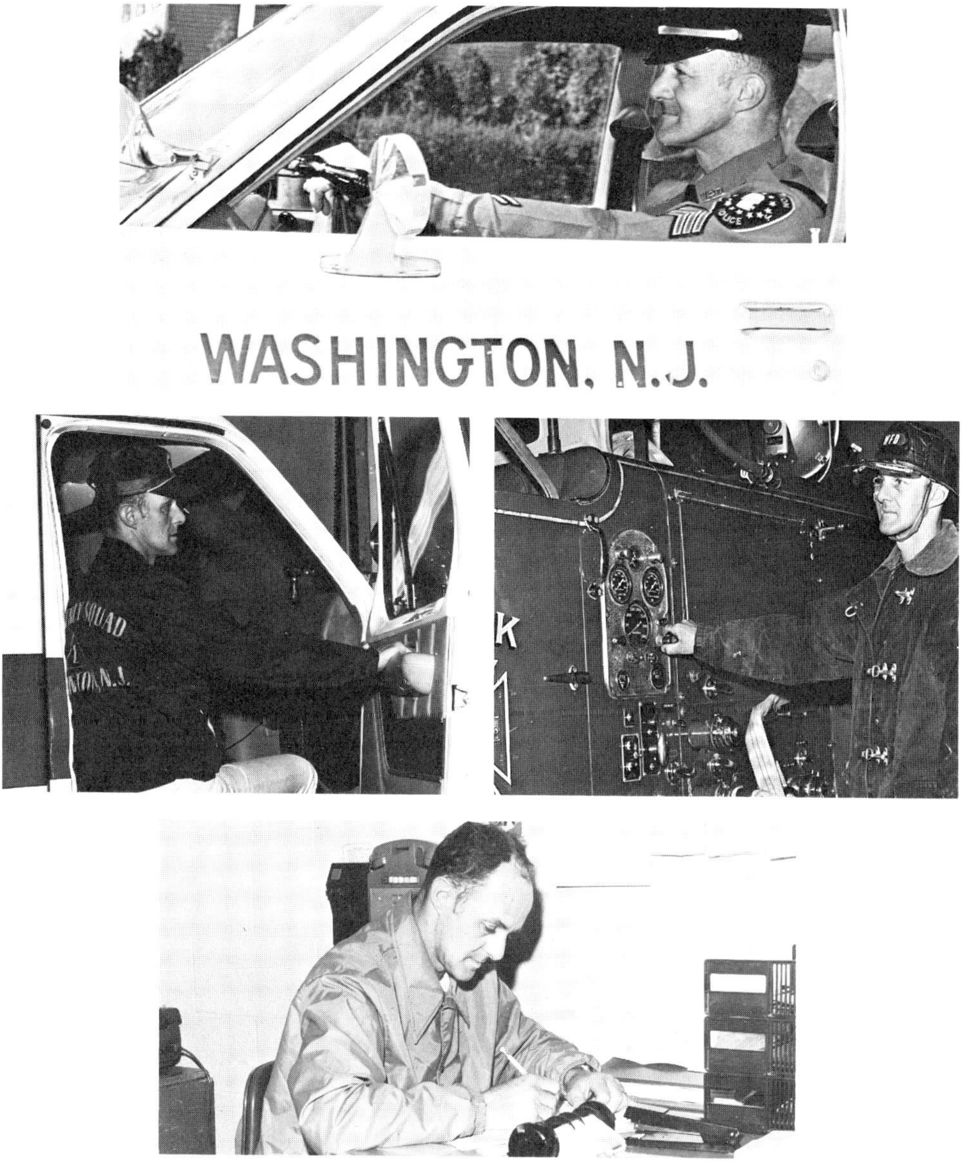

Minassian photos

SUPER VOLUNTEER — *William Brewster is shown at work in top picture. He is a borough police sergeant. Most of his spare time is devoted to volunteer service. He is shown in lower pictures entering ambulance as an emergency squadman, operating fire truck controls as a fireman, and at his desk planning the activities of the Police Athletic League.*

Dale Coban and Richard Thompson.) Brewster was the squad's treasurer and a duty crew chief.

In addition to attending the meetings and drills of both organizations and answering both types of calls when he was not on police duty, Brewster found time to guide the activities of the Police Athletic League, enabling hundreds of young people to participate in many kinds of organized sports.

Brewster, along with Stephen Speirs, another sergeant of the Washington police force and an honorary emergency-squad member, spent about three nights a week supervising nine baseball teams for boys, four softball teams for girls, a swim team, several hockey teams, and an annual Easter egg hunt in the borough park. Another chore was fund raising. The borough donated $1,500 toward a PAL budget of $6,000 per year, the balance being raised by the organization itself.

But despite the unusual number of hours Brewster spends in volunteer service, his interest never falters. One year the PAL fell $2,000 short of its financial goal, so Brewster and Speirs took out personal loans at a local bank to make up the difference. The deficit was paid off the following year.

"Somebody's got to do it, so I just pitch in and do what I can," Brewster says in reflecting on his way of life. He is now an honorary squad member, but he still responds to calls when needed. Rosemarie is a member of the fire department's ladies auxiliary. The Brewsters reside in Washington.

In 1984 an effort was made to locate all living old-time squad members. In addition to those already mentioned and the honorary members who appear in a later chapter, the following survive: Don DeBacco, Kent Bergmann, Thomas DeVoe, Dennis Duryea, Daniel Gardner, Harry Garey, William Gild, Frank Hagerman, Raymond Major, Kerry Meichsner, Elmer Neuls, Marinus Peters, Charles Roberts, Donald Sinkway and Ben Tedesco.

Because emergency-squad members were picked from the membership of the fire companies, and only eight from each company were chosen, there was a waiting list for squad membership during the early years. Many firemen became trained in first-aid work and then waited months and sometimes years to become squad members. The first log book shows that several of these firemen aided the squad and responded to calls while they awaited formal membership. They were Douglas Barras, Vernon Geary, Andrew Henderson, William Sheats and Barney Sinkway. Other firemen who helped the squad but did not become members were John Reigel, Wilson Rush and Elton Wright.

At times the squad accepted the help of residents who were not eligible for membership because they were not firemen but who offered their services. They were used for directing traffic at accident scenes, help in lifting patients, and aid with the sometimes strenuous work of extricating victims from vehicles involved in accidents. They were Robert Baldwin, Robert McAllister (manager of the G. C. Murphy store), James McCarty, LeRoy Schamp, Samuel Slater and William Thatcher.

On July 16, 1938, the Boy Scouts were enlisted by Captain Vernon Oakes when the squad was called to Belvidere to help recover a body from the Delaware River. Oakes notified Scoutmaster John Bodine who responded with troop members Alan Castner, Thomas Conroy, Benjamin Ford[1] and Christopher Sinkbeil. Oakes also called the Phillipsburg Emergency Squad. When the body was recovered, the inhalator and artificial respiration were employed in a lifesaving effort, but the victim was pronounced dead by Dr. Jackson of Belvidere.

It is difficult to single out individuals from a group of people who volunteer and serve the public at a great sacrifice to themselves and to their families. There are many who undertake this commitment and then serve beyond the normal call to duty. Washington residents are indeed fortunate because through the years their emergency squad has been in existence so many of its members have distinguished themselves with unselfish service to their neighbors.

These pages have recorded the lives and experiences of some of them, but there are many more. After decades of leaping out of bed at the sound of the whistle in the middle of the night, signaling that somebody, somewhere, is in trouble and needs help, the retired old-timers have earned the privilege of turning over and going back to sleep. But they do so with the knowledge, as they hear the sirens wail in the distance of the cold night, that members of another generation of fabulous volunteers are answering the call, and that they are on their way with better training and more modern equipment than ever before.

[1]Benjamin Ford lost his life in the Korean War.

Washington Emergency Squad Captains 1936-1983

Vernon Oakes
1936-39

Walter Castner
1940-55

Charles Eagan
1956-59

Charles Hubbard
1960-61

Roy Wiseburn
Part of 1962

John H. Hoffmaster, Jr.
1962-63

Howard Bulmer
1964-65

Elvin Shook
1966-67

Vincent Smith
1968-69

George Saunders
1970-71

Paul Gyuricza
1972-73

David Lance
1974-75

John Sozanski
1976-77

Dale Coban
1978-81

Thomas Mason, Jr.
1982-83

Washington Fire Chiefs Who Headed Ambulance Service Before It Was Combined With Emergency Squad 1954 - 1973

John Riegel
1954-55

Alvin Burd
1956-57

Andrew Henderson
1958-59

Ralph Kinsey
1960-61

Melvin Burd
1962-63

Quentin Chambellan
1964-65

Nelson Beam
1966-67

Elias Johnson
1968-69

Vincent Smith
1970-71

John H. Hoffmaster, Jr.
1972-73

Richard W. York photo

OLD-TIMERS' AMBULANCE — *Until 1978 the streamlined Cadillac ambulances were used by the Washington Emergency Squad. They rode very nicely but did not have the interior dimensions and arrangements of the modular and van-type vehicles which replaced them. This 1972 Cadillac is being restored as an antique reminder of the old days.*

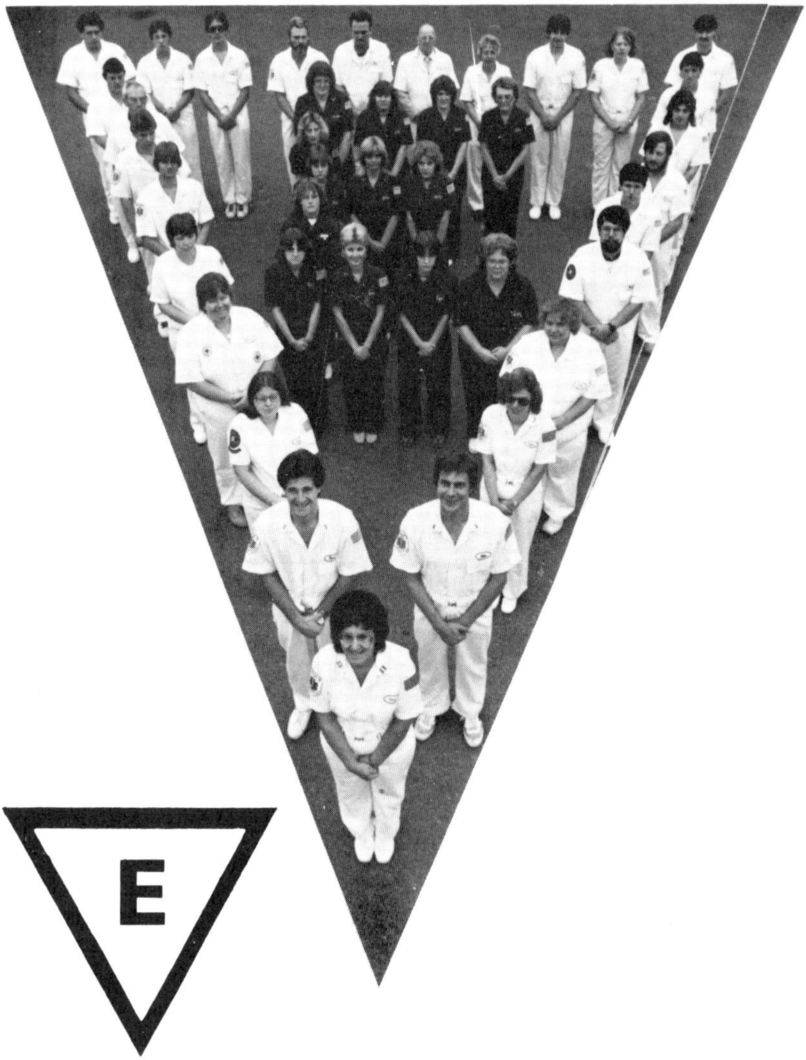

***SQUAD EMBLEM** — The Washington Emergency Squad adopted this emblem when its name was changed in 1936, and it is still in use in 1985. Photographer Richard W. York used squad members for this photograph of emblem.*

6

An Independent Emergency Squad

As the years passed a problem developed. The authorized squad membership of 16, even when augmented with some firemen who were awaiting vacancies so they could join, became insufficent to handle the increasing number of calls.

The fire department is a membership organization and, as such, has its own rules for joining. These rules were created long before there was any thought of providing emergency first-aid service. Because emergency-squad members were appointed only from the membership of the fire companies, and a prescribed number had to come from each company, unnecessary obstacles existed for non-firemen who sought membership in the squad.

First, would-be members had to become firemen and become trained for fire fighting, a kind of training not closely related to emergency-squad work. Then they had to wait until emergency-squad vacancies occurred that could be filled from the particular fire company to which they happened to belong. This process could take months and sometimes years.

As the number of emergency calls increased, the difficulty of always having enough members ready to respond became acute. Women were showing interest in the emergency service, but fire-department membership was an obstacle to them. As one old-timer put it, "There's no reason to teach registered nurses how to climb around on burning buildings in order to make first-aiders out of them."

The problem was solved temporarily, but not satisfactorily, by extending auxiliary membership in the emergency squad to citizens who were not firemen but met all of the requirements for rescue work and served in the same manner as the regular members. They had all of the privileges except one. They could not vote at squad meetings. By the late 1970's the unfairness of this could no longer be ignored, because there were more auxiliary members than there were regular (firemen) members.

The problem was resolved in 1978 when the firemen appeared before the borough council and requested that the emergency squad be recon-

Richard W. York photo

LAST AND FIRST CAPTAIN — *Captain Dale Coban was the last to hold that position while the emergency squad was part of the fire department. He was also the first captain of the independent squad.*

Richard W. York photo

ASSISTANT CAPTAIN — *Donald Butler was the last assistant captain while the squad was part of the fire department and occupied the same position in the independent squad.*

stituted as an independent organization. The requested ordinance was adopted in December of that year. The emergency-squad members responded by creating the Washington Emergency Squad as a nonprofit organization under the terms of the ordinance.

The Siamese-twin separation of the squad from the fire department was amicable. The transition was made easier because Dale Coban and Donald Butler, the captain and assistant captain of the old fire-department squad and, of course, both firemen, assumed the same offices in the newly created organization. The former auxiliary members then joined as regular members with full voting rights.

In order to further assure a smooth transition, the membership voted to extend the terms of all officers for an additional two years through 1981.

Independence has not severed the bond of fellowship between firemen and emergency-squad members. They work together, and together they form a bulwark, protecting their fellow citizens and neighbors from human suffering and property destruction.

With the beginnings of the emergency squad rooted firmly in the fire department, the days when its primary function was to treat injured firemen at the scenes of fires have not been forgotten. The tradition is honored. The squad responds to every structural fire call in case its services may be needed.

Service in either a fire department or an emergency squad is so time-consuming today that few volunteers find it possible to become trained and serve in both, but despite these demands it is interesting to note that the Washington Emergency Squad has three active and three exempt firemen on its active membership roll today. They are James Hudock, an active borough fireman; Martin Nyland, Jr., and John DeFillipis, active township firemen; and Larry Collins, Terry Kresge and A. Fletcher Wright, borough exempt firemen. Thomas Cicerelli is a member of the junior squad and is also a junior member of the township fire department.

The firemen and the squad members are all volunteers—fabulous volunteers.

7

The Fabulous Females

Down through history it has been routinely accepted that women were the caretakers of the injured, the wounded and the sick. We envision women as the members of the tribe whose job it was to care for the sick and injured in pre-historic times. There are legends of women braving the savagery of bloody battlefields in the face of physical danger to rescue and treat the wounded. There are stories, novels and movies about women risking fatal diseases to remain at the bedsides of the stricken.

How did it develop, then, that men were the rescuers and first aiders some halfway into the 20th Century?

It was because firemen, normally the first on the scenes of fires and other disasters, routinely pulled people from burning buildings, icy waters, collapsed structures, wrecked automobiles and downed aircraft. Firemen were organized into departments and trained to respond to alarms. They were easily summoned and able to respond in significant numbers. Heavy rescue had been relegated to them since the days when colonists joined together for the common good and fought fires with bucket brigades.

The evolution of firemen from rescuers to first-aiders was a logical transition. The changes which brought this about included replacement of the horse and buggy with the high-speed automobile and its proclivity for accidents.

It soon became obvious to firemen like Vernon Oakes that first-aid equipment should be carried on fire trucks. Firemen were in a position to provide first aid on the scene while the injured awaited arrival of the ambulance. Then, as firemen saw they could improve the system, they began to develop and operate emergency vehicles and ambulances.

It became the job of the firemen to rescue, treat and transport those injured in disasters. Since only males were firemen, rescue tasks fell to them, and they continued to perform the function for decades in a meritorious fashion.

No one knows when the first female became a member of an emergency squad, but we do know why that occurred and why a gradual shift from exclusively male-operated squads to those including women developed.

It was a change in the economy and a related expansion in the job market. Men, for the most part, no longer worked in the towns where they lived. Employers no longer excused men from work so they could respond to emergency alarms. Jobs became more demanding, and time became increasingly valuable to the average man. For various reasons fewer men were able to volunteer their time for rescue work. At the same time first-aid work itself became more and more demanding. There were pressures to upgrade the medical qualifications of volunteers, and longer and more intense training was required.

Furthermore, since these volunteers had provided such outstanding service to their municipalities, the public became more demanding. It was no longer certain that a real emergency existed when the alarm sounded. Sometimes it was merely a cut finger which could have been taken care of with the application of a simple Band-Aid, but first-aiders never ignore a call.

Ambulance service provided by squadmen increased. The need to transport patients from their homes to hospitals or from one hospital to another became a time-consuming duty. It became evident that some squads were having difficult times answering calls, and it was not long until such information became a matter of public concern.

While no one knows for certain, there were undoubtedly scores of women waiting quietly in the wings for the opportunity to join rescue squads. The decrease in volunteers in the 1960's and 1970's enhanced that possibility.

The acceptance of women was accomplished over a long period of time and in many cases begrudgingly. There are reports some men left or retired from squads earlier than planned simply because they did not want to serve with women.

Today, however, women not only serve on squads but have proven to dubious men they can function as extremely efficient and valuable members. In many instances they have distinguished themselves. Ask any male squad member about the women today, and invariably the answer will be, "We couldn't get along without them." In a few years attitudes have completely changed.

Today the president of the New Jersey State First Aid Council, the highest position in the realm of rescue organizations in the state, is a woman—another first for the female gender. She is Winnie Hartvigsen, resident of Mantoloking and a member of the Dover-Brick Beach First Aid Squad in Normandy Beach, Ocean County.

TOP OFFICIAL — *Winnie Hartvigsen became president of the New Jersey State First Aid Council in 1985, the first woman to hold that position.*

FIRST GIRL TO JOIN *— Marti Leitner was the first female member of the Washington Emergency Squad. She joined as a junior in 1976.*

Minassian photo

She attended the fourth annual presentation meeting of The Vernon Oakes Society in Washington on January 27, 1985, when the society presented $20,000 to the Washington Emergency Squad.

"There is not much history of women serving on emergency squads," notes Hartvigsen, "but each year there are more and more not only becoming members, but officers as well." She points out, for example, that the Brick Township First Aid Squad was formed by women.

"I am visiting each council district this year, and so far I have been received very well. I get a bit of kidding now and again but no feeling whatever of animosity," she says.

The first female member of the Washington Emergency Squad was Marti Leitner. She joined as a junior member in 1976.[1] In that same year Diana Dunlap and Mary Petrick, both registered nurses, became auxiliary squad members. In 1977 Linda Belese was added to the auxiliary membership roll. Sharon Cramsey became a junior member in August 1978. These five were the only females to serve in the squad while it was part of the fire department.

In October 1978, when the squad became independent of the fire de-

[1]The Washington Emergency Squad, because of its fire department origin, was not a leader in the acceptance of female members. Lopatcong Emergency Squad, Inc., broke the ice in 1955 when Grace Pickel, Kay Scarlett, June Streepy and Shirley Willever became the first female squad members in Warren County. Helen Brunner, Adele Clymer, Marie Clymer, Fern Fulmer, Lois Kupcha, Catherine Michalowski, Stella Mount, Naomi Peters, Blanche Ritz, Gloria Schmeltzly, Eleanor Thatcher and Jessie Wolf joined later that year.

partment, the distaff membership continued to grow. Rachael Semonche joined at the first meeting of the independent squad, and Kathleen Adams became a junior that year. In 1979 Debra Armitage became a member, and Andrea Roy and Heather Wollman joined as juniors.

When the first edition of this book was published in 1980, nine of the original 10 women were still serving in the squad and were pictured in a photograph captioned "The Fabulous Females." Today one of them is the 16th captain of the Washington Emergency Squad.

When Mary Petrick, R.N., a graduate of Jersey City Medical Center and an employee in a local doctor's office, made her bid to become a squad member in 1976, she didn't find a welcoming committee. It wasn't really a case of not wanting her as a member; it was that the squad of those days, as part of the fire department, included only firemen as members. But the firemen had created an auxiliary status for non-firemen who wished to serve on the squad. She accepted that non-voting membership.

In 1978, while the squad was still in the fire department, she became the first female officer when elected to the office of secretary. She served in that capacity through 1981. She was then elected lieutenant of the independent squad—its first female line officer—and held that post in 1982 and 1983.

Today Washington residents, both borough and township, are proud to acknowledge the fact that the captain of their emergency squad is a woman—Mary Petrick, R.N. Added to her firsts is the fact of being the first female captain of the Washington Emergency Squad.

Petrick is very much aware of the old attitudes toward women squad members and is willing to discuss them candidly. She says, "I think men on the squad felt women would present problems for the overall operation. They were concerned whether we could lift a stretcher and if we could drive an ambulance. It seemed like a few of the men said to themselves the first time they saw me, 'Oh my God—a woman!'

"Other functions men felt we couldn't handle included lifting and operating Jaws of Life and handling belligerent patients," she says. "As far as lifting patients is concerned, we do that in the hospital every day. We don't have men running around behind us doing the lifting—we do it ourselves," she adds.

The new women members found little or no difficulty handling and operating Jaws of Life. Jaws is a device, powered by hydraulic pressure, used in prying apart wreckage in the extrication of trapped accident victims.

Belligerent men who have had a few drinks too many are usually the ones who resist attempts to treat them or transport them to hospitals. Women, especially those trained for hospital work, find they are often able to calm such individuals better than men, Petrick notes.

For a time after women became involved with the emergency squad, the men would often linger around the squad building after returning from a call, to observe the driving expertise of the female members. "It was quite nerve-wracking in the beginning, especially if we went out with firemen. They would all stand around to see if we could back the ambulance into the bay without wrecking either the vehicle or the building. Sometimes we tried to hurry back ahead of the firemen so we wouldn't be forced to stand inspection," the captain explains.

One of the situations Petrick and others like her must face is the possibility of making some of the male members feel less competent than the registered nurses. "The RN's walked lightly to make sure we didn't make any of the longtime members feel inadequate. In the beginning some of them didn't know we were nurses. That problem, however, is no longer an issue," Petrick says.

"Being elected captain is surely a tremendous hurdle, but acceptance by the rank and file is really the acid test," Petrick comments. "One bitter cold night, after I had been named captain, the driver of a crashed car fled the scene into the nearby woods, and we thought he was lost. I called out the firemen, and there I was, in charge of the entire operation. Each one of those guys was standing there looking at me and wondering what I was going to do. They wondered if I knew what to do and if I could do it.

"We called for Molly, the bloodhound from the Mansfield Township police department. She led us to the home of the victim where he was in bed asleep. His mother told us she hadn't seen him.

"I guess from that night on I had the respect I needed, and I think it may have alleviated apprehensions of a lot of men in both the squad and the fire department about a woman's ability to do the job," Petrick says.

Being a female member of a volunteer emergency squad, however, involves more than just getting the male members to accept the change.

"I realize men in rescue squads and fire departments leave hot meals on the table, respond to calls from church or work, and sometimes are required to practically abandon their families on weekends, but for a woman it involves all that and just a bit more," says Petrick.

"Sometimes when I leave my home, the family's dinner is in the oven or on the stove. I've often called my husband from the hospital and told him to be sure to take the roast out of the oven at a certain time or to go ahead and feed the family. I know sometimes he isn't very happy at not having his wife there to do that for him," she continues.

Furthermore, Mary's son, Robert, 18, is now a squad member, and

Minassian photo

***SQUAD CAPTAIN** — Mary Petrick, R.N., first female captain of the Washington Emergency Squad, also serves as an emergency room nurse on the 11 P.M. to 7 A.M. shift at Warren Hospital, is an instructor of advanced first aid and CPR (cardio-pulmonary resuscitation) for the American Red Cross, and was named Mother of the Year in 1984.*

another son, Thomas, 16, is a junior member. When the alarm sounds, three members of the family respond from the Petrick household. "We know one thing for sure, and that is the fact that anyone who is a volunteer cannot function without the full support and understanding of the family members," Petrick says.

Her talent for running a home and raising children has also been honored. The Warren County chapter of Mothers Against Drunken

Minassian photo

THE FABULOUS FEMALES OF 1980 — *The distaff membership included, from left: Andrea Roy, Kathleen Adams, Debra Armitage, Heather Wollman, Sharon Cramsey, Mary Petrick, Rachael Semonche, Diana Dunlap and Marti Leitner. Roy and Adams were junior members.*

Driving conducted a contest in 1984 in which Mary Petrick was voted Mother of the Year.

In 1985 another responsibility came her way. The Warren County Medical Examiner appointed five registered nurses to newly created positions known as R.N. Medical Investigators. These investigators assist the medical examiner by looking into the circumstances surrounding unusual fatalities and, living in various locations in the county, they are able to arrive at the scenes very quickly. Petrick was appointed to one of these positions, and two of the others were filled by Washington Emergency Squad members Diana Dunlop and Carol Kresge.

A Sunrise Terrace resident, Petrick was born on Long Island and has lived in Washington 18 years. She is married to Joseph Petrick, a carpenter. Besides Robert and Thomas they have a daughter, Peggy, 14, also at home.

Nearly five years have passed since the picture of the nine fabulous females of 1980 appeared in the first edition of this book. What are the nine doing today? The answers, which follow, are interesting.

In the order in which they appear in the accompanying picture, Andrea Roy is studying medical technology at Kean College in Union, New Jersey; Kathleen Adams lives in Richmond, Pennsylvania, and is employed by the Howard Johnson's restaurant chain; Debra Armitage is a New Jersey state trooper; Heather Wollman graduated from Sage College and is now a special education teacher in the Oxford Central School; Sharon Cramsey graduated from Trenton State College as a registered nurse and is a public health nurse in Middlesex County, New Jersey; Mary Petrick, R.N., is an emergency room nurse at Warren Hospital on the "graveyard" 11 P.M. to 7 A.M. shift, an instructor of advanced first aid and CPR (cardio-pulmonary resuscitation) for the American Red Cross (a voluntary position), and captain of the squad; Rachael Semonche is employed at Warren Hills Family Health Center and is a trustee of the squad; Diana Dunlap, R.N., is a nursing supervisor at Warren Hospital, vice-president of the squad, a duty crew chief, and the squad's alternate delegate to the New Jersey State First Aid Council; Marti Leitner, who graduated from junior to active squad membership before the 1980 picture was made, is an engineering assistant at Eaton Manufacturing Company in Whippany, New Jersey, and works as a police dispatcher in Washington on weekends.

These are the fabulous females who paved the way for the many women who serve in the Washington Emergency Squad today.

Royal Photographics photo

BEFORE THE PARADE — *This photograph of squad personnel was taken just before the mammoth 50th-year parade. Identifications of those pictured appear with individual photos on the following pages.*

8

The Washington Emergency Squad Today

Come rain, hail, snow, wind, heat, cold or ice the fabulous volunteers of the Washington Emergency Squad stand ready to provide help when and where needed. Nearly four calls are received every 24 hours. They responded to 1,368 calls in 1984.

Squad members, past and present, represent just about every vocation imaginable. The membership roster has included mechanics, factory workers, gasoline station attendants, letter carriers, undertakers, clerks, housewives, business proprietors and professional people, to name a few. As this is written the squad includes 34 active members — 24 men and 10 women. Three of the women are registered nurses.

Through most of its history the squad enrolled only borough residents as members because it was part of the borough fire department, and its membership was drawn entirely from that department. In 1979 the squad had become an independent organization without legal ties to the fire department, and in 1981 its bylaws were amended to permit the admission of members from Washington Township. The squad is now an enterprise of the two municipalities.

Active membership is open to borough and township residents who are 18 years of age or older. New members are on probation during their first year of service. During that year they receive comprehensive training in first aid and emergency procedures.

The membership elects line officers and desk officers. The line officers are the captain, assistant captain and lieutenant. They are in command of all rescue operations. The desk officers are the president, vice-president, corresponding secretary, recording secretary and treasurer. The desk officers care for the administrative affairs of the organization.

To assure that calls are answered efficiently and to spread the early A. M. calls among the membership, the squad has organized five four-member duty crews, one for each of the nights from Sunday through Thursday. Each duty crew includes four or five members. One member of each duty crew is designated by the line officers to serve as its chief.

Each duty crew responds to calls from 11 P.M. to 6 A.M. on the night to which it is assigned. During the hours covered by duty crews, other squad members respond only to second or third calls that may occur before the duty crew has cleared from a call.

A squad member may volunteer for the duty crew that serves during a night when the member is usually available and is expected to arrange a substitute for any night the member will not be available.

A few squad members are available for daytime calls during weekdays. They do not comprise a duty crew, but they remain alert to calls which originate during the midweek daytime hours. No duty crews are assigned to weekends because there are always enough members available during those periods of time.

Since 1976 junior squad membership has been available to young people who have reached the age of 16. It is customary for a senior member to consult with the parents of a prospective junor member before membership is granted. Two regular squad members serve as advisors to the juniors.

Junior members elect a captain from their own membership. Juniors are subject to the same training as active members and may accompany them on calls if there is enough room available on the responding vehicles. A junior who has completed training by the time he or she becomes 18 years of age may become an active member without the usual probationary period.

The juniors are assigned the duties of cleaning the quarters, vehicles and equipment. They plan and carry out their own fund-raising events in order to help the squad financially. They participate in parades and other events in which the squad is involved. In 1985 the junior roster included seven members—six boys and one girl. Two of the boys reached the age of 18 and became active squad members before the end of the year.

Young people who aspire to become emergency medical technicians, paramedics, doctors or nurses, or who wish to go through life possessing the skills which could enable them to assist in emergency situations which they may encounter, find their experience as junior and eventually senior squad members to be an excellent foundation upon which to build their careers.

The Washington Emergency Squad Auxiliary[1] was organized in March 1979 with a membership of 12. Its purpose is to assist the squad in fund raising and in other ways. Immediately after organizing it started a

[1]The present Washington Emergency Squad Auxiliary should not be confused with the auxiliary squad membership available to non-firemen before the squad became an independent organization.

Richard W. York photo

BUSINESS MEETING — *Mary Petrick, captain; Michael Baylor, lietutenant; Larry Collins, president; and Madelyn Fleming, recording secretary, conduct regular squad meeting at the Vernon Oakes Building.*

Minassian photo

AUXILIARY MEETING — *Members of Washington Emergency Squad Auxiliary meet at The Vernon Oakes Building.*

program of conducting cake sales and raffles in order to build up its treasury. The auxiliary participates with the squad in all parades, celebrations and other special events. The organization's members elect their own officers. The 1985 membership roster includes 21 borough and township residents.

Regular squad business meetings are held on the third Monday of each month, and drills are conducted on the first and second Wednesdays. Officers hold meetings at 7 P.M. on the second Monday, followed by a meeting of the duty-crew chiefs. All squad members are expected to attend at least 50 percent of the meetings and drills and to respond to a reasonable number of calls.

The juniors do not hold regularly scheduled formal meetings, but gather at the Vernon Oakes Building on at least one Sunday each month. The auxiliary conducts business meetings on the fourth Tuesday of each month.

Honorary membership was initiated at the squad meeting in October 1966 when John King and A. Leighton Goberman were elected honorary members. Today any member who has served for seven years may ask for and receive honorary status. Members with less than seven years of service who have performed in an outstanding manner may be elected to the honorary membership roll by unanimous vote of the squad. The 1985 honorary roll lists 22 members, three of whom are deceased.

Honorary members are not required to respond to calls or take further training, but if they desire to answer calls, they are required to maintain the proper certifications. Since honorary membership became available 22 members have become honoraries. Two of them continue to answer calls. Four are deceased.

The Vernon Oakes Society[1] was created by a resolution of the squad in 1981, and its members enjoy a direct affiliation with the squad organization. The purpose of the society is to honor the founder and first captain of the Washington Emergency Squad and to assist the squad financially through its yearly dues of $100 from each member. Starting with a charter membership of 126, its membership roll passed the 200-mark in 1984.

The original resolution provided for a single officer, the director, and Alvin Sloan was appointed to that position. The resolution was amended in 1984 to create the additional offices of assistant director and secretary. Lynn Gulick and Vickie Gulick were appointed to those positions. Officers serve until successors are appointed.

The Washington Emergency Squad and its affiliated organizations comprise a formidable team dedicated to the aid and protection of the people of the Washington area.

---

[1]Complete information about The Vernon Oakes Society is contained in Chapter 12.

STAND-BY SERVICE — *Where there are crowds, there are emergencies, and the Washington Emergency Squad stands by at important events of the Blue Army Shrine near Washington. Rachael Semonche is shown treating a bee sting while township police officer Charles White holds first-aid kit.*

Richard E. Harpster photo

FOOTBALL-GAME DETAIL — *Captain Mary Petrick and Howard Reed are part of crew standing by to assist players or fans should an emergency arise.*

Washington Emergency Squad Active Members 1985

Richard W. York photos

MARY PETRICK, R.N.
Captain
Captain-elect, 1986-87

RUSSELL WILDRICK
Assistant Captain,
Alternate Delegate to NJSFAC
Vice-President elect, 1986-87

MICHAEL BAYLOR
Lieutenant
Assistant-Captain elect, 1986-87

LARRY COLLINS
President, Crew Chief

DIANA DUNLAP, R.N.
Vice-President, Crew Chief

MADELYN FLEMING
Recording Secretary, Crew Chief, Junior Squad Advisor

SANDY MICKALOWSKI
Corresponding Secretary, Trustee, Crew Chief
Trustee-elect, 1986-87

WARREN EASTMAN
Treasurer, Crew Chief
Treasurer-elect, 1986-87

JOSEPH BARTHA

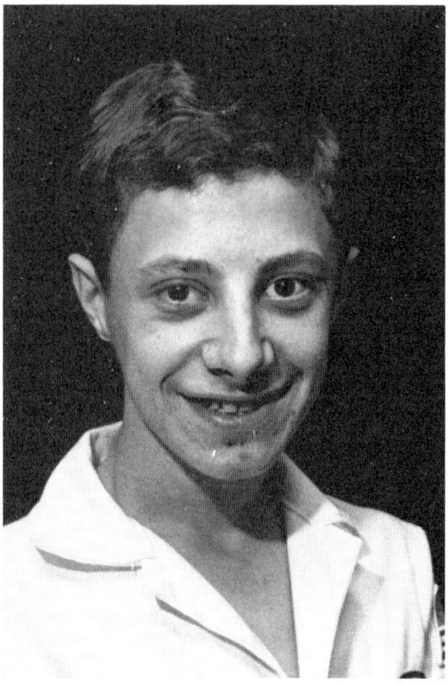

JOHN BLACK

DONNA BOWLBY
Crew Chief
Corresponding-Secretary elect, 1986-87

JEFFREY COOPER

JOHN DeFILIPPIS

BETH EASTMAN

LEONARD HENGST

JUDITH HERRICK

JAMES HUDOCK

CAROL KRESGE, R.N.
Trustee-elect, 1986-87

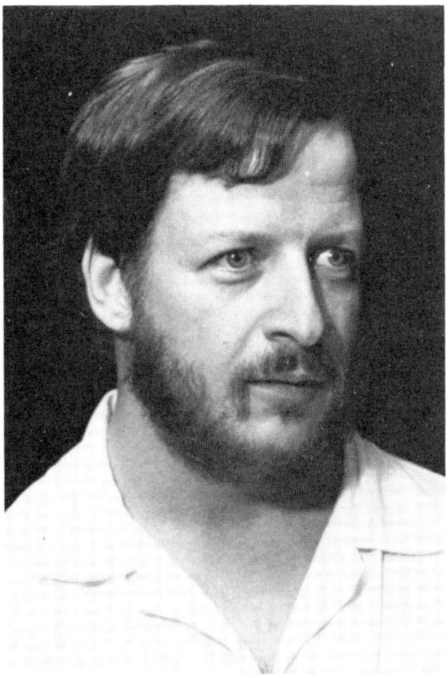

TERRY KRESGE
Delegate to NJSFAC

THOMAS MASON, JR.

ROBERT NYLAND
Trustee

MARTIN NYLAND, JR.
Trustee
Recording-Secretary elect, 1986-87
Trustee-elect, 1986-87

ROBERT PETRICK

BARBARA PLETZER

SCOTT PLETZER

HOWARD REED
Crew Chief,
Junior Squad Advisor
Lieutenant-elect, 1986-87

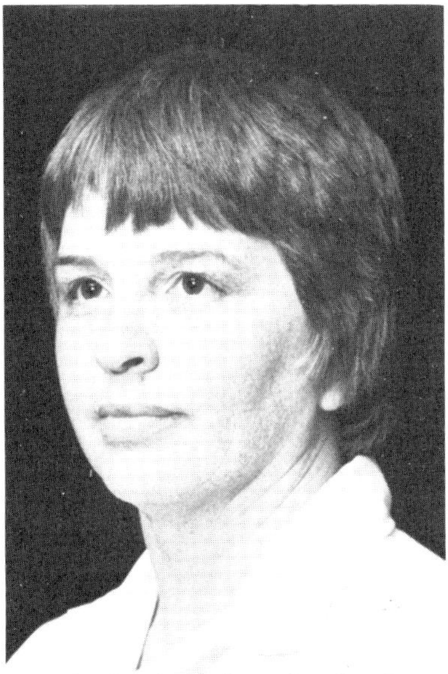

RACHAEL SEMONCHE
Trustee
President-elect, 1986-87

BRIAN SHEA
Trustee
Trustee-elect, 1986-87

GREGORY WARNE

DAVID WENCH

A. FLETCHER WRIGHT

RICHARD YURKOVITCH

TIMOTHY YURKOVITCH

BRIAN ZACHAR

Washington Emergency Squad Auxiliary Members 1985

Minassian photos

BETTY DEEMER
President
Trustee-elect, 1986-87

LYNN SHURACK
Vice-President
Vice-President elect, 1986-87

DENISE FOX
Recording Secretary

MICHELLE STONE
Corresponding Secretary
Trustee-elect, 1986-87

BONNIE BAYLOR
Treasurer, Trustee
President-elect, 1986-87

SANDY BARTHA

PATRICIA BOUCHER

LOUISE FEDOR

EVELYN FOX

SUE FREEZER

HELEN HARTRUM
Trustee
Trustee-elect, 1986-87

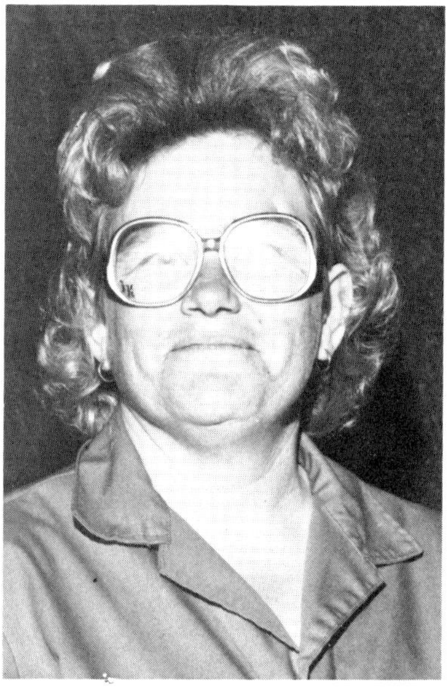

JOANN KOEPKE

KAREN KRESGE

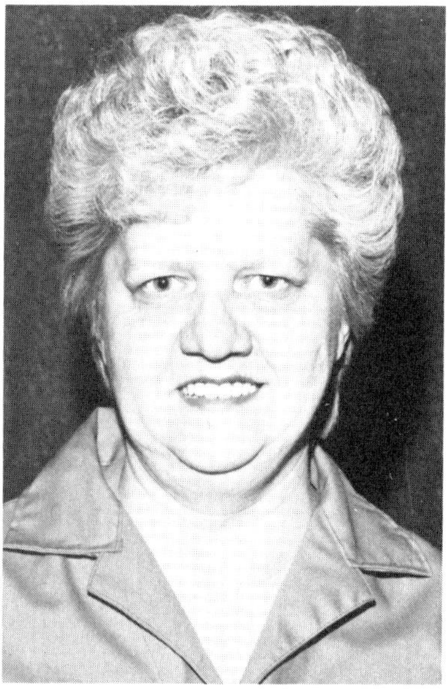

BARBARA KRIES
Corresponding-Secretary elect, 1986-87

MELANIE KRIES
Treasurer-elect, 1986-87

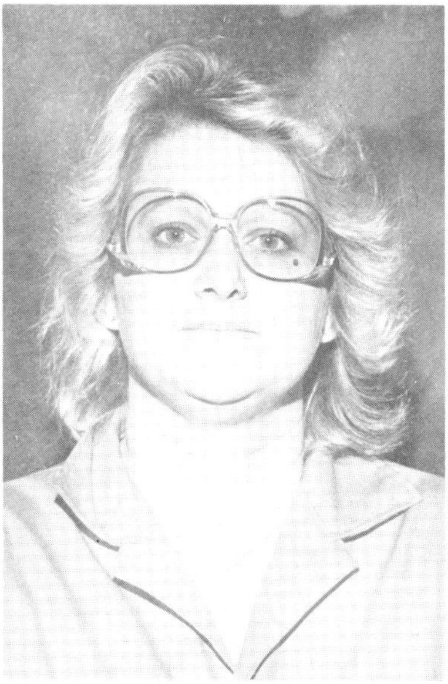

HOPE LaPORTA

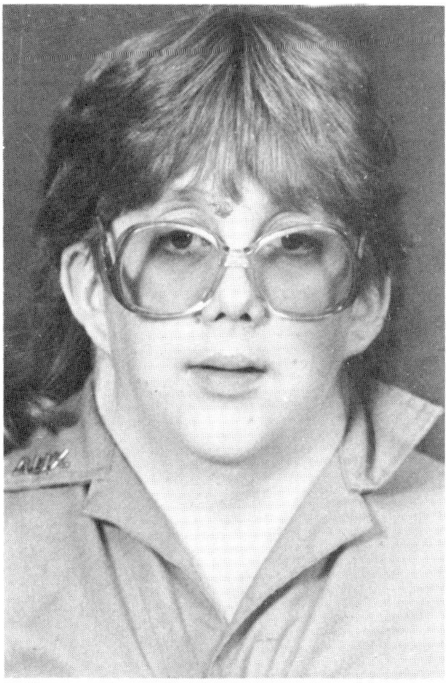

KAREN MINNICK

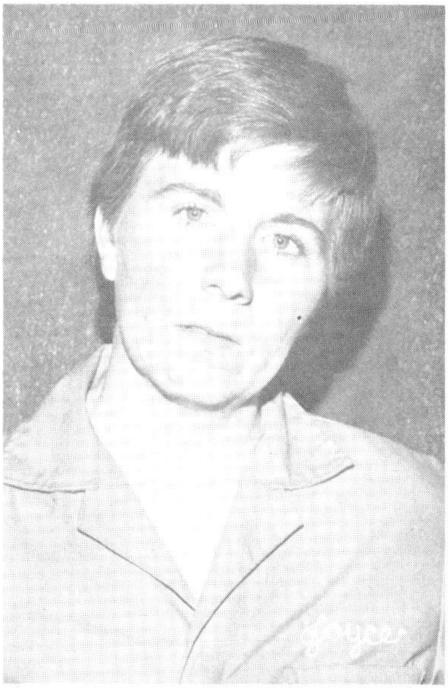

BEVERLY READ

JOYCE SEMON
Trustee
Recording-Secretary elect, 1986-87

PETRA ZIOBRO

MARY MASON
(Photograph not available)

Washington Emergency Squad Junior Members 1985

Minassian photos

JOHN BEREZNEY
Captain-elect, 1986[1]

THOMAS CICERELLI

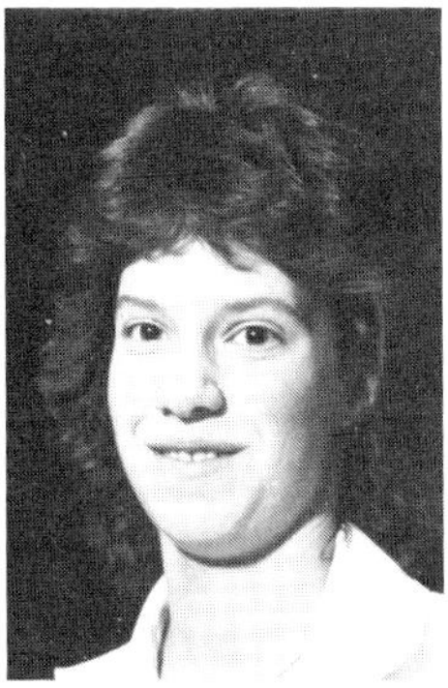

KAREN NUNEMACHER

THOMAS PETRICK

KEVIN RYNO

[1]Scott Pletzer was the 1985 captain. He reached the age of 18 during that year and became an active squad member.

Washington Emergency Squad Honorary Members 1985

Richard W. York photo

RICHARD ADAMS

Richard W. York photo

NELSON BEAM

Richard W. York photo

WILLIAM BREWSTER

Richard W. York photo

HOWARD BULMER

Richard W. York photo

GUY BURD, SR.

Richard W. York photo

ANTHONY DAMELIO (Deceased 1984)

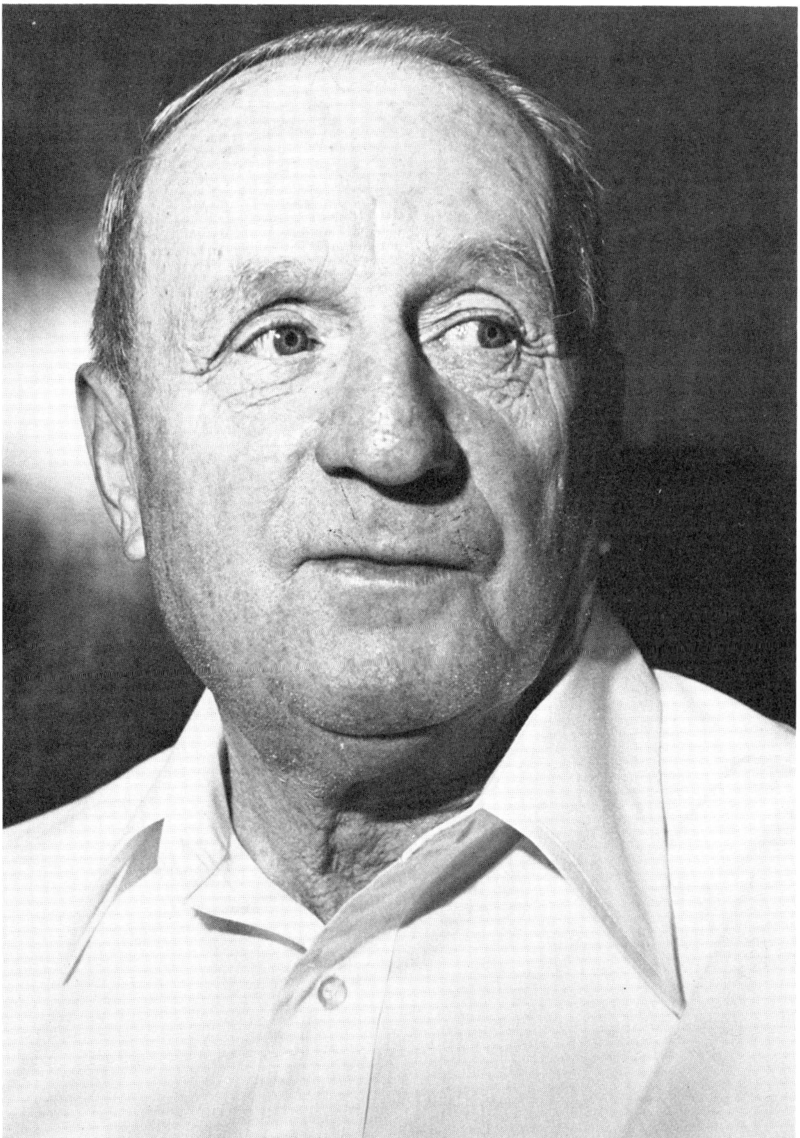

Richard W. York photo

CHARLES EAGAN

Richard W. York photo

JOSEPH EGER (Deceased 1985)

Richard W. York photo

A. LEIGHTON GOBERMAN

Richard W. York photo

PAUL GYURICZA

Richard W. York photo

JOHN H. HOFFMASTER, JR.

Richard W. York photo

CHARLES HUBBARD

JOHN KING *(Deceased 1971)*

Richard W. York photo

DAVID LANCE

Richard W. York photo

LESTER LANCE (Deceased 1983)

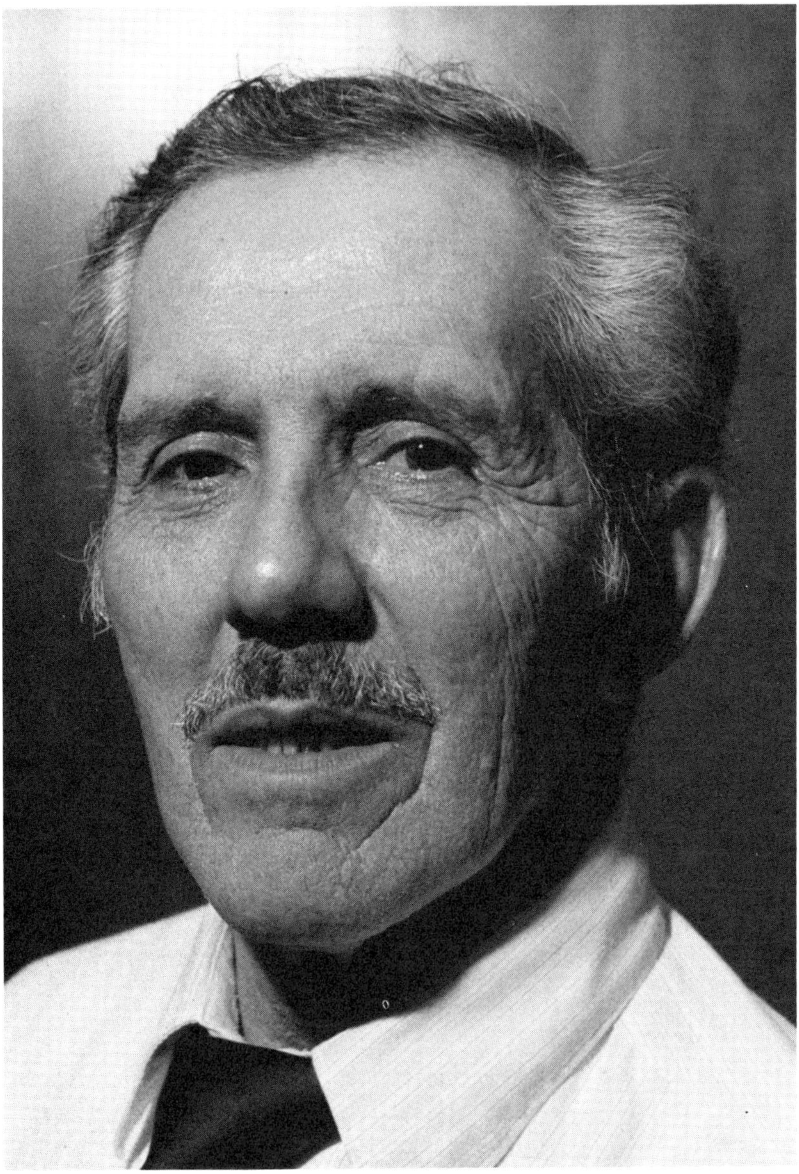

Richard W. York photo

JOSEPH LaPRINO

Richard W. York photo

THOMAS MASON, JR.

Richard W. York photo

JAMES PENCE

Richard W. York photo

VINCENT SMITH

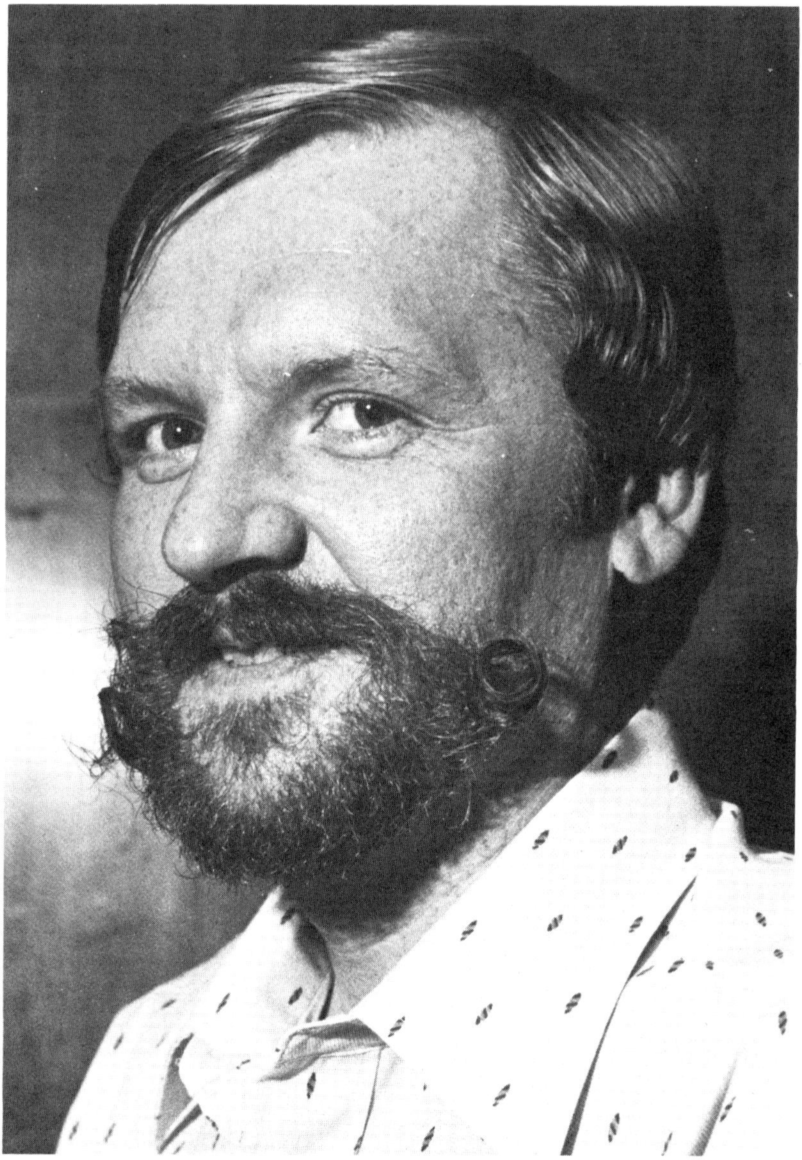

Richard W. York photo

JOHN SOZANSKI

Richard W. York photo

STEPHEN SPEIRS

Richard W. York photo

A. FLETCHER WRIGHT

The Vernon Oakes Society of the Washington Emergency Squad Members 1985

HONORARY

Royal Photographics photo

***DAUGHTER OF FOUNDER** — Mrs. June Oakes Burk is the daughter and only living relative of Captain Vernon Oakes, founder and first captain of the Washington Emergency Squad.*

***AUTHOR OF BOOK** — Richard E. Harpster, author of this book, worked closely with the squad during his career as a newspaper reporter, photographer and writer.*

THE VERNON OAKES SOCIETY

INDIVIDUALS

Mr. and Mrs. Ray W. Afflerbach
☆ Mr. Fred R. Alleman
☆ Mrs. Sophia Andrews
☆ Mr. and Mrs. Homer P. Arena
Mr. and Mrs. David Balfour
☆ Mrs. Fred I. Bodenstein
Mrs. Clark C. Bowers, Jr.
Mr. and Mrs. Clark C. Bowers III
Mr. and Mrs. John W. Bowman
☆ Mr. and Mrs. Richard A. Bowman
☆ Mr. and Mrs. James J. Breslin
☆ Mr. and Mrs. Leonard S. Brown
Mrs. Edward Brugman
☆ Mrs. Alvin Burd
☆ Mr. and Mrs. Harold Burd, Jr.
☆ Mr. and Mrs. Harold Burd, Sr.
Mr. James R. Burd
Mr. John L. Burd
☆ Mr. and Mrs. Robert M. Burd
Mr. John Burton
☆ Mr. and Mrs. Ray Busch
Mr. and Mrs. Anthony Cabone
Mrs. Walter A. Cook
Mrs. Lee Cressman
Mr. Kenneth T. Cunningham
☆ Mr. and Mrs. Samuel Davis
☆ Mr. and Mrs. E. Thomas DeVoe
☆ Mrs. Max S. Dilts
Mr. and Mrs. Walter T. Dunlap
☆ Mr. and Mrs. Sidney Effross
☆ Mr. and Mrs. Jack S. Ferry
☆ Mr. Leon O. Fisher
☆ Mrs. George W. Fleming
☆ Mr. and Mrs. C. Fred Ford
☆ Mr. and Mrs. Willard F. Gibson
☆ Mr. and Mrs. Lynn E. Gulick
Mr. and Mrs. Ray Halpin
☆ Mr. and Mrs. W. Russell Hamlen
Mr. Lester W. Hann
☆ Mr. and Mrs. Richard E. Harpster
Mrs. Ruth Cook Heckman
☆ Mrs. Earle J. Hill
☆ Mr. and Mrs. Klaus Hingst
Sgt. and Mrs. Thomas Holmes
☆ Mrs. Charles J. Jensen
☆ Mrs. Harold W. Jensen
☆ Mr. and Mrs. William T. Kauffman
Mrs. Gertrude Cook Kehler
Mr. and Mrs. John B. LaPorta
Mr. and Mrs. Fred E. Lewis
☆ Mr. and Mrs. Earl Lunger
☆ Mr. and Mrs. Mack McCormick
Mr. and Mrs. Richard C. Meeker
Mr. and Mrs. Arthur D. Merrill
Mr. and Mrs. Kenneth C. Miller
Mr. and Mrs. William A. Miller
☆ Mr. and Mrs. James A. Milson
☆ Mr. and Mrs. Ralph M. Mitchell
☆ Mr. and Mrs. F. J. Mooney
Mr. and Mrs. Barry D. Mueller
Mr. and Mrs. Richard F. Mueller
Mr. and Mrs. Arthur Olson
Mr. and Mrs. Patrick J. O'Malley
Mr. and Mrs. Theodore R. Peyrek
☆ Mr. Robert L. Plenge
☆ Mr. George D. Polt, Jr.
Joyce and Gordon Pyle
Mrs. Margaret H. Randall
☆ Mrs. Thomas W. Roberts
☆ Mrs. Matilda O. Roseberry
Mr. and Mrs. Orville L. Rupell, Jr.
☆ Mr. and Mrs. Ace Rush
Mr. and Mrs. Wilson R. Rush
Mrs. Frank A. Saubier
Mr. Frederick J. Schlink
☆ Michael R. and Nancy J. Gianni Schmidt
☆ Mr. and Mrs. Leonard R. Schumann
☆ Mrs. Pence Skinner
Mr. and Mrs. Felix Slean
☆ Mr. and Mrs. Alvin Sloan
☆ Mr. and Mrs. Charles C. Smith
☆ Mrs. Harry L. Smith
☆ Mr. and Mrs. Larry K. Smith
☆ Mr. and Mrs. Henry Steinhardt
Mrs. Nelson Stem
Mr. and Mrs. Vernon O. Stettler
Mr. and Mrs. Donald Strelecki
☆ Herbert Trubek
☆ Mrs. Ritter L. Vaida
Mr. and Mrs. George C. Van Horn
Mrs. William H. Varney
☆ Nancy and Joe Vlossak
☆ Mrs. Clark C. Willever
☆ Mr. and Mrs. John Wilson
☆ Mr. and Mrs. Leonard C. Ziegler

PROFESSIONALS

Marc Neal Abo, M.D., and Mrs. Abo
☆ Arthur L. Alexander, Esq.
☆ Frank J. Bartolini, M.D., and Mrs. Bartolini
☆ Jerome V. Baucom, Esq., and Mrs. Baucom
☆ Charles Biggs, P.E., and Mrs. Biggs
Richard D. Birkins, Jr., D.D.S., and Mrs. Birkins
☆ Harold R. Bloom, D.D.S., and Mrs. Bloom
☆ Hon. Clark C. Bowers
Broscious and Cooke, Esqs.
☆ Hon. and Mrs. Martin Bry-Nildsen, Jr.
Susan D. Bullock, D.M.D., and Mr. Alan Bullock
☆ Ray C. Cooper, M.D., and Mrs. Copper
Ernest F. Duh, Esq. and Mrs. Duh
Henry W. Eckel, Jr., Esq. and Mrs. Eckel
☆ Jesse Espinola, M.D., and Mrs. Espinola

☆ Felix P. Foschetti, Jr., D.O., and Mrs. Foschetti
☆ Frank J. Gilly, M.D.
James E. Goodwin, M.D., and Mrs. Goodwin
☆ William R. Griffith, D.D.S., and Mrs. Griffith
☆ John E. Hampton, M.D., and Mrs. Hampton
Gunnar M. Henning, D.C., and Mrs. Henning
Howard A. Herman, D.M.D.
Hodakowski and Detrano, CPA's
K. S. Kim, M.D., and Mr. Yang Kim
Stanley M. Kozakowski, M.D., and Mrs. Kozakowski
☆ Charles M. Lee, Esq., and Mrs. Lee
☆ McGinn and Ours, Esqs.
Rev. Dr. and Mrs. J. Mark Odenwelder
☆ Vincent E. Paolicelli, R.A., and Mrs. Paolicelli
Plaza Medical Associates
☆ Cesar Ravanzo, M.D., and Mrs. Ravanzo
☆ Robert L. Schumann, Esq.
Drs. Mohan and Rani Sehdev
Harry K. Seybolt, Esq., and Mrs. Seybolt
☆ H. J. Shin, M.D., and Mrs. Shin
Roger J. Skoog, Esq., and Mrs. Skoog
☆ Harold S. Sloan, LL.D., D. Sc.
Joseph P. Sofia, D.D.S.
☆ Edward E. Stover, Esq., and Mrs. Stover
☆ A. Frederick Uhler, O.D., and Mrs. Uhler
Louis Wasser, V.M.D., and Mrs. Wasser
☆ Stanley E. Yellin, M.D., and Mrs. Yellin

BUSINESSES

Alert Answering Service of Washington
☆ Arctic Foods
Ashman's Auto Body
☆ Breslin-Pritchard Agency, Inc.
☆ Castle Press Publications, Inc.
☆ Gene Castner, Contractor
☆ Century 21 Banks E. Moyer Agency
Clyde's Auto and Truck Repair
☆ Dean Appliance Co.
Duryea Agency of Hunterdon
Duryea's AMC Jeep Renault
Fatima Travel, Inc.
Ken Fisher, Electrical Contractor
☆ Fliegauf Jewelers
☆ Flowers By Theo
☆ Ford Funeral Home
☆ Fox's Liquor Store
Galloway's Tire Associates
Hackettstown Glass and Lock Co.
☆ Howard's Radio and TV Service
Arnold J. Howell, Realtor
J & D Auto Body
☆ Jerry's Meat Market
Lin Supply Company
☆ Masenior's Washington Greenhouses
☆ Mike's Auto Body Shop
Minassian Studio & Camera Shop
Mueller's Feed and Garden Center
Opdyke's Sales and Service
Petty's Auto and Tire Center
Radio Shack
Rossi Pontiac Buick GMC Inc.
☆ S.E.A. Automotive Distributors, Inc.
Shangri-La Restaurant
Shelby's
☆ Smith Motor Co.
☆ Somerset Tire Service, Inc.
☆ Stew's Auto Body Shop
R. J. Strunk, Excavating Contractor
Taylor Rental Center
Villa Furniture
Richard Warnkin, Excavator
Warren County Auto Parts
☆ Warren County Liquors
☆ Warren County Pharmacy
☆ Warren Lumber, Inc.
☆ Washington Auto Parts
Washington Diner
☆ Washington Hardware Co., Inc.
Washington Locksmith
Williams Paper Products
Zachie's Restaurant

FINANCIAL INSTITUTIONS

City Federal Savings and Loan Association
☆ First Fidelity Bank
☆ Midlantic National Bank
☆ Summit Federal Savings and Loan Association

INDUSTRIES

☆ American Can Company
☆ BASF Wyandotte Corporation
Candle Artisans, Inc.
☆ Hedges and Brother, Inc.
☆ Ingersoll-Rand Co.
Leacock & Co., Inc.
☆ Treitler-Owens, Inc.
Turbine Alloy Corporation
☆ Washington Mechanical, Inc.
☆ The Witte Company, Inc.

RELIGIOUS ORGANIZATIONS

Blue Army Of Our Lady Of Fatima
First Baptist Church of Washington
First Presbyterian Church
Jewish Center Of Northwest Jersey
Mt. Pisgah A.M.E. Church
St. Peter's Episcopal Church
United Methodist Church
Washington Assembly Of God Church

CIVIC AND FRATERNAL ORGANIZATIONS

Loyal Order Of Moose, Lodge 512
Mansfield Lodge 36, F.&A.M.
Washington American Legion, Post 103
Washington Area Chamber Of Commerce
Washington B.P.O. Elks Lodge 1563
☆ Washington Centennial Foundation
☆ Washington Junior Woman's Club
☆ Washington Kiwanis Club
☆ Washington Lions Club
Washington Rotary Club
☆ Washington Woman's Club

IN MEMORIAM

☆ Mrs. Arthur L. Alexander
☆ Mrs. Alice C. Axford
Mr. James Balfour
☆ Mr. Fred I. Bodenstein
Mr. Clark C. Bowers, Jr.
☆ Mr. Albert O. Crobaugh
☆ Mr. Max S. Dilts
☆ Mrs. Leon O. Fisher
☆ Mr. Charles J. Jensen
☆ Mr. Ralph D. Latham
☆ Mrs. Blanche E. Ley
☆ Mr. and Mrs. Kenneth C. Riley
☆ Mr. Thomas W. Roberts
Robert S. Rush, Esq.
Mr. Robert W. Skinner

☆ Charter Members

***SOCIETY EMBLEM** — Upon joining The Vernon Oakes Society, members receive membership plaques bearing this emblem.*

Ricahrd W. York photo

SOCIETY OFFICERS — *Alvin Sloan, former mayor of Washington, standing, is the founder and director of The Vernon Oakes Society. Vickie Gulick is secretary. She is the daughter of the late Walter Castner, a fireman for 40 years beginning in 1929, chief of the department in 1936 and 1937, and the second captain of the emergency squad. He succeeded Vernon Oakes in that position and served as captain for 15 years—longer than any other captain—and then became a dispatcher in 1951, retiring in 1971. Lynn Gulick is the society's assistant director. He was an active member of the Washington Fire Department for 10 years and a member of the emergency squad for three of those years.*

Richard W. York photos

CHRISTMAS PARTY — *Squad youngsters gather around tree in the Vernon Oakes Building in December 1984. Surrounding photos: Santa Claus (sometimes known as Dr. Gunnar M. Henning) greets excited clientele.*

Richard W. York photos

***THE SCRAMBLE IS ON** — The pinata is broken and the candy is eagerly pursued. Surrounding photos: Santa trades confidential information with true believers. Lower right: Captain Mary Petrick asks for two new ambulances, and she gets them!*

Is it ticking?

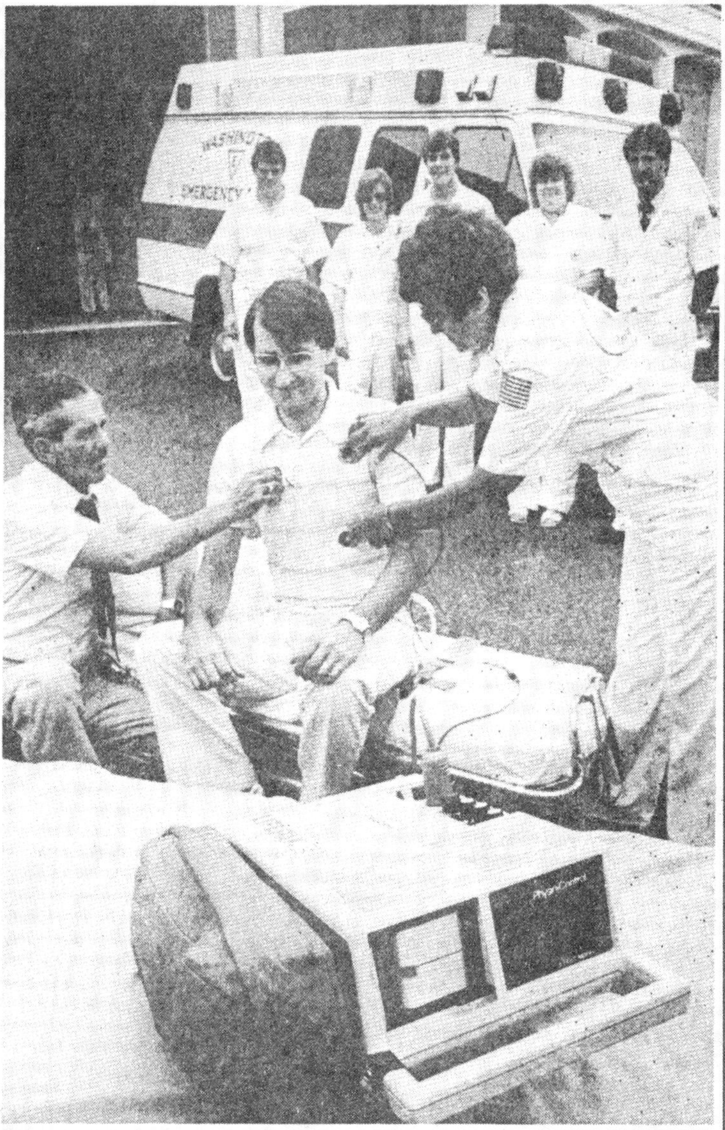

Express photograph/MIDIC CASTELLETTI

Washington Borough Manager Alan Fisher is a volunteer patient for Mayor Joseph LaPrino, left, and Mary Petrick, R.N., Washington Emergency squad lieutenant, in a trial run of Lifepak 5, a portable cardiac monitoring device. The borough, which purchased the $4,500 unit and the ambulance, background, for the squad, is the first in Warren County to acquire the Lifepak 5, enabling personnel to take electrocardiogram readings of patients with chest pains, trauma or respiratory distress and report to emergency-room doctors at a hospital. Watching demonstration at rear are, from left, squad members Brian Shea, Maddy Fleming, Mike Baylor, Diana Dunlap and Russ Wildrick.

The Express, August 31, 1983

9

Training

According to the American Red Cross, first aid is "the immediate and temporary care given the victims of an accident or sudden illness until the services of a physician can be obtained." But the variety of accidents and sudden illnesses is numberless, and each requires its own kind of temporary care. In each case the first-aider must be able to determine what is to be done and then do it. Extensive training and experience are required to acquire the knowledge, the technical skill, and the maturity of judgment to perform these tasks effectively.

In order to give the reader some idea of the scope on basic first-aid instruction, the following outline of selected subjects is taken from the textbook *First Aid and Emergency Rescue* by Lawrence E. Erven, published by Glenco Press in 1970.

1. *Anatomy*—Cells, Tissues, Bones, Joints and Ligaments, Muscles and Tendons, Skin, Internal organs.
2. *Common Disabilities*—Shock, Fainting, Hyperventilation, Choking, Strangling, Snow blindness, Particle in eye, ear or nose, Nosebleed, Diabetic coma.
3. *Bone, Joint and Muscle Injuries*—Fractures, Dislocations, Sprains, Strains, Contusions.
4. *Wounds*—Abrasions, Lacerations, Punctures, Crushed wounds.
5. *Internal Disorders*—Heart attack, Brain injuries, Abdominal pains, Asthma, Emphysema.
6. *Heat and Cold Injuries*—Burns and Scalds, Chemical burns, Sunstroke, Heat exhaustion, Frostbite.
7. *Inhalation of Gasses*—Smoke, Carbon monoxide, Amonia, Fire gasses, Nitrous fumes, Petroleum vapors, Hydrogen sulphide.
8. *Bandaging*—Compresses, Dressings.
9. *Transportation*—Fireman's carry, Seat carry, Pack-strap carry, Incline drag, Blanket drag, Stretchers, Litters.
10. *Poisons*—Irritants, Depressants, Excitants, Emetics, Demulcents, Antidotes.
11. *Emergency Childbirth*—Stage of labor, Umbilical cord, Care of

baby, Miscarriage, Abortion, Complications.

12. *Rescue Skills and Techniques.*

There are two training programs approved by the New Jersey State First Aid Council. One is offered by the New Jersey State Department of Health and is known as EMT (emergency medical technician). This is the official United States Department of Transportation course for emergency care and transportation of the sick and injured. The total course consists of about 25 training sessions involving 89 hours[1] in the classroom and 10 hours in the hospital emergency room for a total of 99 hours.

The course is given by the department under the sponsorship of existing institutions. In Warren County the sponsoring institution is the Warren Hospital, and all classes are held there.

Teaching is done by paid instructors and supervised by a paid coordinator.[2] Dorothy Zito, of Columbia, New Jersey, is the Warren County coordinator, and her staff includes two head instructors, seven regular instructors, and three aides. If aides aspire to become instructors, they may accomplish this by training and passing tests given by the New Jersey State Department of Health.

Included in the EMT course are from 10 to 15 lectures given by doctors, for which they receive a modest fee of $25 per lecture.

For the convenience of the students, basic instruction during 1985 was given in two classes on Sundays which lasted from 9 A.M. to 4:30 P.M. Refresher courses were given on Friday evenings from 7 P.M. to 10:30 P.M. The days and times of instruction may vary from year to year but always occur from January to May.

Upon completion of the training and the passing of a state examination, students are accredited emergency medical technicians.

The functions of the emergency medical technician are as follows:

1. Prompt and efficient care of the patient before transport.
2. Control of the accident scene.
3. Extrication (light) and preparation of the patient for transport.
4. Safe and efficient transport and continuing care of the patient on the way to the hospital.
5. Orderly transfer of patient and patient information to hospital

---

[1]The basic course was formerly 79 hours. Ten hours have been added for training in the use of mast trousers, a device that has raised the survival rate of trauma patients from 20% to 70%.

[2]A minimum of 60 students is required to qualify for state financing. On an occasion when enrollment dropped below that figure and the state assistance was cut off, the instructors completed the course without remuneration. The County of Warren helped with enough funds to purchase small equipment, pay the doctors for lectures, and pay the travel expenses of the instructors.

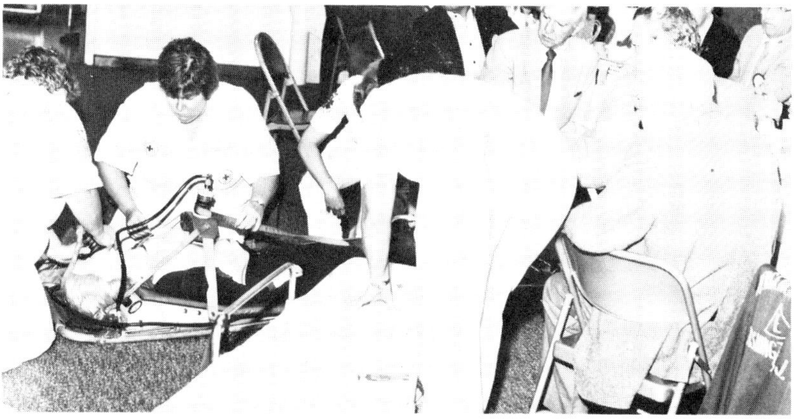

Minassian photo

***CPR DEMONSTRATION** — Squad members demonstrate life-saving techniques at service clubs as part of training and public-relations program. Pictured demonstration was given at a meeting of the Washington Kiwanis Club in 1985.*

emergency department.

6. Communications.
7. Reporting and record keeping.
8. Care of the vehicle and equipment.

The other approved training program is known as the five-point course. Instruction is given by qualified volunteer[1] Red Cross instructors or other instructors appropriate to the subjects being taught. The usual class session occupies four hours and is divided into two periods of two hours each. Classes are held at the headquarters of squads or at other suitable locations. The times of the classes are arranged to suit the convenience of the instructors and students.

There are two American Red Cross chapters in Warren County. The Phillipsburg chapter covers that municipality, and the Warren chapter covers the rest of the county. Donald Butler[2] is chairman of the board of

[1]Red Cross volunteers are sometimes paid under special circumstances when they give up paid employment in order to instruct classes. In some cases a department of government or a corporation will pay a Red Cross chapter for instruction of employees and the chapter will pay the volunteer instructors.

[2]Donald Butler joined the Washington Fire Department and became an auxiliary member of the Washington Emergency Squad in April 1973. He became a regular member of the squad when a vacancy occurred in January 1974. He served in the squad for eight years and was assistant captain from 1978 through 1981. After serving as safety-service chairman of the Warren Chapter of the Red Cross for three years, he became the chairman of its board in 1980.

the Warren chapter.

The training of emergency-squad members in the Warren chapter's area is supervised by the chapter's safety-service chairman, Robert Biamonte, chief of the Hackettstown Emergency Squad. The first-aid chairman is James Patrick, now of Belvidere, who was a member of the Easton, Pennsylvania, chapter when he resided in that city. Water safety instruction is in the charge of Deborah Miller, physical education teacher at Hackettstown High School and an associate professor at Centenary College. There are 115 volunteer Red Cross instructors in the Warren Chapter.

Included in the roster of the Washington Emergency Squad are eight members who are both EMT and five-point certifed and 11 more who are five-point certified. Also included are five CPR (cardio-pulmonary resuscitation) instructors and one advanced first-aid instructor.

The five-point program:

1. *Advanced First Aid* taught by American Red Cross volunteer instructors.

2. *Cardio-Pulmonary Resuscitation* taught by American Heart Association or American Red Cross volunteer instructors.

3. *Emergency Childbirth* taught by doctors.

Marilyn Cressman photo

JAWS DRILL *— Extrication practice with Jaws of Life equipment takes place on lot in rear of squad building.*

4. *Light Extrication* taught by New Jersey Department of Transportation instructors.

5. *Defensive Driving* taught by insurance company instructors.

Upon completion of the course in one of the five points, the student is certified by the instructor teaching that course. When the courses of all five points are satisfactorily completed, the volunteer is awarded a certificate signed by the squad captain and the mayor of the municipality in which the squad is located.

First-aid work requires keeping abreast of the latest techniques and procedures. For this reason all volunteers must take refresher courses at designated intervals.

In addition to the two basic-training programs,there are several opportunities for volunteers to increase their knowledge of first-aid and rescue work, and many of the volunteers take advantage of these programs.

Warren Hospital sponsors bimonthly seminars for emergency-squad personnel. The needs are established by a committee of emergency-squad members. The hospital's patient and community-health education department, of which Patricia A. Mathews, R.N., M.A., is coordinator, arranges the speakers and presentations.

The hospital is also the county training center for MAST (military antishock trousers) that is now included in EMT instruction. It conducts training programs for both EMT's and five-pointers and provides training materials to Hackettstown Community Hospital to assure the standardization of training in the county. The same hospital department also acts as the liaison with the squads and coordinates communciation in connection with the educational seminars, disaster drills, etc.

Hackettstown Community Hospital conducts seminars on medical subjects and invites the members of rescue squads to attend the ones which contain information that will be helpful to them.

The Northampton County Rescue School provides special training in mountain and silo rescues.

In nearby Hunterdon County the West Jersey Search and Rescue Team specializes in the types of rescues which its name implies.

The Hurst Rescue Division of the Hale Pump Company, providers of equipment to fire departments and rescue squads, conducts training sessions to assist its customers in the use and maintenance of the equipment it sells. In the summer of 1985 three members of the Washington Emergency Squad, John DeFilippis, James Hudock and Gregory Warne, made the trip to Swedesboro in southern New Jersey and attended an all-day training session in light and heavy extrication. The seminar included four and a half hours of classroom instruction followed by the use of equipment on wrecked cars in a nearby junkyard. The Washington men

Reinhold Radke photo

HOSPITAL SEMINAR — *Dr. Stanton H. Sykes addresses members of various rescue organizations at Warren Hospital seminar.*

returned with certification as operators of heavy extrication tools.

The Hammonton Rescue School in Atlantic County has trained several Warren County squad members in heavy-rescue procedures.

Some members of the Hoffmann-LaRoche squad have gone an even greater distance to the Dover, Delaware, State Fire School for special training in confined-space rescues.

Comprehensive water-rescue instruction is available from the national scuba program of the YMCA located in Atlanta. The pool of the Easton YMCA is made available to Stephen Hardick, of Phillipsburg, who has trained many rescue-squad members. A basic course of from six to eight hours of instruction is available, as well as an advanced course, intended for students who are already trained in water rescue, which includes diving and the handling of unusual water-rescue situations.

In a rural area such as Warren County, farming creates hazards of its own. Pesticides can poison, feed grinders can mangle limbs, tractors and other machines can capsize, and animals can injure humans.

In March 1985 the Washington Emergency Squad and the Warren Hills Chapter of the Future Farmers of America gave a farm rescue demonstration on the property of Frank A. Rymon & Sons, a farm-machinery dealership south of Washington.

The purpose was twofold: to teach farmers how to prevent farm-related accidents and to instruct rescue personnel how to respond appropriately when such accidents occur. Every farmer in Warren County was invited by the FFA and the county agricultural extension office to attend. The Washington squad was joined by squads from Belvidere, Bloomsbury, Lebanon Township and Mansfield Township. More than 100 people, including farm families and squad personnel, attended the demonstration.

Captain Mary Petrick of the Washington Squad cautioned the farmers to make sure someone is alerted when they are going into fields, to wear well-fitted clothing, and to teach every family member how to turn off each piece of equipment. Squad member Robert Nyland, who is a past state president of the FFA, was assisted by Rick Yurkovitch, another squad and FFA member, in demonstrating methods of freeing injured people from machinery.

The squad and the FFA are working through the North Hunterdon Training Group of High Bridge to develop a course that will provide area squads with certified instruction in farm rescue. They had previously completed a drill on the farm of Leonard Hengst, a Washington Township dairy farmer who is a former FFA member and one of the organizers of the program. Squad members who participated in both events are now certified in farm rescue.

Express photo

FARM-SAFETY DEMONSTRATION — *Squad member Leonard Hengst, left, and Mark Fournier demonstrate the proper use of a chain saw."*

Early in 1979 state legislation was proposed that aimed at standardizing and professionalizing first-aid services. This legislation would have required every member of any squad to be an emergency medical technician graduate and to work only under the direction of a paramedic. The state was to be divided into districts with one hospital designated to handle emergency cases in each district. Each emergency vehicle would be equipped to communicate with its district hospital while on the road.

Many rural squad members felt that while such a program might be appropriate and desirable in cities and heavily populated areas where many hospitals are close together, in rural areas it would require squads to transport patients greater distances, increase travel time needed to deliver patients to hospital emergency rooms, make it difficult for volunteers who cannot train at the specific times the EMT classes are held, and burden taxpayers—already suffering from excessive taxation —by making necessary the augmenting of volunteer crews with paid paramedics, all to the harm of patients and the general public. They viewed the suggested program as an opening wedge for the replacement of volunteers with paid civil servants, a situation that few municipalities wanted or could afford. They also considered the proposal to be an unwarranted threat to home rule.

When the proposed legislation was being discussed by the state legislators, rural first-aid and ambulance squads appeared in Trenton in force and emphatically expressed their opposition. The controversial legislation was postponed.

The successful protest had been organized by the New Jersey State First Aid Council. The Washington Emergency Squad had joined the council in 1956 but did not continue its membership the following year. After the 1979 controversy in Trenton, the squad members voted to rejoin and support the organization.

Squad members are very much aware of the need for adequate and continuing training and spend much time and go to great lengths to get it. The New Jersey State First Aid Council has done much to improve the opportunities for training, and the squads have demonstrated their desire to constantly improve the knowledge and abilities of their members.

Royal Photographics photo

WASHINGTON EMERGENCY SQUAD VEHICLES *— From left: 1963 emergency-truck body on 1973 Ford chassis, 1978 Cayel Craft ambulance on Ford chassis, 1985 Cayel Craft ambulance on Ford chassis, 1983 Ford van ambulance, support vehicle converted from 1971 International ambulance in 1983 and 14-foot aluminum boat. Since this photograph was taken, the 1978 Cayel Craft ambulance was replaced with a similar 1985 vehicle.*

10

Vehicles and Equipment

The most conspicuous pieces of equipment belonging to an emergency squad are its vehicles. They are also the most costly and, in many cases, the shortest lived. Their design, maintenance and the equipment they carry has much to do with the performance and safety of any squad, and the Washington Emergency Squad has put its many years of experience in the field to good use in the development of better and more economical conveyances.

The squad keeps five vehicles in service. They include an emergency truck, two first-line ambulances, a smaller van ambulance, and a support truck. Each unit is the latest in a series that has shown development and improvement through the years, and an examination of the forebears is interesting.

In the 47 years since its rescue equipment was moved from the cabinet on the running board of the fire department's ladder truck, the Washington squad has used a series of four emergency trucks. The 1937 Dodge with its homemade body was replaced with a 1952 Ford after being in service for 15 years. The second truck was replaced with a 1963 Ford after serving for 11 years. Ten years later a 1973 Ford chassis replaced the 1963 model at a cost of $6,927, and nearly $9,000 was spent on the body which was updated and refurbished. As this is written, that truck is still in service. It was overhauled and repainted again in 1983. Meticulously maintained and kept up-to-date, this truck is still winning first prizes in competition with the newest trucks in judging at many parades.

The mileage covered by the emergency truck is always much less than that covered by the ambulances because the truck returns to the base directly from the scene of each call while the ambulance must make round trips of at least 20 miles to a hospital. The mileage on the truck has been curtailed even more by a change in the method of handling calls. The truck now responds only to calls involving highway accidents or other emergencies where extrication devices, floodlighting or other specialized equipment may be required. Modern ambulances carry all of

FIRST EMERGENCY TRUCK *— The 1937 Dodge with homemade body carried Otto Eger's fire bell on front bumper.*

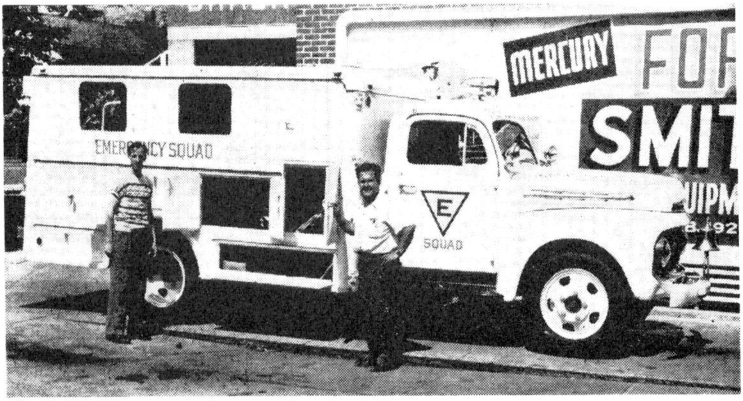

REPLACEMENT TRUCK *— A 1952 Ford became the second truck to be owned by the squad. Squad member Joseph Eger, left, and Ford dealer Charles Smith stand by truck before it was delivered. Otto Eger's fire bell survived the change and is shown on front bumper.*

THIRD TRUCK *— The fire bell was a casuality when this change was made. The 1963 Ford was equipped with a winch, leaving no room for Otto Eger's masterpiece. Squad has had to manage without a bell ever since.*

Richard W. York photo

NEW CHASSIS *— A new 1973 Ford chassis replaced the older one and the body was upgraded and moved over. Color of vehicle was changed from white to red.*

Richard W. York photo

STILL GOING STRONG — *Emergency truck with 1963 body and 1973 chassis, repainted in present squad colors, is meticulously maintained. It wins prizes in competition with the newest vehicles.*

the equipment and supplies required for home and workplace accidents and illnesses, while in earlier days they were used almost entirely as a means of transporting patients. The emergency truck carried oxygen and nearly all equipment and supplies, a fact which required it to respond to every call. Today the majority of calls do not require the use of the truck at all.

The present prize-winning truck, with its 11-year-old body and 22-year-old chassis, has only 12,000 miles registered on its odometer, and there are no immediate plans to replace it.

Old-timer Charles "Buss" Eagan recalls that even in the earliest days the squad vehicles carried equipment that was sophisticated for those times.

The first truck was equipped with two-way radio communication, but, of course, it was not as good as the equipment in use today. A single frequency was used by the squad, the police department, and the fire department. Today the fire departments of the county have a band for their own use. The first truck also carried the Davis Inhalator which was mentioned in a previous chapter.

The second truck was equipped with a portable "iron lung" machine which could force a patient to breathe. It was powered by either 110-volt power, the battery of the vehicle, or by a hand-cranked mechanism. This machine could be strapped to the patient. This truck also carried a self-starting generator to furnish current for floodlights. It could be started from the dashboard of the truck while the squad was arriving at the scene of an emergency. It was not necessary for the squadmen to jump out of the truck to start the generator after they arrived.

In 1959 the squad obtained a "shock unit." This was a device that sent a force of electricity into a patient's body to reactivate a heart that had stopped beating. Similar equipment is often seen today on television. Eagan says, "This piece of equipment was later pulled off the market because the company that manufactured it had problems with government regulations. We were ordered by the United States Department of Health, Education and Welfare to destroy it, and we took a loss of some $600."

The need for a boat to use in water-rescue operations became apparent during the early days of the Washington Emergency Squad. William Sheats, who joined the squad during its first year, was an avid and well-equipped fisherman. He donated one of his boats to the squad, and the squad members built a trailer on which to haul it. This boat, which was made of wood, served until 1970. In that year the squad purchased a new 14-foot aluminum boat and trailer which are still in service today.

The present emergency truck carries a generator with six quartz floodlights, reels of electrical cables, portable generator, Jaws of Life and O-cutter, Portapower extrication device, chain saw, air chisel, two Scott packs, resuscitator, trauma kit, basket stretcher, burn pack, come-alongs, large tool roll with assorted hand tools for vehicle rescues, small tool roll, long and short back boards, climbing ropes, back pack with first-aid supplies for off-road rescues, flares, assorted splints, various axes and pry bars, assorted wood blocks for stabilizing vehicles, and a host of smaller items.

The two first-line ambulances are both Cayel Craft bodies on Ford chassis, one delivered early in 1985 and the other later in the same year. The newer one is the 17th ambulance to serve the Washington area, and its lineage goes back to the beginning of ambulance service in Washington in 1936. The American Legion began service that year and used a series of two vehicles, described earlier in this book, until the fire department instituted its service in 1954 with a used Buick which served temporarily until a new 1954 Cadillac was delivered. New Cadillacs replaced older ones in 1959, 1966, 1967,[1] 1972 and 1976. Then came the first modular ambulance in 1978—a Cayel Craft body on a Ford chassis. That vehicle was replaced with the present one.

The predecessors of the other 1985 Cayel Craft go back to the year 1974 when an increasing number of calls caused the firemen to place a third ambulance—a new Cadillac—in service. This was replaced in 1979 with a used 1977 Chevrolet modular ambulance which was purchased from the West Orange First Aid Squad. In 1982 the Chevrolet was replaced with a new small Ford modular vehicle. In 1985 the Ford was sold to the Oxford Emergency Squad, giving way to the present Cayel Craft because a decision had been made to keep two large first-line ambulances in service, each capable of carrying five patients.

These ambulances are equipped with Lifepak-5 heart monitors, heart-lung resuscitators for automatic cardio-pulmonary resuscitation, on-board suction units, portable suction units, various sizes of Philadelphia cervical collars, large first-aid kits, Hare traction splints, long back boards, XP-One boards, airway kits, blood-pressure kits containing stethoscopes and various sizes of cuffs, emergency-childbirth packs, 2000-liter bottles of oxygen capable of supplying all on board, oxygen masks and canulas, tool rolls for automobile extrication, flares, rechargeable flashlights, ambu-bags used for ventilation, portable stretchers, locked cabinets with intravenous supplies in case a doctor is at the scene, blankets, sheets, towels, assortments of splints, and many other

---

[1]The purchase of the 1967 Cadillac was made necessary because of a highway accident in which the 1966 model was damaged.

Richard W. York photo

A "SQUARE ONE" *— A modular ambulance is compact on the outside and roomy on the inside. This Cayel Craft, the first modular ambulance of the Washington Emergency squad, was built to the squad's specifications and is mounted on a 1978 Ford chassis. The vehicle served for seven years and was traded on a new one late in 1985. With the introduction of the modular ambulances, the streamlined Cadillacs became obsolete.* *(See picture on Page 91.)*

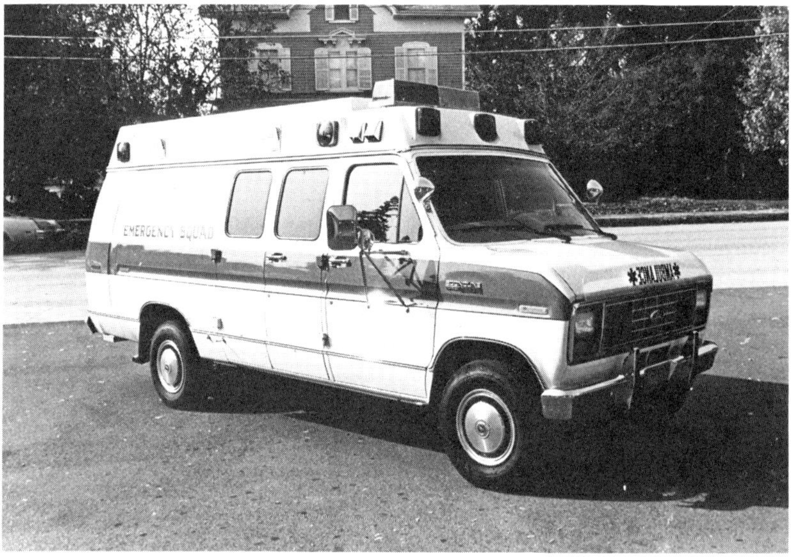

Richard W. York photo

***VAN** — This vehicle, smaller than the other ambulances, is used mainly for transportations. It is a 1983 Ford.*

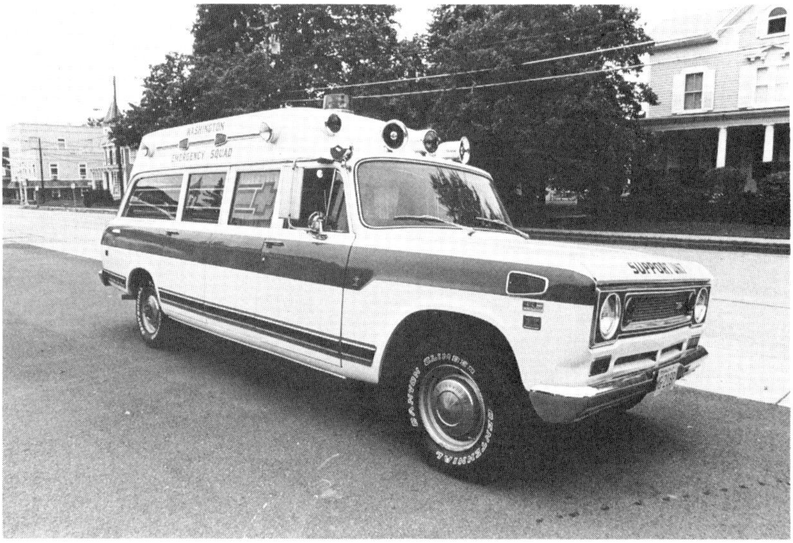

Richard W. York photo

***SUPPORT VEHICLE** — This International ambulance was purchased new in 1971 and was converted to a support vehicle in 1983.*

small items.

The small van ambulance is a 1983 Ford capable of carrying two patients. Its predecessor dates back to 1971 when the firemen purchased an International to use as a second ambulance. The present vehicle is used mainly for non-emergency transportation service and secondary trips when patients, previously taken to hospitals by the squad, must be transported to other hospitals for specialized tests or treatments. These secondary trips include runs to Allentown, New York City, Philadelphia and sometimes much greater distances, and are often followed by similar trips to return the patients to the original hospitals.

In order to be available for emergency service at times when three ambulances are needed, the van carries substantially the same equipment as the first-line ambulances except that it lacks Lifepak-5 heart monitor and heart-lung resuscitator.

The support truck is the former International ambulance which has been converted to its present use. It is equipped to tow the trailer and boat, and it carries life jackets for water rescues, an extra supply of tools, and other items with which to back up the other vehicles. Consideration is now being given to the replacement of this aging vehicle, probably with a four-wheel-drive truck.

For many years the squad vehicles and equipment were maintained by member Guy Burd, Sr., who recently acquired honorary status. Today

Royal Photographics photo

MAINTENANCE MEN — *Squad members Howard Reed, left, and Martin Nyland, Jr., perform the routine maintenance chores on all of the vehicles.*

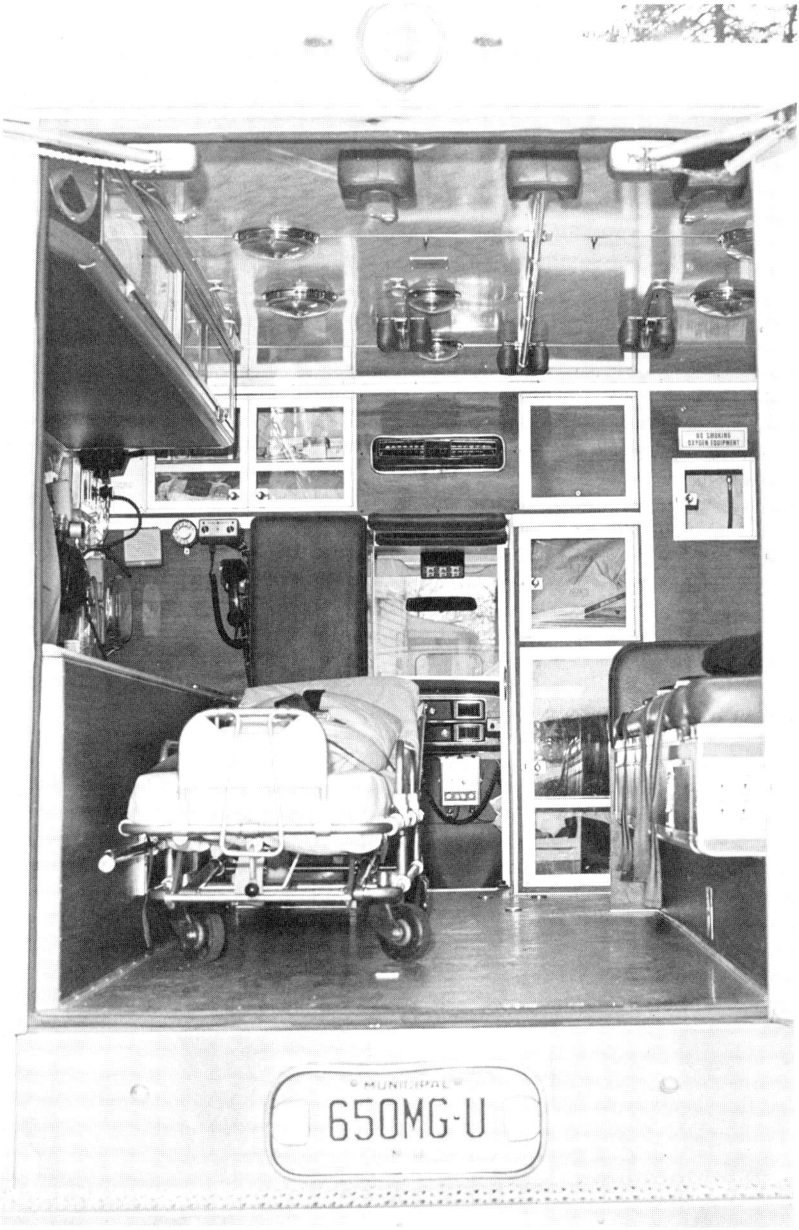

Minassian photo

EMERGENCY ROOM ON WHEELS — *Interior of modular ambulance has floor space and ceiling height to permit treatment of patient with life-supporting equipment while on way to hospital. Vehicle shown is Washington squad's first Cayel Craft ambulance in 1978.*

members Howard Reed and Martin Nyland, Jr., are in charge of all vehicle and equipment maintenance. Much of the work is done by them, often with the help of other members. They have firsthand knowledge of every piece of equipment owned by the squad, from Jaws of Life down to blankets and splints. Major vehicle repairs are performed by local garages. Assisting in the maintenance of equipment other than the vehicles are John DeFilippis, Robert Petrick, Thomas Petrick, Richard Yurkovitch, and Timothy Yurkovitch.

The sleek, streamlined Cadillac ambulances have nearly become things of the past, and square modular or van-type vehicles are used almost exclusively today. Their square conformation provides a floor area and ceiling height that allow attendants to stand and walk around while administering to patients. They also provide ample room for the convenient storage of the large amount of sophisticated equipment carried by today's modern ambulances. These vehicles are small emergency rooms on wheels.

When the change from streamlined to modular ambulances was taking place, the Washington Emergency Squad, with a history dating back to the early days of volunteer squads and a membership with a combined experience of some 200 years of driving and riding ambulances, decided to go back to the drawing board and attempt to create the optimum ambulance. The membership worked with the manufacturer of Cayel Craft bodies, and the result was the first modular ambulance of the squad. It was placed on a 1978 Ford chassis. This was a remarkable vehicle and served the squad for eight years before it was traded with more than 100,000 miles on its odometer.

The squad had set out to create a vehicle that would endure in a man-

Richard W. York photo

***EXCITING MOMENT** — Squad members Michael Baylor and Brian Shea arrive from Rock Rapids, Iowa, with new Cayel Craft ambulance in January 1985.*

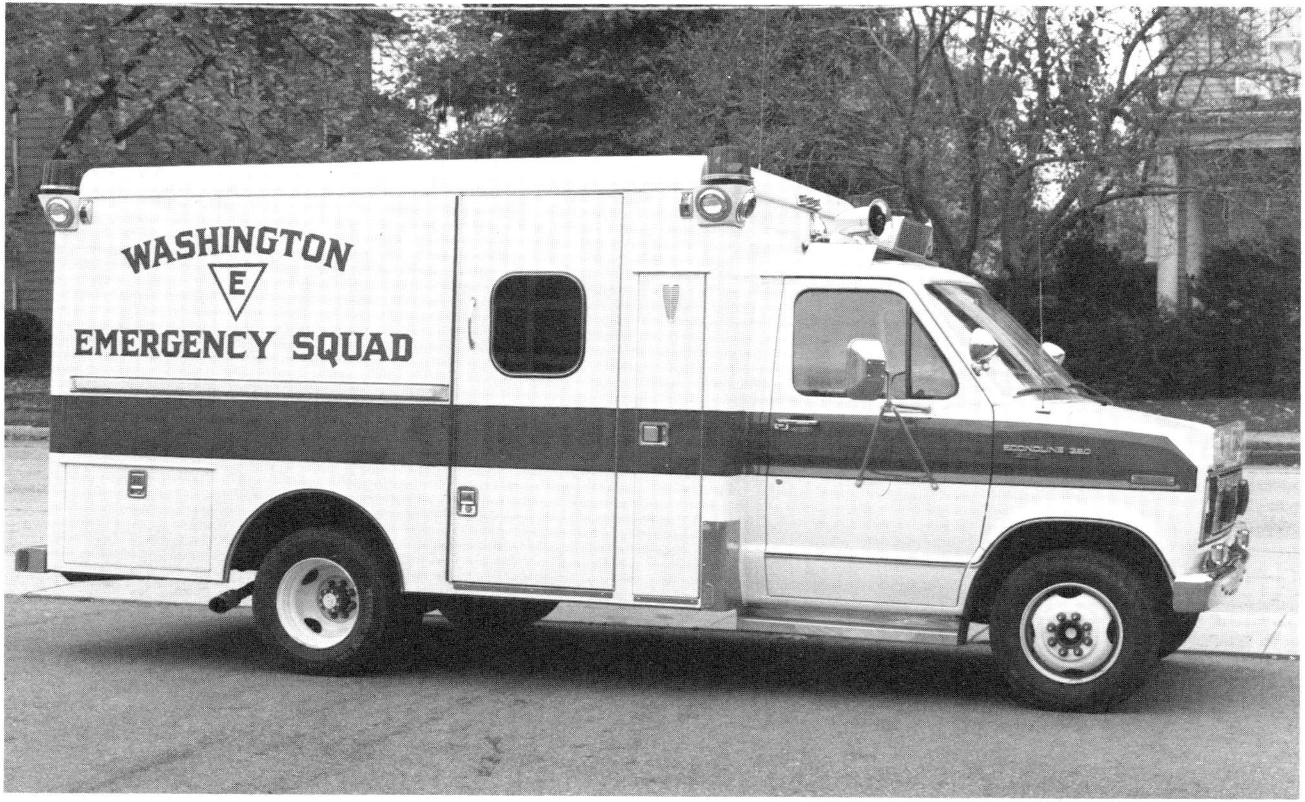

Royal Photographics photo

NEW FIRST-LINE AMBULANCE — *In January 1985 this new Cayel Craft ambulance with stainless-steel body replaced a small Ford van when it was decided to operate two fully-equipped first-line ambulances. Van was sold to Oxford Emergency Squad.*

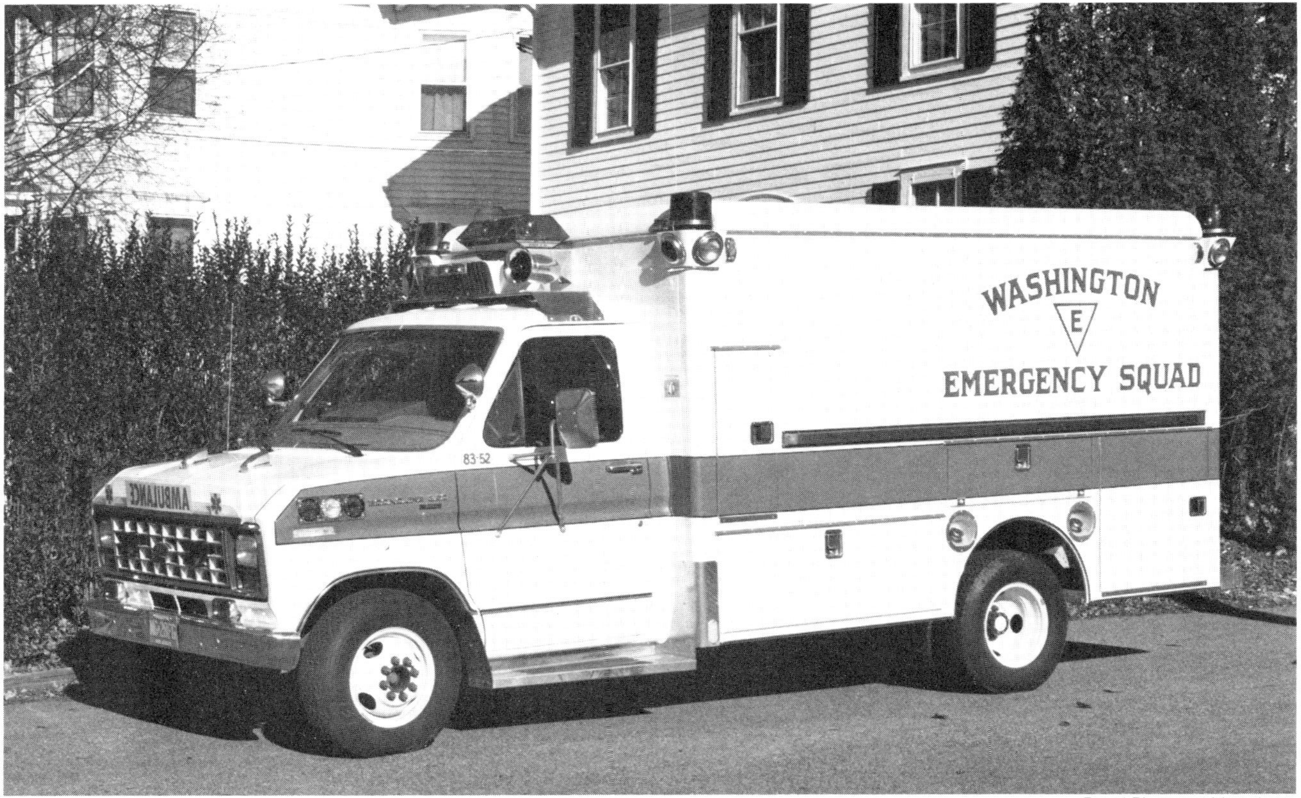

Royal Photographics photo

NEWEST AMBULANCE — *In November 1985 this new stainless-steel Cayal Craft replaced the aging 1978 model vehicle. Old vehicle had recorded more than 100,000 miles on its odometer but brought a generous trade price because its steel body was galvanized. The new ambulance is the 17th to serve the Washington area.*

ner that would bring a high price when traded in, and with a body of such quality it could be used for additional years on a new chassis if desired. For reasons of maximum structural strength and safety, a steel body was preferred to aluminum, but as most motorists know, the enemy of steel is rust. The Cayel Craft body was offered with galvanized steel, a fact that appealed to the Washington squad members. The manufacturer co-operated with the ideas that had been generated by the long experience of this squad, and the resulting vehicle turned out to be a consistent prize winner.

When the squad decided to replace two ambulances in 1985, its members went back to the drawing board again. The fact that they succeeded the first time was evidenced by the small number of changes that were made in the new vehicles. The biggest change was the use of stainless steel in the new Cayel Craft bodies, a fact that affords even better rust protection than the formerly used galvanized steel with, of course, no sacrifice of strength and safety. The skills and experience of the membership of this squad and those of the well-established body builder combined to create a vehicle that stands out in a crowd and a model that has become admiringly known as "the Washington ambulance." From its beginning the Washington Emergency Squad has earned the reputation of being among the first to obtain the latest and finest equipment. The creation of this outstanding ambulance is in keeping with that tradition.

Since 1981 Allentown and Sacred Heart Hospital Center has maintained a helicopter transport service for critically ill and injured patients. It is known as MedEvac, and it is available to emergency squads in cases where faster transport than can be accomplished by ambulances may save lives of patients.

MedEvac provides 24-hour-a-day, seven-day-a-week emergency transportation-by-air services for critically injured persons needing acute care at accident scenes primarily within a 60-mile radius of Allentown. It also serves a much larger region for interhospital patient transfers.

On-scene requests make up about 70% of the MedEvac missions and include auto accidents, industrial accidents, burns, penetrating trauma, and limited-search-and-rescue operations. Squads summon MedEvac to emergency scenes when the amount of time needed to transport a patient by ground transportation to an appropriate facility may pose a threat to the patient's life; when weather, road conditions or other factors affecting the use of ground transportation may seriously delay the patient's access to advanced life-support care; when the ambulance unit does not have the skills or equipment needed for the case at hand; and when, if

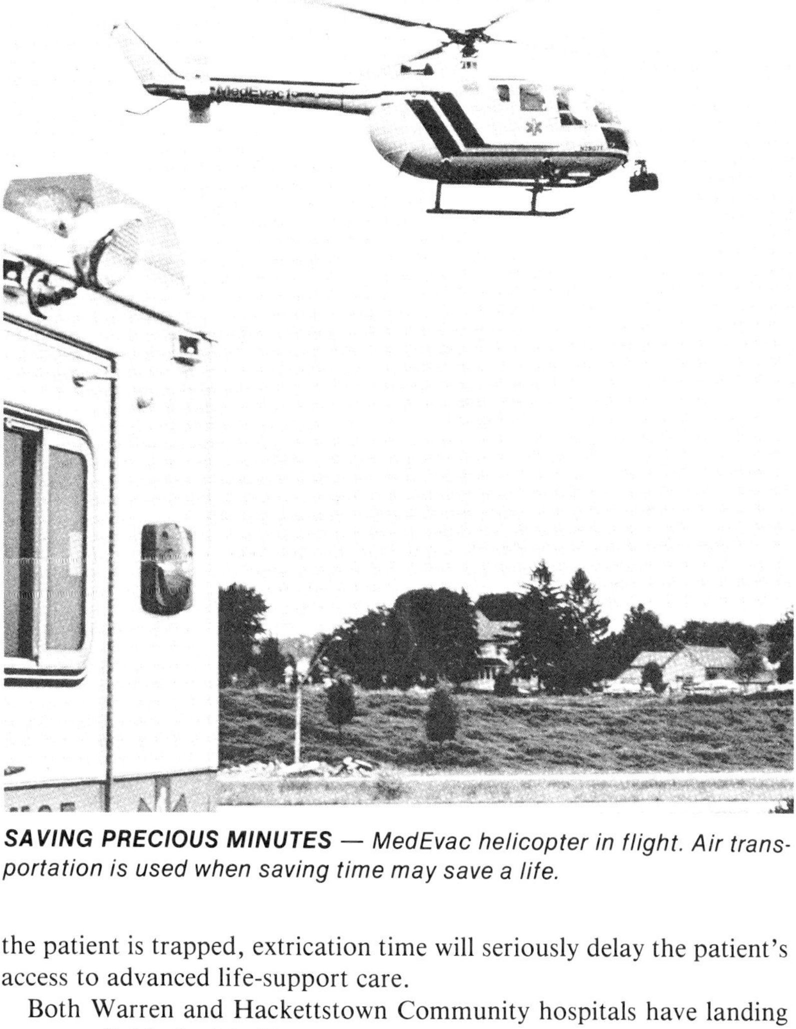

***SAVING PRECIOUS MINUTES** — MedEvac helicopter in flight. Air transportation is used when saving time may save a life.*

the patient is trapped, extrication time will seriously delay the patient's access to advanced life-support care.

Both Warren and Hackettstown Community hospitals have landing areas available for MedEvac.

The emergency squads make available the vehicles, equipment and personnel that can cope with most emergency situations, but in the special cases where time is the essence for the saving of lives, the MedEvac helicopter adds another very important dimension to the services that are available.

FIRST BOROUGH BUILDING — *This property, on the southwest corner of Belvidere Avenue and West Church Street, was purchased from the Peter R. Winter Benevolent Association for $7,500 in 1874. The larger building became the first Borough Hall. Remodeled several times, it served the borough for 96 years. It is now the Mueller Building.*

11

The Squad Building

The first meeting of the Mayor and Common Council of the Borough of Washington was held at a local hostelry, the Washington House, on April 18, 1868. Subsequent meetings were held in various locations, frequently at the private business office of the mayor in office at the time.

Every municipality needs adequate quarters in which to have its council and various board meetings and to house the vehicles and equipment of its street, police, fire and other departments. The excellent Municipal Building and emergency squad building in Washington are the result of more than a century of increasing needs and measures taken to meet them.

In 1873 the organization of the Excelsior Fire Company and the purchase of a Babcock fire engine created an immediate need for a building. On April 1 of that year, council ordered that a building be sought in which to house the engine.

The quest for a building did not succeed at first. On May 15 council decided to obtain a plan and cost estimate of a building containing a meeting room. On June 3 it was decided to build such a structure. On June 17 a committee was appointed to seek a suitable lot.

The committee did not succeed. It was discharged on June 24 and replaced by a new committee on July 1. A. R. Strader, secretary of the Excelsior Fire Company, appeared before council on July 19 and stressed the urgency of the provision of a building for the Babcock engine.

A special council meeting was held on October 16 at which it was decided to purchase a property at the corner of Belvidere Avenue and West Church Street from the Peter R. Winter Benevolent Association for $6,000 cash and the assumption of a $1,500 mortgage. An existing building was suitable for the needs of the borough, and a house on the corner of the property could be rented out.

Title problems caused some delay in the purchase, but in May 1874 the borough leased the property and made minor alterations to the building

COSTLY FIRE — *The Borough Hall was gutted by fire in 1913. Borough records were saved, but fire-company documents were destroyed.*

***REBUILT AND ENLARGED** — Old walls were re-used in construction. House was razed to make room for larger main building. Fire bell is visible in tower atop building.*

in order to gain occupancy pending the delivery of a deed.

The third floor of the main building was rented for a few months to the Washington Cornet Band as a practice room, after which the area was set aside for the firemen and became known as Firemen's Hall.

The property served the borough and its fire companies for 96 years. In 1908 council appointed a committee to consider the possibility of constructing a new municipal building, but for financial reasons the project was abandoned in favor of the construction of a sewer system and sewage disposal plant.

A building project was carried out after the Borough Hall was gutted by fire in 1913. Reconstruction included the original brick walls. The house on the corner of West Church Street was razed to make room for an addition to the larger structure.

In the later years more improvements were made. A refurbishing in 1937 included the provision of quarters for the emergency truck and ambulance on the West Church Street side of the building and the in-

Easton Express photo

FIRST SQUAD QUARTERS — *Entrance to emergency truck and ambulance bays on West Church Street side of old Borough Hall in 1954. The fire department ambulance had replaced the Community Ambulance Squad, but sign over door had not yet been changed. This photo was taken when the new 1954 Cadillac ambulance arrived, replacing temporary used Buick. A. Fletcher Wright, left, the former fire chief, extends congratulations to John Riegel, 1954 chief (in cab), while Alvin Burd, 1954 assistant chief, stands between them.*

***IMPROVEMENTS** — Overhead doors on vehicle bays, repainting, new letters on facade and provision for emergency truck and ambulance quarters on West Church Street were included in remodeling in early 1950's. Tower and fire bell were removed from roof when fire whistle was installed.*

stallation of overhead doors in all of the vehicle bays.

An emergency squad requires centrally located quarters in which to house its vehicles and equipment, and to provide an area in which to hold meetings and conduct practice drills and first-aid classes with the vehicles close by.

The room provided by the municipality on the West Church Street side of the old Borough Hall in the early days of the emergency and ambulance services was a makeshift arrangement. It was barely large enough for the two vehicles in service at the time and afforded little room for equipment storage and none at all for meetings or training sessions.

The firemen decided to purchase a property for the purpose of providing adequate quarters for their emergency and ambulance vehicles. When the Atlantic Refining Company offered the rear portion of its filling station property at the corner of West Washington and South Lincoln Avenues for sale in 1948,[1] the firemen purchased it with funds they had raised.

---

[1]The Cornish piano and organ factory formerly stood on that lot.

Minassian photo

***PREPARATION FOR FUTURE** — In 1948 the firemen purchased this lot on South Lincoln Avenue, where the Cornish piano and organ factory once stood, for a future emergency squad building. They sold the lot to the Washington Parking Authority when the new Municipal Building was built.*

For want of funds the construction of a building had to be left for the future. In the meantime the firemen leased the land to the borough for use as a much needed parking facility with the understanding that the parking would give way to the firemen's fund-raising carnival during one week of each summer.

The firemen held back from undertaking a building project because the borough council had its own building plans under consideration. The borough owned the former Hotel Windsor property, located diagonally across the street from the old Borough Hall at the intersection of Belvidere Avenue and East Church Street. That land had been purchased as a site for a municipal building as authorized by a referendum several years before, but this project had also been left for the future. Crowded conditions in the old municipal offices were now hastening the construction date.

In 1970 the new Municipal Building became a reality. A spacious area was provided for the fire trucks and emergency vehicles. With sufficient

Old postcard courtesy of Barry Mueller

MUNICIPAL BUILDING SITE — *Voters approved purchase of the Hotel Windsor on the northeast corner of Belvidere Avenue and East Church Street in 1944. Purchase was made the following year at a price of $16,000. The building was razed, and the land became a parking lot until the Municipal Building was built in 1970.*

Richard W. York photo

NEW MUNICIPAL BUILDING — *In 1970 the four fire-truck bays and two emergency-vehicle bays on Belvidere Avenue were adequate, but not for long.*

Richard W. York photo

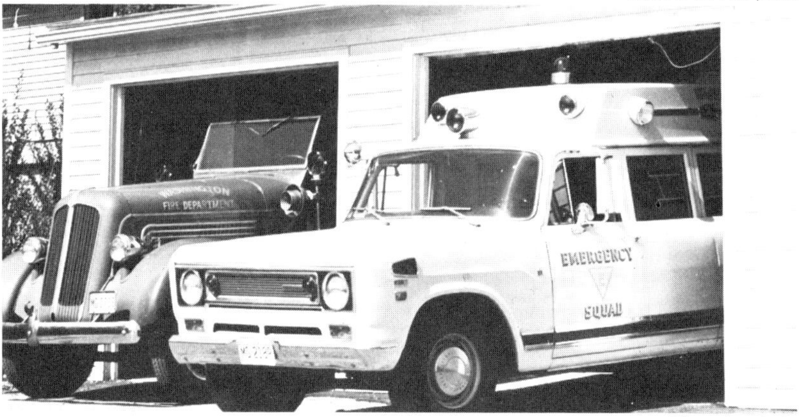

Minassian photo

Richard W. York photo

RUNNING OUT OF ROOM *— By 1979 three vehicles were being kept in space meant for two, a fire truck and an emergency vehicle were being kept in a frame building at another location, and a Cadillac ambulance was left outdoors.*

Richard E. Harpster photo

***LUCKY BUY** — This property, next to the Municipal Building on Belvidere Avenue, was vacated by the Washington Clinic when it moved to the new Warren Hills Family Health Center. The firemen lost no time in buying it.*

space now available for all of their requirements, the firemen sold their South Lincoln Avenue property to the Washington Parking Authority, and it became a permanent unit in the downtown parking system.

But the solution to the problem of space proved to be a temporary one. Population grew and the number of emergency calls increased. Within nine years the fire department purchased an aerial truck, and the emergency squad was operating three ambulances instead of one. Three emergency vehicles were now housed in an area meant for two, a fire truck and an ambulance were kept in a frame building nearby, and one ambulance had to remain outdoors. The vehicle area in the Municipal Building was so crowded that prompt accessibility to one of the ambulances was lacking, and no space was available near the vehicles for drills and classes.

Once again the firemen conducted a search for a suitable property on which an emergency-squad building could be built. The search came to

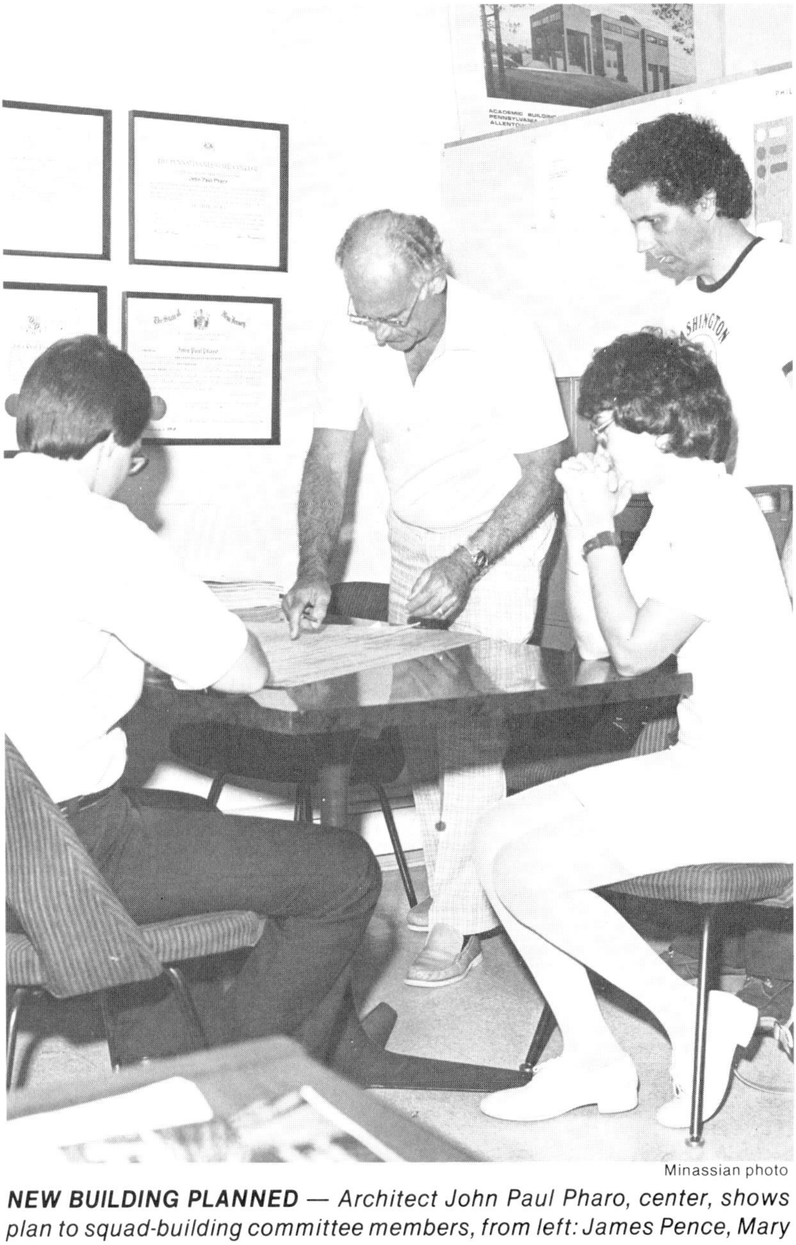

Minassian photo

NEW BUILDING PLANNED — *Architect John Paul Pharo, center, shows plan to squad-building committee members, from left: James Pence, Mary Petrick and Captain Dale Coban.*

***CONSTRUCTION PROGRESS** — Various stages in construction of the new squad building were photographed by member Guy Burd, Sr.*

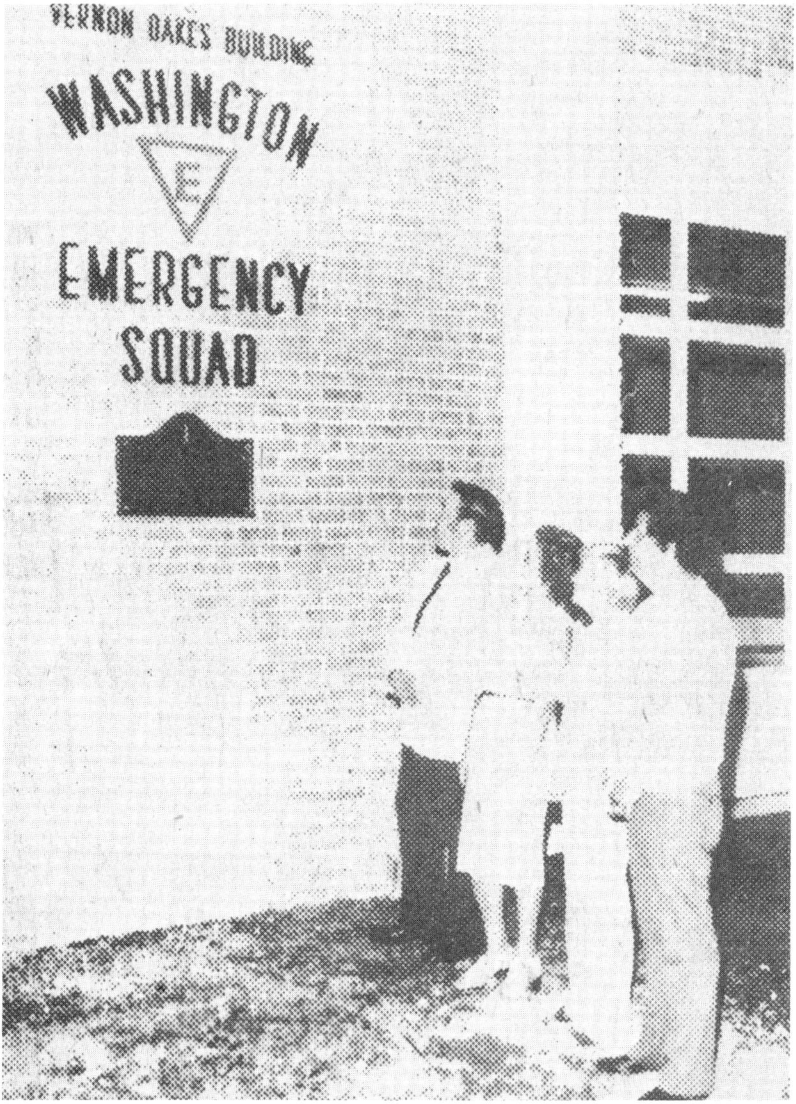

Forum photo

***BUILDING NAMED** — A ceremony in 1982 marked the designation of the structure as the Vernon Oakes Building in memory of the squad's founder and first captain. From left: Gene Castner, contractor who built the structure; Mrs. June Oakes Burk, daughter of the late Captain Oakes; Judy Coban, president of squad auxiliary; and Dale Coban, squad captain. Letters were donated by Castner.*

MAYOR CUTS RIBBON — *Building was dedicated on October 1, 1982. From left: Lieutenant Mary Petrick, President Terry Kresge, Mayor William Haller, Assistant Captain Russell Wildrick and Captain Thomas Mason, Jr.*

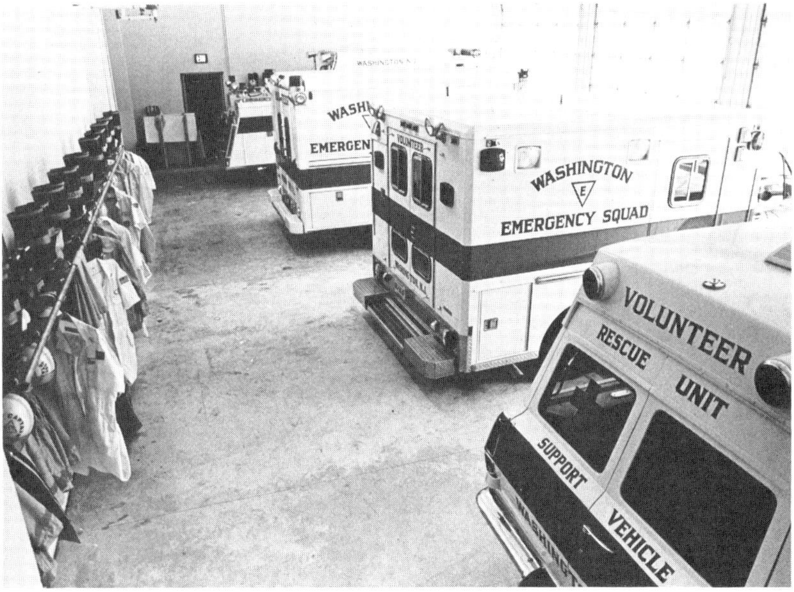

Richard W. York photos

***FEATURES OF BUILDING** — Meeting room, top, and vehicle room. Next page, from top: supply room, office and kitchen.*

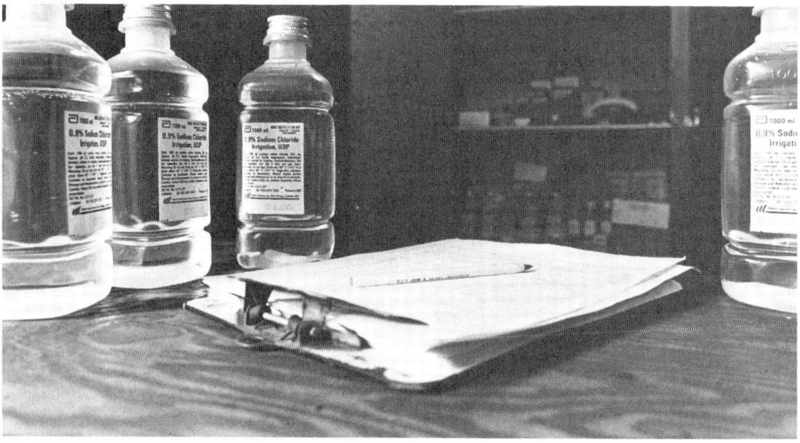
1000 ml
0.9% Sodium Chloride
Irrigation, USP

Royal Photographics photo

***THE VERNON OAKES BUILDING** — Structure is decorated to celebrate the 50th year of the Washington Emergency Squad in 1985.*

an abrupt and very happy ending when the Washington Clinic moved out of its building on Belvidere Avenue, next door to the Municipal Building. The property, extending all the way through to Taylor Street, was ideal for the purpose, and the firemen grasped the opportunity to purchase it.

Before arrangements could be made to construct a building, the amicable separation of the fire department and the emergency squad had occurred. The fire department and the squad agreed to own the property jointly, with the fire department using the rear half with frontage on Taylor Street and the squad using the front half fronting on Belvidere Avenue. The squad immediately got its building plans under way.

Captain Dale Coban, Donald Butler, Guy Burd, Sr., Thomas Mason, Jr., James Pence and Mary Petrick were appointed to serve as a building committee. John Paul Pharo was commissioned as the architect, and Gene Castner was selected as the contractor to build the structure.

A fund-raising drive was organized,[1] and ground was broken in 1979. A cornerstone was laid, behind which a copy of the first edition of this book was imbedded. Work proceeded as funds became available.

In September of 1981, with the outside walls completed, the squad conducted a ceremony for the purpose of naming the building. Decision had been made to name it the Vernon Oakes Building, and the letters on the facade were donated and installed by contractor Gene Castner. Also installed was a bronze plaque, donated by the squad auxiliary, containing the First Aid Squad Prayer.

Participating in the ceremony were June Oakes Burk, daughter of the late Captain Vernon Oakes; James Burk, her husband; Castner; Dale Coban, squad captain; and Judy Coban, president of the squad auxiliary.

The project was completed during the summer of 1982, with squad members doing much of the interior work. A dedication ceremony was held on Sunday afternoon, October 1, 1982. June Oakes Burk was guest of honor. Mayor William Haller cut the ribbon, and former Mayor Alvin Sloan was master of ceremonies for the program that followed. The public had been invited, and the large audience included past and present squad members, auxiliary members, juniors, representatives of other emergency squads, and public officials.

The Vernon Oakes Building is greatly admired, serves the needs of the squad very well, and represents an important milestone in the history of the Washington Emergency Squad and the Washington area.

---

[1]See Chapter 12.

Minassian photo

FUND-RAISING MINSTREL SHOW — *This show, in late 1940's, was one of the last in a long series. Front row, from left: Rick Stevens, Robert Levine, Elmer Neuls, Harry Garey, Samuel Levine and Roger Seaman. Second row: James Keenan, Doris Opdyke, Jack Rush, Dorothy Opdyke and Charles Wright. Third row: Harry Shrope, Melvin Burd, Jerry Wilkins, Joseph Ragno, William Sheats, Thomas DeVoe, Russell Beam, Ralph Kinsey, James Plotts, William DeMont, Joseph Eger, A. Fletcher Wright and Harold Sheats. Back row: William Allen, Walter Castner, Charles Wright, Kenneth Cregar, William Gild, Elvin Shook, Robert Gardner, Fred Glosser, Charles Eagan and Quentin Chambellan. Girl in front of interlocutor is unidentified.*

12

Financing and Fund Raising

The financial needs of the Washington Emergency Squad are formidable. Vehicles must be replaced frequently because of the large number of miles travelled. When a newer and better piece of lifesaving equipment becomes available, this squad is among the first to acquire it. All sorts of costly supplies, ranging all the way from tires to oxygen, require a continual flow of cash.

In earlier days financial needs were more modest. A fine new ambulance could be purchased for less than $10,000. The firemen and the Legionnaires raised funds by sponsoring annual outdoor carnivals in the summer and producing home-talent minstrel shows in the winter.

The minstrel shows ran for two or more nights in a local theater or school auditorium and were fun events for the audience and cast alike. They were always sellouts and provided substantial profits to be used for the fire department and its emergency squad or for the American Legion Ambulance Corps. Several local people developed into stars, and their antics were anticipated by eager ticket buyers. ''Bab'' Oakes was the interlocutor in the firemen's shows and Harvey Mowder in the Legion performances. After the death of Oakes, Bob Groat, Al Sloan or Russ Beam occupied the center chair and performed the straight-man chores in the firemen's shows.

Many of the end men achieved local stardom, and the names of ''Snub'' Dixon, ''Buss'' Eagan, Jim Ervin, Russ Gibson, Bill Gordon, Pete Hoppaugh, Joe Miller, Jimmy Ryan, ''Tuffy'' Sheats, Harry Shrope, George Snyder and ''Abbie'' Wright are a few that come to mind. Hit soloists included ''Shine'' DeMont, Raymond Eckhardt, Art Fliegauf, Elwood Sliker and Herbie Smith. The Washington Glee Club membership contributed heavily to the chorus and furnished many of the outstanding soloists.

The performers—over the years there were many more than can be recalled here—and the audience had a big night at every performance. The last show was always long remembered, and the next one was eagerly anticipated.

Richard W. York photo

***POTATO-PEELING DETAIL** — Preparing fund-raising dinner to be served in the firemen's hall at the Municipal Building. From back: Harold Radcliff, Jody Fritts, Rudolph Bescherer and Sharon Sozanski.*

The firemen ran many special fund-raising campaigns to provide for the purchase of vehicles and other large and costly items of equipment. This method of funding purchases is no longer practical because the need for the replacement of a vehicle now occurs nearly every year. Today's fund raising is a continual effort to meet the needs of the squad, and particular items of equipment are no longer identified with any campaign. When the Municipal Building was built, carnivals, minstrel shows and drives for specific pieces of equipment were discontinued, and the firemen made use of the excellent kitchen and dining facilities in their new Firemen's Hall to raise needed funds. Public dinners are served twice each year, the hall is rented for private parties, and banquets are catered. The financial needs of the fire companies are met in this manner, but when the emergency squad became a separate organization it had to devise its own methods of raising funds.

The financial needs of the Washington Emergency Squad now approach $100,000 per year if the funds are to be on hand for the purchase of the next ambulance when needed. The squads income comes from many sources. A substantial sum comes from the people who are helped. There are nearly 1,400 of them each year, and many express their appreciation by sending contributions to the squad.

The Borough of Washington furnishes gasoline and insurance to the squad and pays for the utilities in the Vernon Oakes Building. Until the squad outgrew its quarters in the Municipal Building, the borough housed the squad's vehicles and equipment there. The borough also makes an annual cash contribution to the squad ($12,220 in 1985), and the township makes a cash contribution ($7,000 in 1985). The County of Warren contributes $800 per year to the Washington squad, as it does to every rescue squad in the county.

Late in 1969 a decision was made to send an annual appeal for funds by mail to all businesses, industries and residents of the area served by the squad. The first mailing was sent in 1970, and the plan has been continued ever since. The response is always generous, but it is far from sufficient to meet all of the needs, so the squad is continually devising new methods of attracting funds.

From time to time on a Sunday or other day when highway traffic was heavy, squad members would conduct a "coin toss" in which motorists could contribute to its work. All squad vehicles were placed on display at the intersection of state highway Routes 31 and 57. Signs were placed along the highways for about a quarter of a mile in each direction. These signs, placed several hundred feet apart, said: "Fund Drive Ahead" . . . "Washington Emergency Squad" . . . "Help Us Help You" . . . "Thank You." At the traffic light the squad personnel, dressed in their white coveralls, received money handed to them or tossed into containers.

Motorists are very much aware that they may need the services of a volunteer rescue squad at any moment, and they are generous when they encounter the roadside fund-raising efforts of these organizations. Operators of tractor-trailer rigs, who as professional drivers know how vital emergency aid can be, are generous contributors, and the Washington Emergency Squad helps many of them.

The highway collections provided nearly $12,000 toward the cost of the squad's new building.

However, many friends and supporters of the squad feel that it is an imposition on the volunteers for them to be required to spend weekends and holidays collecting funds on the highways, so other fund-raising methods are now being used. The last highway "coin toss" conducted by the Washington squad was in 1981.

The squad members run several games at the annual fairs on Fourth of July afternoons in connection with the Washington Celebrates America celebrations.

Members and organizations within the squad have been inventive in devising fund-raising devices. A. Leighton "Hap" Goberman, retired businessman and honorary squad member who still responds to calls when needed, grew a crop of shamrocks in his back yard. He gave them

Minassian photo

HIGHWAY COLLECTION *— Motorists are given opportunity to contribute to service which they may need at any time. Signs tell the story, and ambulance serves as appropriate reminder.*

EIGHTEEN WHEELS, FOUR WHEELS, OR THREE WHEELS — *They are all willing to contribute. Kathleen Adams does the collecting.*

Minassian photos

Minassian photo

***FOOD CONCESSION** — Auxiliary members sell hot dogs and refreshments on East Washington Avenue during merchants' sidewalk sales.*

to the squad members on St. Patrick's Day, and the members sold them in the business section of the town and netted $314.

The squad's auxiliary runs rummage sales, bake sales and other events to benefit the treasury of the squad.

In 1978 the junior members conducted a car wash in front of the Municipal Building vehicle bays which was very successful. Car washes have become frequent events in front of the new Vernon Oakes Building. Although they are juniors' projects, many regular squad members join in to help.

The juniors run occasional raffles, one of which occurred in December 1984 with a "Boom Box" cassette player as the prize.

The Vernon Oakes Society[1] has become one of the most important sources of funds for the Washington Emergency Squad. The January meetings of the society, at which its members' checks are presented to the squad, have become larger each year and are now important civic events.

In January 1982 twenty society members and guests comprised a committee that attended the squad's regular meeting. The meeting was interrupted for the presentation of the checks. The theme of the presentation was based upon a membership promotion previously created by the society. The society was characterized as a "cash cow." Illustrated by a cartoon, when fed $100 by a society member, the cow produced

[1]More information about The Vernon Oakes Society appears in Chapter 14.

Minassian photo

***CAR WASH** — Juniors get lots of help from regular members with car wash in front of the squad building on Belvidere Avenue.*

Minassian photo

***JUNIOR RAFFLE** — "Boom Box" cassette player is the prize in raffle held at Radio Shack store. From left: Juniors Scott Pletzer and Thomas Cicerelle, and Lisa DeMonti watch Alvin Sloan draw winning ticket. Captain Mary Petrick and store proprietor Michael DeMonti hold bag filled with chances. Prize is on shelf in back of Petrick.*

A WONDERFUL ANIMAL!

FEED THE CASHCOW $100 AND SHE PRODUCES $10,000 FOR THE WASHINGTON EMERGENCY SQUAD

This advertisement contributed by a friend of the Washington Emergency Squad.
Cartoon through courtesy of Lebenthal & Co., Inc.

When he's not answering police, emergency or fire calls, squad treasurer Bill Brewster spends a lot of time milking the cashcow. Mary Petrick, the squad's energetic secretary, spends most of her time watching Bill do the milking (when she's not answering emergency calls or working at her profession as a Registered Nurse. On the wall is portrait of Vernon "Bab" Oakes, who founded the Washington Emergency Squad, the first in Warren County and one of the first in the United States.

MEMBERS OF THE VERNON OAKES SOCIETY KEEP THIS COW WELL FED.
WE HONOR THE MEMORY OF «BAB» OAKES, WE KEEP BILL WORKING
AND WE KEEP MARY HAPPY!

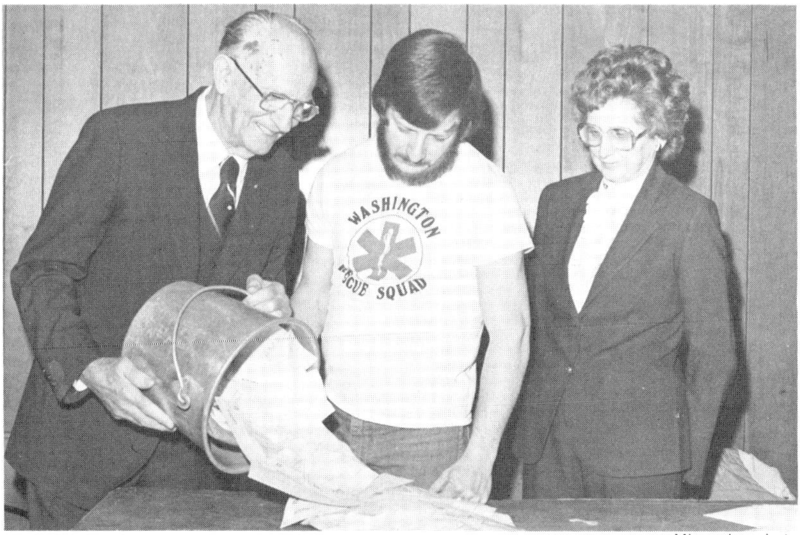

Minassian photo

***CASH COW PRODUCES** — Judge Clark C. Bowers, charter member of The Vernon Oakes Society, pours checks of society members from milk pail as squad president Terry Kresge and Mrs. June Oakes Burk look on.*

thousands of dollars for the squad. The cartoon depicted William Brewster, squad treasurer, milking the cow with Mary Petrick, the secretary, looking on. A picture of the late Vernon Oakes adorned the wall in back of the cow.

At the meeting Clark C. Bowers, former county judge and a charter member of the society, "poured" the checks out of a milk pail into the hands of Terry Kresge, squad president. Former Mayor Alvin Sloan, founder and director of the society, had sought 100 charter members but, by the time the meeting was held, checks from 121 members added $12,100 to the squad treasury.

The January 1983 presentation produced $12,600. A Christmas tree was decorated with 126 checks from society members and presented to the squad by Fred R. Alleman, secretary of the Washington Area Chamber of Commerce and a charter member of the society.

In January 1984 the presentation event was "old-timers night." The meeting room was filled to capacity despite sub-zero weather. All early squad members were invited. Fifty of them attended and were presented with society plaques. New Jersey State First Aid Council 10-year-service pins were presented to 29 former and present members. Certificates were awarded to former and present members in recognition of outstanding service.

Lorraine Fleming, a charter member of the society, presented the original incorporation certificate of the American Legion Ambulance Corps to John Hoffmaster, Legion post commander and former squad

Marilyn Cressman photo

VALUABLE CHRISTMAS TREE *— Fred R. Alleman, right, secretary of the Washington Area Chamber of Commerce and charter member of The Vernon Oakes Society, presents Christmas tree decorated with society members' checks to Captain Thomas Mason, Jr., as Mrs. June Oakes Burk observes.*

Marilyn Cressman photo

RECEIVES PHOTO OF SQUAD FOUNDER — *Mrs. June Oakes Burk receives photograph of painting of her father from Alvin Sloan in recognition of her interest in the Washington Emergency Squad. She is an honorary charter member of The Vernon Oakes Society.*

Marilyn Cressman photo

OLD-TIMERS NIGHT — *Meeting room is filled for the third annual presentation meeting of The Vernon Oakes Society in January 1984.*

Marilyn Cressman photo

***MAIN SPEAKER** — Charter member Larry K. Smith tells of his experience when the Washington Emergency Squad helped him at the scene of an accident.*

Marilyn Cressman photo

***OLD CHARTER** — Charter member Mrs. George W. Fleming gives corporation papers of the American Legion Ambulance Corps, for which her late husband was attorney, to John Hoffmaster, Legion Post commander and former squad captain.*

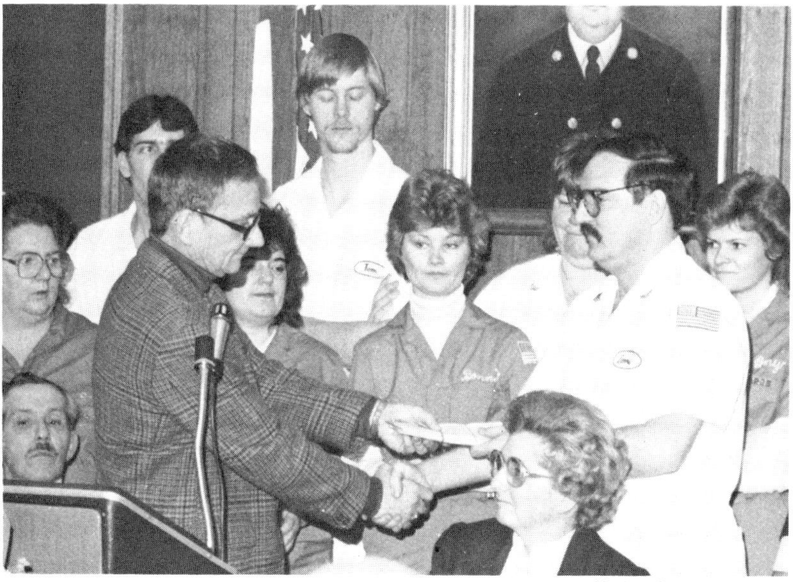

Marilyn Cressman photo

***PRESENTATION** — Charter member Larry K. Smith presents $16,000 in checks from society members to Larry Collins, squad president.*

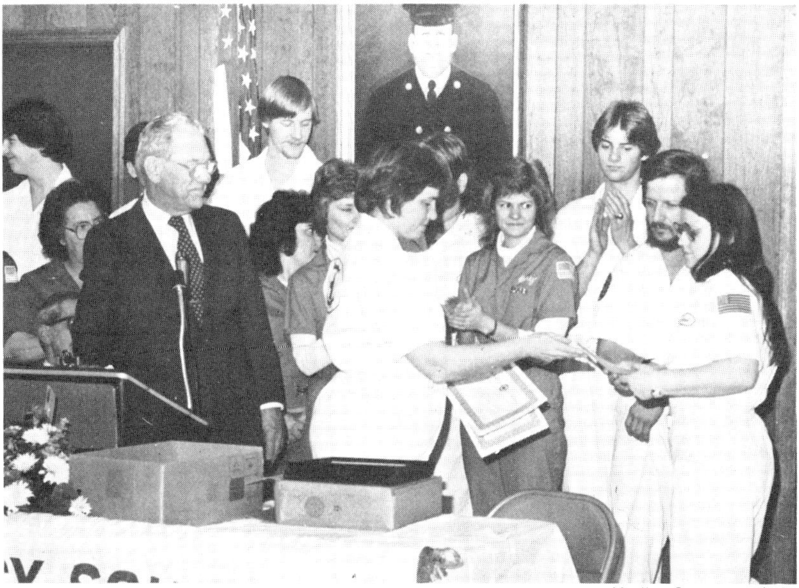

Marilyn Cressman photo

***SERVICE AWARDS** — Five-year service certificates and 10-year service pins are given to members by Rachael Semonche, squad trustee.*

Marilyn Cressman photo

***BOROUGH MANAGER** — Alan Fisher acknowledges introduction.*

Marilyn Cressman photo

***PROUD FATHER** — Paul Leitner is introduced with his daughter, Marti, who became the squad's first female member in 1976.*

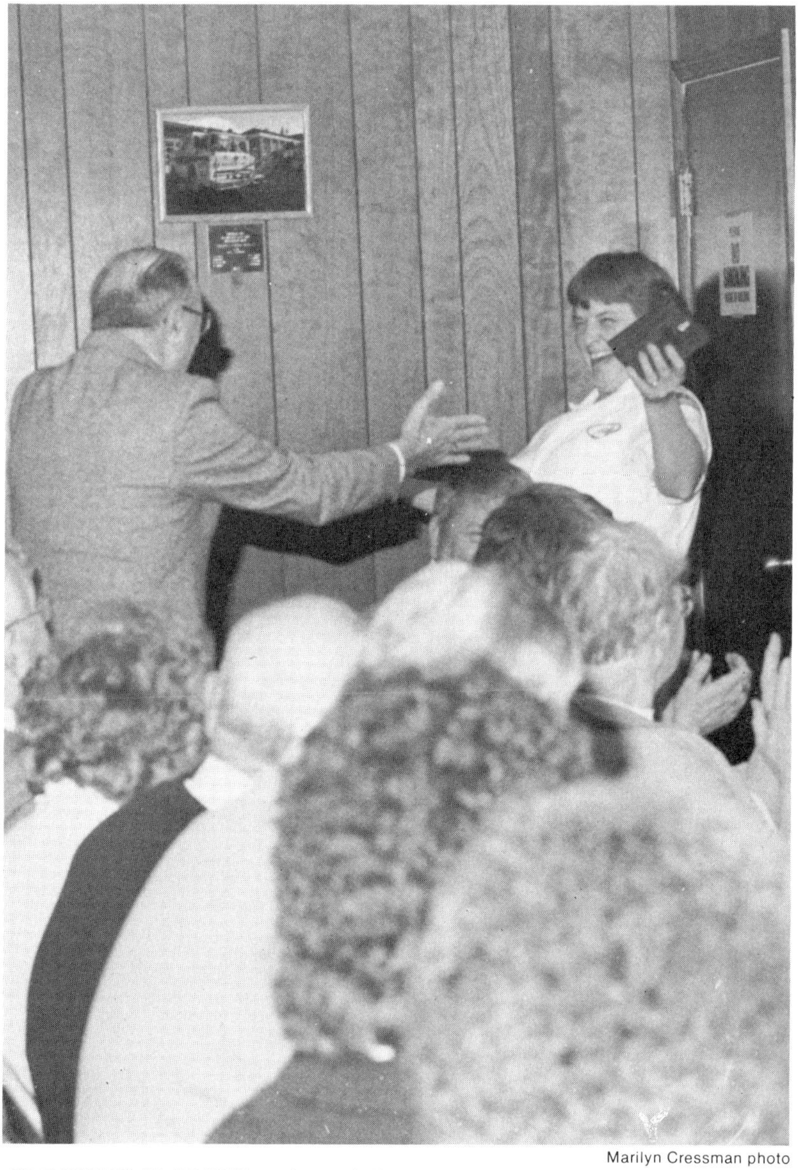

Marilyn Cressman photo

OLD-TIMER PLAQUES — *Joseph Eger, one of more than 50 old-timers being honored, is about to receive his plaque.*

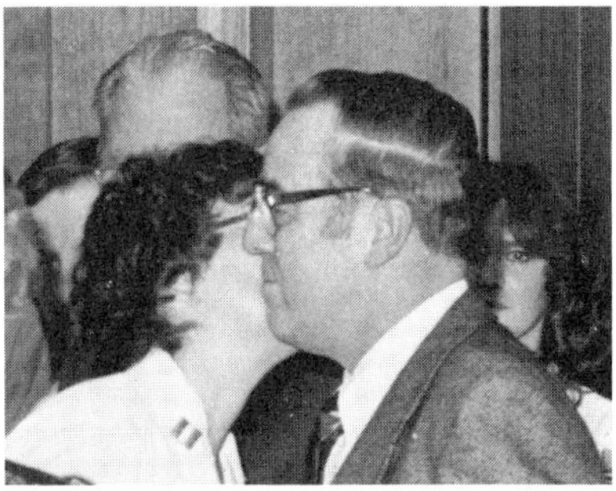

Marilyn Cressman photos

AS THE EVENING PROGRESSES *— Top left: Joe Eger receives plaque (and more) from squad trustee Rachael Semonche. Top right: David Lance, former fire chief and squad captain, receives plaque from Captain Mary Petrick. Middle: Guests examine old photographs of squad activities and calls. Bottom: Refreshments are enjoyed by all.*

Express photo

WHY IS THIS MAN SMILING? — Lieutenant Michael Baylor holds $20,000.00 in checks of $100.00 each from members of The Vernon Oakes Society.

captain. Mrs. Fleming's husband, the late George W. Fleming, an attorney and former mayor of Washington, had handled the incorporation of the Legion corps. Hoffmaster turned the document over to the squad for preservation with its historic memorabilia.

The checks from society members—this time there were 160 totaling $16,000—were presented to Larry Collins, squad president, by society member Larry K. Smith who had recently been the victim of a serious traffic accident. Smith had been treated at the scene and transported to Warren Hospital by the squad. He praised the squad's work and told the audience: "The apparent cost of membership in The Vernon Oakes Society is a privilege, not at all a cost. This money means that these people, our neighbors, will be able to provide for us the kind of care and treatment we would actually demand if we or our family would be in jeopardy of life. This money is not charity in any sense of the word. It is our responsibility to these volunteers to make certain they can continue to protect us against trauma and death."

The afternoon of Sunday, January 27, 1985, was the time of the largest presentation in the four-year history of the society.[1] With a membership roll that had passed the 200 mark, the organization's donation to the squad was more than $20,000.

The presentation was made by Washington Mayor Nancy J. Gianni Schmidt, a charter member of the society. Included in Mayor Schmidt's

---

[1]This meeting was used by the squad to be the time and place for the kickoff of its 50th-year observance. See Page 239.

***WROTE TRIBUTE** — Washington Mayor Nancy J. Gianni Schmidt, a charter member of The Vernon Oakes Society, presented $20,000 in members' checks to the squad. Her presentation remarks included tribute she had composed in honor of all volunteers.*

presentation address was the following which she had composed in honor of the members of the Washington Emergency Squad and fabulous volunteers everywhere:

VOLUNTEERS

V is for the VALUE they place on human life.

O is for the OATH they take to serve their community.

L is for the LABOR of love they perform.

U is for the UNDERSTANDING they have of the needs of others.

N is for the NUMBER of ways they volunteer their services.

T is for the TIME they devote to helping others.

E is for the EMPATHY they demonstrate.

E is for the EMERGENCIES to which they are always ready to respond.

R is for the RESCUES they so ably perform.

S is for the SQUAD they join in order to help their neighbors.

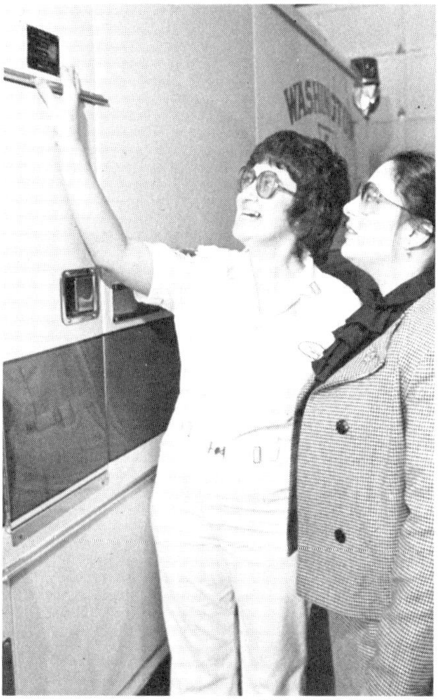

***DEDICATION PLAQUE** — Captain Mary Petrick shows Washington Mayor Nancy J. Gianni Schmidt plaque on new ambulance which had been dedicated to Alvin Sloan earlier in the evening.*

Richard W. York photo

The highlight of the program was the unveiling and placing in service of a new ambulance. To the obvious surprise of Alvin Sloan, the vehicle was dedicated to him and carried a plaque containing the following words:

IN HONOR OF
MR. ALVIN SLOAN
for his
SINCERE DEDICATION
to the
WASHINGTON EMERGENCY
SQUAD
January 27, 1985

The Washington Emergency Squad is particularly proud of its training program, the quality and scope of which make the squad eligible for grants-in-aid from the Institute for Instructional Improvement, Inc., a New York nonprofit educational organization. Several grants have been made to this squad during past years.

Richard W. York photo

NATIONAL BOOK PROJECT — *Participation of the Washington Emergency Squad in proposed book about rescue squads in the United States is discussed at squad meeting in 1979. From Left: Dale Coban, captain; Larry Collins, president; James Daniel, Reader's Digest roving editor; and William Brewster, treasurer.*

Richard W. York photo

LOCAL BOOK PROJECT — *The preparation of the first edition of this book is discussed during luncheon meeting at the Washington Diner. From left: Richard E. Harpster, author; James Rush, squad member; Herbert Trubek; Guy Burd, Sr., squad member; and Dr. Harold S. Sloan.*

One of these grants made possible the publication of the first edition of this book, and a subsequent grant has funded the publication of this edition. The entire receipts from the sale of both editions benefit the squad.

In 1978 Dr. Harold S. Sloan, a friend and supporter of the squad, read a brief squad history that had been written by Captain Vernon Oakes in 1939. Dr. Sloan suggested that a book containing the entire history of the Washington Emergency Squad should be published because this squad is the oldest in its area and one of the oldest small-town volunteer squads in the nation.

When the book-publishing project was envisioned, the advice of James Daniel was sought. Daniel, a resident of Weston, Connecticut, served as mayor of that municipality and is a retired member of its volunteer fire department and its emergency squad. He was a roving editor of Reader's Digest, for which he had written many articles. One of these was ''How Good Are Your Volunteer Firemen?'' That article praised the performance of the volunteers and also touched on the subject of emergency

Richard W. York photo

***BUILDING FUND RAISERS** — From left: Alvin Sloan, building fund committee member; Rev. M. E. Farr, committee chairman; and Joseph Sloat, committee treasurer.*

squads. It received national attention. Washington firemen used reprints of the article as part of their successful campaign for an affirmative vote in the referendum which resulted in the construction of the new Municipal Building.

Daniel visited the Washington Emergency Squad at its March meeting in 1979. He was impressed with what he saw. He has considered the possibility of writing a comprehensive book about volunteerism and, with the help of the Institute for Instructional Improvement, Inc., has researched the subject. It is hoped that such a book will be published in the future.

The need for a squad building created an immediate requirement to raise more than $170,000. Such a need occurs only once in a lifetime but, when added to all of the other necessary fund raising, was a challenge of staggering proportions. A group of local citizens came to the rescue. They proposed that the squad members be relieved of the task and that a citizens' committee should raise the money for them.

A committee was organized. Headed by Rev. Maurice E. Farr, it included Robert W. Burd, W. J. Choborda, Charles J. Jensen, Alvin Sloan, Joseph Sloat and Herbert Trubek. Its efforts were successful in raising much of the money required for the building and the financing of the balance.

Occasionally local organizations or individuals have donated needed items of equipment. The Washington Rotary Club furnished jackets to

Richard W. York photo

***SOLICIT INDUSTRIES** — Robert Burd (left) and Joseph Choborda, industrial co-chairmen.*

Richard W. York photo

***SEEK GIFTS** — Herbert Trubek (left) and Charles Jensen, special gifts co-chairmen.*

Richard E. Harpster photo

***PRESENTS JACKETS** — Martin Bry Nildsen, Jr., left, 1956 Washington Rotary Club president, presents jackets for squad members. Receiving sample jacket are Assistant Captain Charles Hubbard and Captain Charles Eagan of the Washington Emergency Squad.*

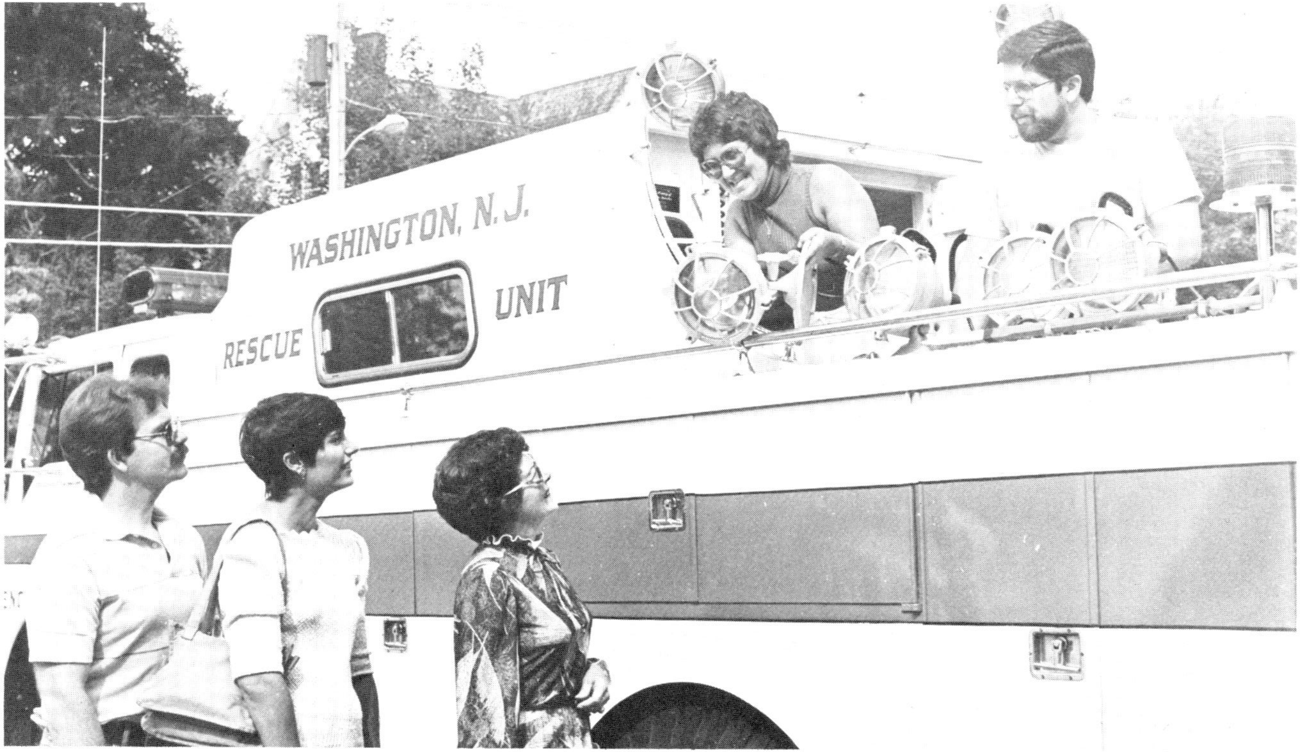

Richard E. Harpster photo

DONATION OF EQUIPMENT — *New quartz floodlights for emergency truck were given to the squad in 1984 by four members of the Saunders family in memory of the late George Saunders, Jr., squad captain. From left: George Saunders III, Mrs. George Saunders III, and Mrs. George Saunders, Jr. Not shown is Robert, brother of George III, who was serving in the Navy when picture was taken. Captain Mary Petrick and squad maintenance man Martin Nyland, Jr., on truck, admire the new equipment.*

the squad in 1956 at a cost of $400. Martin Bry-Nildsen, Jr.,[1] president of the club, made the presentation at a banquet held at Kapler's Hotel in Oxford in November of that year. The gift was accepted by Captain Charles Eagan and Assistant Captain Charles Hubbard of the squad.

In 1984 the family of the late George Saunders, squad captain in 1970 and 1971, donated a set of quartz floodlights for the emergency truck as a memorial to the deceased official.

Several residents of the area served by the squad have remembered the organization in their wills, and the custom of suggesting in newspaper obituary notices that contributions be made to the Washington Emergency Squad as memorials to the deceased is becoming more popular than ever and provides an additional source of needed funds.

The raising of the money needed to equip, supply and carry on the services of the Washington Emergency Squad is a problem that never goes away, but it is a problem that has been met, so far, by the squad membership and its thousands of friends and supporters. It has been met so well that the squad can be depended upon to provide the best trained personnel, using the latest and finest equipment, to meet just about any sort of emergency that can befall the people of the Washington area, and there is no reason to believe that this financial support will falter or the services performed by the squad will ever be anything short of the best.

[1]Martin Bry-Nildsen, Jr., is a retired Superior Court judge.

Richard W. York photo

BIG WINNERS — *Lieutenant Michael Baylor, Captain Mary Petrick, Assistant Captain Russell Wildrick, and Robert Petrick hold trophies won by squad in 1984 Hampton parade. The Washington Emergency Squad wins many awards in competitive events.*

13

Recognition of Excellence

One of the biggest sources of pleasure and pride in serving volunteer fire departments and emergency squads comes from taking part in—and hosting—the parades. The parades in Washington and vicinity are annual folk events attended by large and admiring crowds. In these days of passive television viewing there's still a big thrill in seeing men and women marching smartly in uniform, flags whipping in the breeze, and the stirring sound of drum and bugle corps temporarily drowning out the background noises of ordinary life. On these occasions chrome and brass, polished to the nth degree, take on the gleam of precious metal.

Audiences wonder "how do these folks put on such a show?"

The answer is complex, but it tells something about how volunteer organizations operate to the benefit of the public. Being unpaid, volunteers are particularly interested in the appreciation of their peers, the volunteers in other communities. So when any department or squad announces an upcoming parade and issues invitations, they are gratefully received because of the chance to see other departments and squads on display and to make comparisons. The hope always is that you will learn something that you can put to use to the advantage of your operation, and that you, perhaps, can contribute something new and better to others, as well.

If these considerations are not enough, there is a very practical one: a department or squad that accepts the invitation to go out of town to create a gala event for a neighboring community knows that when, in due time, it wants to put on its own show and issues invitations, other communities will reciprocate by sparing the time and going to the expense and trouble to participate. The principle, "you scratch my back and I'll scratch yours," operates across the board in human affairs and it's not to be ashamed of, especially since there's nothing like a parade for letting a town know what it is getting for the money it contributes to support a volunteer organization.

For days before a parade, visitor and host volunteers are busy getting

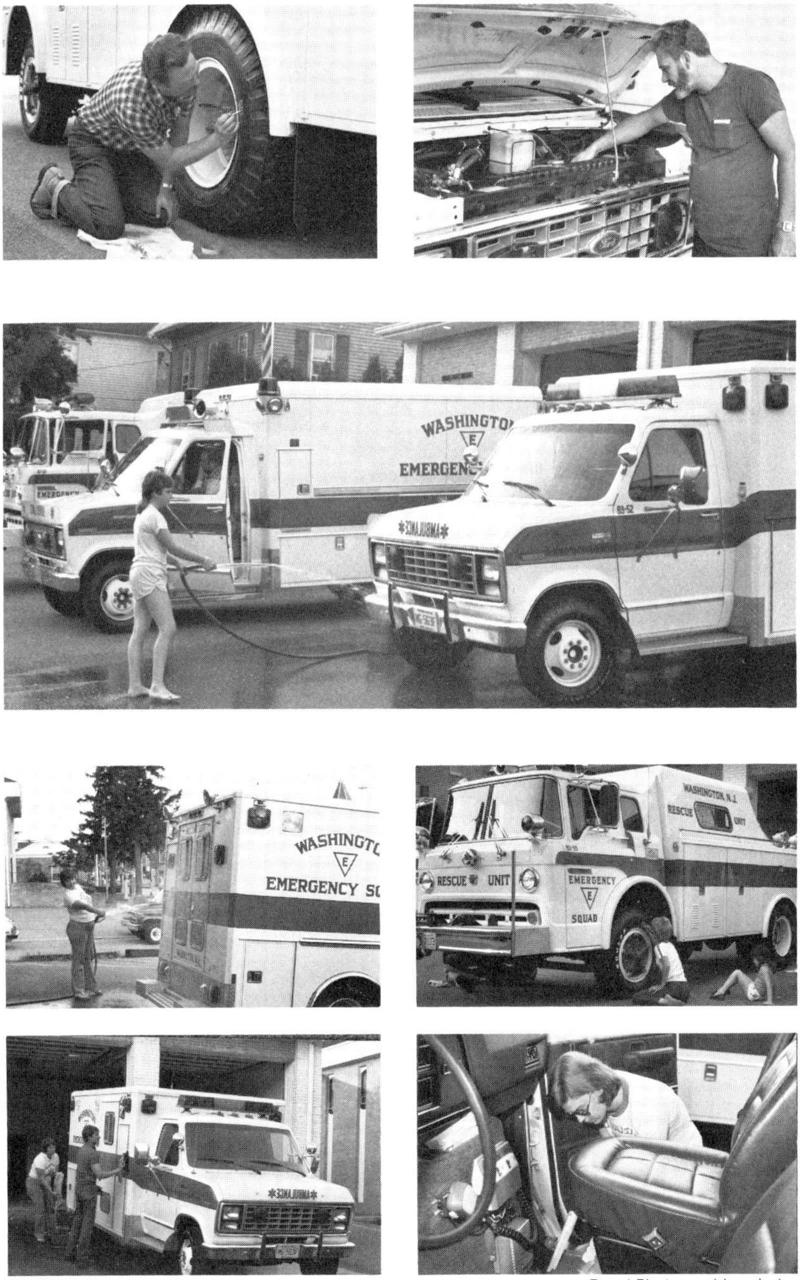

Royal Photographics photos

***THE NIGHT BEFORE** — Everything must be spotless as squad members prepare for tough competition.*

LOCAL PARADE — *Squad marches on Belvidere Avenue.*

ON EAST WASHINGTON AVENUE — *Washington was host of big parade in the 1960's. 1966 Cadillac ambulance follows 1963 emergency truck.*

WASHINGTON CELEBRATES AMERICA *— Squad marches on Carlton Avenue in annual July 4th parade.*

Washington Firemen Cited Best

POHATCONG TOWNSHIP — Twenty firefighting companies and 10 emergency squads from five New Jersey and Pennsylvania counties showed their colors in the annual Fire Prevention Week Parade last Saturday afternoon.

Some 1,500 people lined the streets of Huntington to watch 83 pieces of firefighting and rescue equipment roll by. Marching bands added a musical flair to the yearly event and various organizations joined the procession.

The event was sponsored jointly by the Huntington Volunteer Fire Company No. 1 of Pohatcong Township and the township's Fire Prevention Board. The companies and squads in Saturday's parade represented the counties of Warren, Hunterdon, Northampton, Lehigh and Bucks.

Winning the trophy for the best overall fire company was the Washington Borough Fire Department. The Huntington Volunteer Fire Company made this award in memory of Donald Galloway and William Gies, two men who were active in the company.

Other prize winners were as follows:

Best fire company with 20 or more men in line of march: Washington Borough.

Best fire company with less than 20 men: Lopatcong Township Fire Department, first place; Quakertown Fire Company, second place; Alpha Fire Company, third place.

Best fire apparatus: Washington Borough, first; Lopatcong Township, second.

Best Ladies Auxiliary: Lopatcong Township, first; Washington Borough, second.

Best emergency or rescue squad: Washington Emergency Squad, first; Lopatcong Emergency Squad, second; Phillipsburg Emergency Squad, third.

Best squad apparatus: Washington Borough, first, Lopatcong Township, second.

Best organization of the children's groups: Pohatcong All-Girl Drill Team, first, Cub Pack No. 56 of Pohatcong Township, second, Pohatcong Cheerleaders, third. Additional trophies were given to the following children's groups for their participation: Brownie Troop No. 289 of Pohatcong Township, Stanton Studio of Dance of Phillipsburg, the Firthtown Drill Team and Cub Pack No. 15 of Alpha.

Best fire prevention float or display: Forks Township Fire Department.

Best comic unit: West Jersey Shrine Club.

FAMILIAR HEADLINE *— A frequent winner, the Washington Squad took many prizes in big 1979 Huntington parade including best emergency squad and best squad apparatus.*

their uniforms cleaned, polishing all the metal, waxing all the paint, blacking all the tires, and checking to be sure all the myriad items of gear are in place. The night before, the volunteers are up to all hours, and if, as often happens, there's a call to be answered and equipment must roll, somebody has to come back to the headquarters and do the job all over again. Even during a parade, the host department may get a call and have to peel off the line of march at the next intersection, sirens sounding. If it's a minor emergency, they'll be back, often before the parade is over. But sometimes they miss their own party.

The culmination of the festivities is the presentation of trophies for the best appearing, best equipped, best auxiliary and other firsts, seconds and thirds. These trophies may appear to be baubles, but the men and women take them with great seriousness, bearing them home and displaying them in the trophy cases of their meeting rooms with pride. Because volunteers forego any financial compensation, they particularly cherish their trophies, which are tangible symbols of the high quality of their service to the public. Oscars and Emmys have nothing on the volunteers' humbler trophies.

Because pictures of parades speak for themselves, there is no need to devote more of this chapter to the printed text.

Richard W. York photo

***PRIZES WON** — Cabinet in the Vernon Oakes Building holds trophies won by squad since it became an independent organization in 1978.*

Royal Photographics photo

SIGN OF THE TIME—*Gene Castner, the contractor who built the Vernon Oakes Building, installs sign marking beginning of the squad's 50th year in June 1985. From left: Mary Petrick, squad captain; Bonnie Baylor, auxiliary treasurer; Michael Baylor, squad lieutenant; Betty Deemer, auxiliary president; and Barbara Pletzer look on.*

14

The Fiftieth Year

Vernon "Bab" Oakes completed his plan for a volunteer rescue squad in 1936, and the first missions were carried out during that year. The year 1985 is the Washington Emergency Squad's 50th year of service to the community.

By the end of 1936 the squad had been summoned to the scene of five emergencies—the first one in Hackettstown. There was almost no limit to the territory served by the squad because it was the only one available to answer calls from a vast area.

Today the squad responds to nearly 1,400 calls each year—most of them in Washington borough and township. The rest of Warren County is served by 12 other squads within the county and four neighboring squads located just outside of the county lines. The number of calls answered in Warren County each year is now approaching the 8,000 mark.

Because Oakes was the pioneer in the field and the Washington Emergency Squad is the original volunteer rescue organization that predated all of the others now serving the county, elaborate plans were made to celebrate the 50th year of service. This resulted in many honors being bestowed upon the Washington squad and its members, but the squad membership feels strongly that honors conferred under these circumstances really belong to all volunteers everywhere. It is in this spirit that the Washington squad has accepted the accolades that have come its way in 1985.

The January 1985 meeting of The Vernon Oakes Society was chosen to be the time and place for the kickoff of the 50th-year observance. At this meeting Mary Petrick, the squad captain, outlined the activities scheduled for the year-long celebration. Included in the plans were the sale of commemorative coffee cups, mugs and first-aid kits; a dinner-dance to be held at the National Guard Armory on May 4; a raffle with a new Ford Mustang automobile as the main prize; a series of 50-50 drawings over a 10-week period; a mammoth parade to be held on September 7; and the publication of this 50th-year edition of *Your*

STATE OF NEW JERSEY
OFFICE OF THE GOVERNOR
TRENTON
08625

THOMAS H. KEAN
GOVERNOR

January 25, 1985

TO THE MEMBERS OF THE WASHINGTON EMERGENCY SQUAD:

Sacrifice is the true test of dedication. There are few who are called on more than our volunteer rescue squad members to help their fellow citizens in distress at all hours and under all conditions.

Members of the Washington Emergency Squad have been performing this service now for the past 50 years and performing it in a manner that demonstrates the true spirit of dedication. This celebration is an appropriate time for all of us to acknowledge how profoundly we benefit from your spirit of public service and your sincere concern for your fellow man. Fidelity to the principles of your organization that you have exhibited will serve as inspiration to those who will follow.

My sincere congratulations for superior performance and my best wishes that success will continue to crown your efforts.

Sincerely,

Thomas H. Kean
Governor

Fabulous Volunteers.

The Washington Emergency Squad Auxiliary announced its own series of fund-raising events to take place during the 50th year celebration. These included a bake sale in April, a craft show and sale in May, a spaghetti dinner in June, and a Halloween dance.

Many prominent citizens and organizations chose this meeting as their opportunity to honor the squad. Attending in person and addressing the audience were: Winnie Hartvigsen, president of the New Jersey State First Aid Council, Inc.; Senator Wayne Dumont, Jr.; Assemblyman Garabed "Chuck" Haytaian; Assemblyman Richard A. Zimmer; Freeholder Director Irene Mackey Smith; Freeholder and Washington Township Committeeman Kenneth C. Miller; Mayor Nancy J. Gianni Schmidt of the Borough of Washington; Councilman Donald Strelecki of the Borough of Washington; and Rev. Maurice E. Farr, pastor of the First Presbyterian Church of Washington.

Also attending were Sheriff Edward G. Bullock of Warren County, Deputy Mayor Richard C. Meeker of the Borough of Washington, and Councilman and former-Mayor Joseph LaPrino of the Borough of Washington.

Letters were received from New Jersey Governor Thomas H. Kean, United States Senator Frank Lautenberg, United States Representative James A. Courter, and United States Representative Marge Raukema.

The meeting was conducted by former-Mayor Alvin Sloan, director of The Vernon Oakes Society, and the audience was welcomed by Russell Wildrick, assistant captain of the Washington Emergency

Richard W. York photo

***WELCOME** — Assistant Captain Russell Wildrick greets the audience.*

Richard W. York photo

***OUTLINES CELEBRATION** — Captain Mary Petrick announces 50th-year events to come.*

Richard W. York photo

FOURTH MEETING — *Public officials join Alvin Sloan, society director, at the 1985 meeting of The Vernon Oakes Society.*

Richard W. York photos

***NOTABLES ATTEND** — From left, starting with top photos: Alvin Sloan, master-of-ceremonies, and Garabed "Chuck" Haytaian, state assemblyman; Wayne Dumont, Jr., state senator, and Richard Zimmer, state assemblyman; Irene Mackey Smith, director of Warren County Board of Chosen Freeholders; Kenneth Miller, freeholder and member of the Washington Township Committee; Donald Strelecki, Washington borough councilman; Nancy J. Guianni Schmidt, Washington borough mayor; and Winnie Hartvigsen, president of the New Jersey State First Aid Council.*

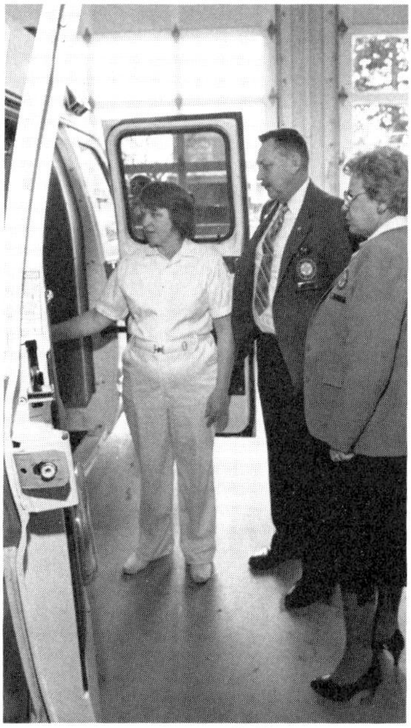

Richard W. York photos

***AROUND THE ROOM** — Clockwise from top left: Lester "Buck" Hann, ambulance driver of the 1930's; ambulance driver of the future; NJSFAC president Winnie Hartvigsen, Captain Mary Petrick and author Richard E. Harpster discuss emergency squad work; squad member Rachael Semonche shows ambulance equipment to Mr. and Mrs. Hartvigsen; squad member Terry Kresge explains heart-lung resuscitator to James Burk and June Oakes Burk; James Burd, member of The Vernon Oakes Society, joins society secretary Vickie Gulick and society assistant director Lynn Gulick in observing mannequin representing accident victim who has been prepared for transportation to hospital.*

Squad.

Resolutions and proclamations praising the squad and recounting its history were received. The New Jersey Senate adopted a resolution, sponsored by Senator Walter E. Foran, which reads as follows:

> WHEREAS, The Washington Emergency Squad of Warren County was organized in 1936 and is one of the oldest small-town volunteer rescue squads in the United States; and,
>
> WHEREAS, The Washington Emergency Squad has, throughout its long and successful history, faithfully and courageously served the citizens of its community through the dedication and skill of its many volunteers who stand always ready to respond to need; and,
>
> WHEREAS, The Washington Emergency Squad is recognized for its exemplary record of leadership, community support and exceptional volunteer training; and,
>
> WHEREAS, In June 1985 the Washington Emergency Squad will begin its 50th year of distinguished community service and will celebrate this milestone through a variety of special events; now, therefore,
>
> *Be It Resolved by the Senate of the State of New Jersey:*
>
> That this House hereby honors and congratulates the Washington Emergency Squad, and pays tribute to its brave and dedicated volunteers, past and present, who have sacrificed personal safety in responding to the needs of their community; and,
>
> *Be It Further Resolved,* That a duly authenticated copy of this resolution, signed by the President and attested by the Secretary, be transmitted to the Washington Emergency Squad.

A similar resolution, sponsored by Assemblymen Garabed "Chuck" Haytaian, Robert Littell, Karl Weidel and Richard A. Zimmer, was adopted by the New Jersey Assembly.

The Warren County Board of Chosen Freeholders adopted a resolution which was moved by Director Irene Mackey Smith and seconded by

Freeholder Kenneth C. Miller. It was presented to the squad in the form of a plaque by Director Smith. The resolution reads as follows:

WHEREAS, The Vernon Oakes Society of the Washington Emergency Squad was formed to help finance the Washington Emergency Squad and is named in honor of its founder and first captain and former fire chief, and

WHEREAS, The Vernon Oakes Society's gift to the Washington Emergency Squad will be a donation of $20,000.00 representing $100.00 contributions by each of over 200 members of The Vernon Oakes Society in honor of the 50th Anniversary of the Washington Emergency Squad,

NOW, THEREFORE, BE IT RESOLVED that the Washington Emergency Squad is hereby congratulated for their fifty years of devoted service to the residents of the Washington area, and they are also commended for the humanitarian and compassionate deeds and life-saving achievements they have performed over the past fifty years.

The Mayor and Common Council of the Borough of Washington adopted the following resolution declaring 1985 a year of celebration of the 50th anniversary of the Washington Emergency Squad, a copy of which was presented to the squad by Councilman Donald Strelecki:

WHEREAS, the Washington Emergency Squad, in conjunction with The Vernon Oakes Society, will be holding a Fiftieth (50th) Year preview ceremony on January 27, 1985; and

WHEREAS, The Vernon Oakes Society, through the generosity of its members, will be making its fourth (4th) annual presentation to the Emergency Squad on the date noted above; and

WHEREAS, both the Washington Emergency Squad and The Vernon Oakes Society are owed an expression of appreciation by the community which they serve;

NOW, THEREFORE BE IT RESOLVED, by the Washington Borough Council, that the best wishes of the community be extended to the Washington Emergency Squad as they start their fiftieth (50th) year of service and to The Vernon Oakes Society for their continued financial and moral support to the Squad and its members. Further, the Council declare the year 1985 as a year of celebration within the Borough of the Fiftieth (50th) Anniverary of the Washington Emergency Squad.

Mayor Richard D. Fifield of Washington Township issued the following proclamation designating 1985 as Washington Township Emergency Squad Semi-Centennial Year in that township:

WHEREAS, the WASHINGTON EMERGENCY SQUAD was founded in June of 1936 with the avowed purpose of providing quality volunteer emergency medical care for the people of the Washington area, including Washington Township; and

WHEREAS, for the past fifty years the WASHINGTON EMERGENCY SQUAD has faithfully fulfilled that goal to the benefit of all residents of the Washington area, including Washington Township; and

WHEREAS, the WASHINGTON EMERGENCY SQUAD was the first emergency-aid company to be formed in Warren County, providing a model for other similar organizations throughout the area;

NOW, THEREFORE, I, RICHARD D. FIFIELD, Mayor of the Township of Washington in the County of Warren and State of New Jersey, do hereby proclaim the year 1985 as

WASHINGTON EMERGENCY SQUAD
SEMI-CENTENNIAL YEAR

in the Township of Washington, in the County of Warren and State of New Jersey, and call upon all residents to support the WASHINGTON EMERGENCY SQUAD in its endeavors in 1985 and the years to come.

The dinner dance at the National Guard Armory on Saturday, May 4, was a festive event attended by more than 500 guests who had paid $50 per couple for tickets which included chances on the Ford Mustang automobile and several other prizes. The drawing was one of the

Reinhold Radke photo

ARRIVALS AT DINNER-DANCE — *Armory is quickly filled as guests sit down for 50th-year dinner.*

Reinhold Radke photos

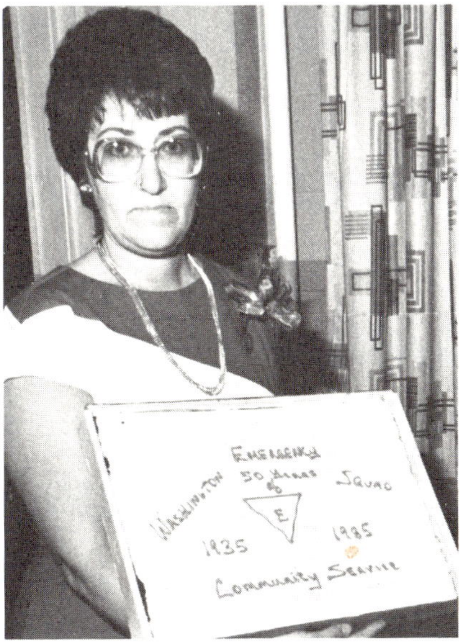

PROGRAM UNDER WAY — *Clockwise from top left: Captain Mary Petrick addresses audience; former Captain Thomas Mason, Jr. speaks; Sandy Mickalowski draws ticket stubs for prizes including new Ford Mustang car; Captain Petrick shows specially decorated cakes.*

Richard W. York photo

THE GRAND PRIZE — *Mr. and Mrs. Wayne Fleming and Wayne, Jr., show the Ford Mustang car which they won.*

highlights of the evening. The car was won by Mr. and Mrs. Wayne Fleming of Washington.

The mammoth parade on Saturday, September 7, included 200 fire and rescue vehicles from more than 100 fire departments, rescue squads and other organizations. It is estimated that 1,000 people were in the line of march. Alvin Sloan was grand marshal, and June Oakes Burk, daughter and only living relative of the late Captain Vernon Oakes, was guest grand marshal. Eighty-three trophies were awarded to outstanding participants.

The parade, which started at 1 P.M., was the first of a day-long series of events including stretcher and crutch races, a bucket brigade involving filling barrels with water, and a dunking booth occupied by squad captains. All events took place at the property of St. Joseph's Catholic

***EVERYBODY LOVES A PARADE** — This girl is obviously no exception.*

Royal Photographics photo

Royal Photographics photo

Royal Photographics photo

***MONUMENT DEDICATION** — Above: Before start of 50th-year parade, squad members dedicate memorial honoring deceased honorary member Joseph Eger. Memorial features bell that was installed on first emergency truck by Joe's brother, Otto, in 1937. Otto created automatic device to ring bell.*

***FESTIVE CARGO** — Left: Content of ambulance is appropriate for the occasion.*

Royal Photographics photo

***PARADE UNDER WAY** — United States Army color guard takes the lead.*

Washington Messenger photo

***VEHICLE OF THE 1930's** — Pontiac roadster, owned and driven by Paul Macomber, transports Grand Marshal Alvin Sloan and Assistant Grand Marshal June Oakes Burk. Car was popular model when the Washington Emergency Squad was organized.*

Royal Photographics photo

SQUAD COLOR GUARD — *From left: Sandy Mickalowski, Robert Nyland, Brian Zachar and Donna Bowlby.*

WASHINGTON'S PRIDE *— From top: Captain Mary Petrick, squad members and auxiliary members precede the squad's vehicles in line of march.*

Royal Photographics photos

Royal Photographics photo

***WAITING TO BE WON** — Trophies which will soon be presented to deserving winners.*

Washington Messenger photo

***MIGHTY WURLITZER** — Ancient band-organ carried on equally old International truck, owned and driven by Charles A. Hildebrant of Oldwick, New Jersey, unrolls many familiar tunes.*

Center, the termination point of the parade.

While the squad was doing its celebrating, its auxiliary conducted some additional events of its own, the largest auxiliary event being a Halloween dance at the Washington Elks hall on Saturday, October 16.

As this book goes to press, two more events have been planned and will take place before the anniversary date. During the spring of 1986 a dinner-dance will be held, and the public will be invited to an open house at the Vernon Oakes Building.

Fiftieth years are not celebrated very often. The events marking the half-century mark of the Washington Emergency Squad will long be remembered by all residents of Warren County.

Royal Photographics photos

***HALLOWEEN DANCE** — Top: Sad wallflowers occupy table at the Elks hall during Halloween dance of the squad's auxiliary, while happy celebrants enjoy the dance floor.*

Richard E. Harpster photo

***FIRE GONG**—At the turn of the century a Washington resident could summon volunteer firemen by striking a gong with a sledgehammer. It was located at the square. Similar gong, in photograph, is located in front of Chester, New Jersey, firehouse.*

***FIRE BELL** — This bell, originally located in tower atop the old Borough Hall, brought out the firemen from 1909 until nearly 1920 when the porcelain plant was built and its factory whistle took over the job. The bell is now a monument on the Belvidere Avenue side of the Municipal Building.*

Richard W. York photo

15

The Dispatching Service

As long as there have been volunteers ready and willing to help their neighbors, there have been methods for summoning them when needed. The need for efficient communication in police, fire and emergency work can be vividly pictured by contrasting the procedure used today, as described in the first chapter of this book, and the primitive methods of a half century ago, as told in the second chapter.

Going back even further to the turn of the century, the volunteer firemen were called out with what might be described as a do-it-yourself dispatching system. The essential element was a heavy wooden frame from which a large rim of metal, usually the rim from the wheel of a railroad locomotive, was suspended. Hanging by a chain from the side of the frame was a large sledgehammer. When struck the rim became a powerful gong. A gong of this type has been preserved and is on display in front of the Chester, New Jersey, firehouse.

When a fire occurred in Washington, anyone who was available ran to the square, where one of these gongs was installed, and beat the metal ring with the sledgehammer. The alarm would bring all of the volunteers within earshot on the double. The first to go into action was Charles Carling. He would run to the livery stable on Belvidere Avenue, across from the firehouse, get the fire horses, lead them across the street, hitch them to the steamer, and take off for the scene of the fire. The other firemen followed with the hose carts, which were pulled by hand.

In 1909 the improvised gong was replaced with a large fire bell that was installed in a tower on the roof of the Borough Hall. A rope, with which the bell was tolled, was available to any person who wished to summon the firemen. That bell is still on display in front of the fire bays of the present Municipal Building on Belvidere Avenue. The following inscriptions are cast on its surface:

PROPERTY OF
THE BOROUGH OF WASHINGTON
WARREN CO., N.J.

COUNCIL 1900
CHAS. B. SMITH, MAYOR
J. DEWITT GROFF, PRES.
CHAS. M. HULL
A. C. GODFREY
ELMER E. WYCKOFF
EDWARD S. SHURTS
AARON H. VOUGH

G. C. LOSEY, CHIEF FIRE DEPT.
A. J. CRAFT, TOWN CLERK

MC SHANE BELL FOUNDRY CO.
BALTIMORE, MD

When the Washington Porcelain Company built its plant on Willow Street prior to 1920, the building included a factory whistle with a piercing sound and a wide range of audibility. The use of the fire bell was discontinued, and factory personnel would blow the whistle when requested to do so. The chore was assumed by office employees during the day and by the watchman at night. The whistle was activated by steam from the factory boiler, and it sounded similar to the present Washington Township fire whistles. In the middle of the night it sounded even more eerie, if that is possible to imagine. If you needed the firemen, you called the factory on your own—there were no organized dispatchers.

In 1931 the borough council adopted an ordinance creating the first dispatching service. This was the first such service in any small community in northern New Jersey or eastern Pennsylvania. The ordinance provided for the employment of a chief apparatus driver who reported to the Borough Hall at the time the clerk's office closed. He took the fire and police calls that came in by telephone until the office reopened the next morning and around the clock on days the office was closed. He had two days a week off, at which times a substitute took over his duties. Continuous dispatching service was thereby provided. Elton "Elt" Wright, a fireman, was the first to be appointed to the new position.

The chief apparatus driver doubled as janitor and maintenance man of the borough building and was provided with a small bedroom where he could sleep between fire and police calls.

When a fire call came in, the chief apparatus driver would blow the whistle, open the doors of the fire bays, start the motors of the fire trucks, and drive them out onto the sidewalk. When a police call was received, he turned on a circuit of lights which flashed from power poles at various locations. The patrolman on duty, upon seeing the flashing lights, would go to the Borough Hall for instructions about the call.

Following the adoption of civil service, the position of chief apparatus driver was eliminated and replaced with the classification of building service worker, but the duties remained the same.

At the same time the service was established, an air horn and a compressed air system with which to operate it were installed in the borough building. From that time on the factory whistle blew only at midnight on New Year's eve. The new horn was equipped with a coding device which allowed the firemen and the public to know the location of a fire by the number of blasts of the horn.

After the Washington Emergency Squad started to accept calls other than fires in 1936, a shrill whistle (probably originally steam-operated) was installed on the compressed air system at the Borough Hall. That was known to firemen and squadmen as the "peanut whistle" and was used to call out the squad. The "peanut whistle" could not always be heard in some locations, and it was replaced with an air horn after a short time. The air horn for the emergency squad had a deeper tone than the one for the fire department, and the volunteers could easily distinguish one from the other. Later the second horn was eliminated and a coded signal (twelve blasts of the fire horn) was used for the emergency squad.

In 1966 a Plectron system was installed. This is a communication system that connects the dispatcher directly to the homes of firemen and emergency-squad personnel, permitting the volunteers to hear the alarms that concern them without being annoyed with the other messages that are sent via radio. It also permits the summoning of the squad during the late night hours without sounding the fire whistle.

Wright retired in 1956 and his relief man, Walter "Toppy" Castner, who was also a fireman, was appointed to the full-time job. Castner retired in 1970.

Meanwhile, in the planning for the new Municipal Building in 1969, Kenneth Greer, the borough's first municipal manager; Chief of Police E. J. Skoog; and Mayor Roger Masenior had noted the number of calls was increasing. Anticipating the needs of the future, they insisted dispatching was already too much of a distraction to the borough clerk and more than should be expected of a sleeping building-service worker.

***FIRST DISPATCHER** — Elton Wright was appointed to the position of chief apparatus driver in 1931, providing the first full-time dispatching service in the entire area. Wright slept at the Borough Hall.*

***SECOND DISPATCHER** — Walter Castner assumed the duties on Elton Wright's days off and was appointed to the full-time job when Wright retired in 1956. Castner served until the present dispatching service was created in 1971.*

They proposed a full-time dispatching service.

Mayor Masenior presented the recommendation to the borough council, which at that time included Stanley Brewster, Charles Hubbard, Frederick Kleen, Jr., Arthur Olson, Edward "Pat" Sheeran and George Thompson. They agreed unanimously, and provision for a full-time dispatching service was included in the plans for the new Municipal Building which was completed in 1970, and the service was inaugurated on November 17 of that year.[1]

The service was organized by the borough manager and placed in the charge of the chief of police. Later, arrangements were made with other municipal and county departments to use the service. This not only spread the overhead cost but provided much-improved communication

[1]In 1985 the communications system was further improved with the addition of Motorola Minitor paging equipment. A pocket-size Minitor radio unit is carried by each squad member at all times. All squad calls are transmitted to these units by a special transmitter, and squad members are alerted to a call when not at home and when out of range of the audibility of the fire horn.

among the police, fire and emergency organizations of the participating municipalities and county departments.

The first full-time dispatchers were Earl French, who had been serving on Walter Castner's days off under the old system, and Gloria Hagerman, Anna Stem and Kathryn Stettler, who were recruited from the police department's school crossing-guard service.

Stettler resigned in 1972 and was replaced by Lee Boehning who served until 1978. Stettler returned later that year.

French (now deceased) retired in 1975, and Carol Southerland received the permanent appointment the following year.

Stem retired in 1980 and was replaced by Mark Beckert, who served for two years and was followed by James Hudock. At the end of 1984

SOUNDING ALARM *— Elton Wright, chief apparatus driver, inserts brass disc in control-box mechanism before pulling lever to sound coded air-horn alarm. Device is still being used.*

Minassian photo

Richard E. Harpster photo

Minassian photo

***SAW THE NEED** — From left: In 1969 Mayor Roger W. Masenior; Washington's first borough manager, Kenneth Greer; and Chief of Police Elbert Skoog proposed the full-time dispatching service that exists today. Service was inaugurated in 1971.*

Hudock resigned in order to join Morris County Communications, a dispatching service in Washington Township, Morris County. He was succeeded by Barbara Ball who was in turn succeeded by John Yerance, Sr., in 1985.

The regular dispatchers, Hagerman (who is now the senior dispatcher), Southerland, Stettler and Yerance, are backed up by eight relief personnel who serve when needed. They are Larry Adams, Dale Bulmer, Marti Leitner, James McDonald, Michael Patchunka, Dennis Ryan, Kenneth Snover and Jeffrey Wright.

Radio dispatchers are the nerve center of any municipality. They are people who need to remain calm during the times they are handling hysterical callers or when irate (and sometimes obscene) telephone calls are received. Their responsibilities require that they function with a considerable amount of common sense, efficiency and patience.

It is not uncommon for dispatchers to receive calls from very lonely, aging people who just want to hear someone else's voice to break the monotony of their days. Some calls require extraordinary measures and expertise in knowing what type of assistance should be dispatched. Some calls are baffling, some are funny, but most are serious.

Anna Stem, now retired, recalls a variety of incidents that occurred during her tenure as a dispatcher. For example, take the night she received a call from a young girl. The child told the dispatcher her house was on fire, she lived in Washington Township, and her mother and father were not home. She hung up before giving the location of her residence.

Anna immediately alerted township police, the telephone operators, and the state police. She also contacted the police in Washington Township, Morris County, in case the young girl had called from there. A panic situation existed for a time, with police and telephone operators trying to locate the child's home.

The episode ended happily, however, except for the young girl who made the telephone call. It turned out that she was upstairs, safely in bed, while her parents were downtstairs, totally unaware that their daughter was telephoning the dispatcher for unneeded help. Needless to say, the incident resulted in stern disciplinary measures to the young caller.

Anna recalls that dispatchers were often called by near-hysterical mothers who had accidentally locked their keys and their babies in cars. Then there were calls for policemen to come because skunks were in yards or to remove bats from houses, and it was not unusual for dispatchers to be asked to summon assistance to round up escaped cows, horses or pigs. Other calls requested that frightened cats be removed from tall trees.

Many callers berated the dispatchers because they had been given parking tickets, but by the time the matters had been referred to the patrolmen who issued the tickets or to the chief of police, the callers had usually calmed down, having taken out their anger on the dispatchers.

Anna remembers occasions when dispatchers in Washington have received fire calls for Asbury Park, a shore community in Monmouth County. Apparently the problem arises because of the close proximity of the village of Asbury in Franklin Township.

One day a woman walked into the Municipal Building, asked for the assistance of the emergency squad, and then gave birth to her baby in the lobby.

A considerable amount of abuse was heaped on the dispatchers during times of floods and heavy snowfalls. During these periods it was not unusual for them to receive telephone calls which included profane and obscene language. People demanded that their cellars be pumped out at once or that their streets be cleared of snow immediately.

Sometimes dispatchers sat with babies, and even cats and dogs, while police were looking for places where they could be cared for properly. There were occasions when youngsters came into the Municipal Building to report that they were lost.

Once Anna received a call that a boa constrictor was sighted on Broad Street. Sure enough, the reptile was a reality and was captured by a patrolman and handed over to a local pet store.

During one of the borough's minor floods, a dispatcher had to argue

Richard W. York photo

DISPATCHER AT WORK *— Dispatcher Anna Stem receives one of the 42,203 calls which were handled in 1979.*

with an irate Phillipsburg resident that his 30-foot boat was not required for assistance.

Anna was a very popular and highly respected dispatcher. Her ability, courtesy and compassion are well-known to her many friends and to all who had occasion to call the dispatching service during the thousands of hours she was on duty.

After she ended her career as a dispatcher in 1980, her colleagues and friends crowded Firemen's Hall to honor her at a retirement dinner. The committee in charge of the event was chaired by Gloria Hagerman, and Chief of Police E. J. Skoog was master of ceremonies. The guest of honor was showered with gifts, and the evening of good-fellowship will long be remembered.

Today's dispatchers, in addition to handling calls over eight telephone lines, take appropriate action in response to many fire and burglar alarm systems.

Washington borough dispatchers handle calls for the Washington Police Department, Washington Fire Department, Washington Emergency Squad, Washington Township Police Department, Washington Township Fire Department, Oxford Township Police Department, Oxford Township Fire Department, Broadway Fire Department, and Mountain Lake Fire Department. They also monitor radio transmissions from the Warren County Prosecutor's office and the Warren County Sheriff Department, and they answer calls for those departments after office hours and on holidays and weekends. Since the middle of 1985 they have handled calls for the Warren County medical examiner.

Scores of citizens listen to police calls on home receivers, and they often provide helpful information. If a patrolman asks the dispatcher for the location of a certain house, and if the dispatcher is unable to provide the information, a caller may provide directions to the site. Such

READY FOR CALL *— Terry Kresge is an emergency squad member and a fireman. He relaxes with the evening newspaper but, like all volunteers, is ready to respond to any call that may come over the Plectron at his side.*

Richard W. York photo

Royal Photographics photo

***THE DISPATCHERS** — Washington's four full-time dispatchers are, clockwise from top left: John Yerance, Sr., Gloria Hagerman, Kathryn Stettler and Carol Southerland. Hagerman is senior dispatcher.*

***COMMANDS DISPATCHERS** — Anthony J. Terminelli, chief of police, is in charge of the Washington dispatching service.*

Royal Photographics photo

assistance is always welcomed.

The wisdom of the 1969 decision to create a full-time dispatching service is obvious today. Chief of Police Anthony J. Terminelli reported calls handled in 1984 as follows: Washington Borough, 33,166; Washington Township, 11,011; Oxford Township, 5,388; Broadway Fire Department, 14; Mountain Lake Fire Department, 11; Warren County Prosecutor's Office, 98; Warren County Sheriff Department, 17.

These 49,705 calls could hardly have been handled during the spare time of a busy borough clerk and a sleep-in apparatus driver![1]

---

[1]Services for summoning aid using sophisticated communications technology are now available to shut-ins and elderly persons who live alone and might have difficulty in reaching a telephone. One of these,the Communi-Call system, is available at moderate cost through the Warren Hospital. All subscribers' medical summaries and emergency instructions are stored in a support-center computer and are available for retrieval 24 hours a day. A subscriber may initiate a call to the support center with a small remote transmitter worn on the person or with a call button on the communicator unit in the home. Two-way communication is thereby established between the homebound subscriber and the support center. The support center then acts appropriately to notify friends, neighbors or the local dispatching service. John A. DeMarrais, Warren Hospital administrator, says, "We are responding to the needs of an increasingly large group of patients who might otherwise require institutional care solely because they have no one or cannot afford to hire someone for 24-hour care."

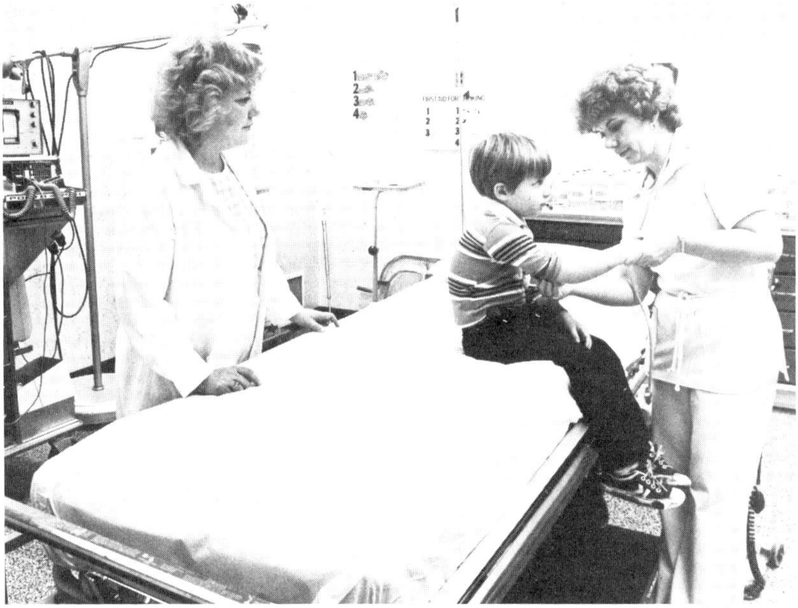

Reinhold Radke photo

***WARREN HOSPITAL EMERGENCY ROOM** — Most cases handled by the Washington Emergency Squad are taken here.*

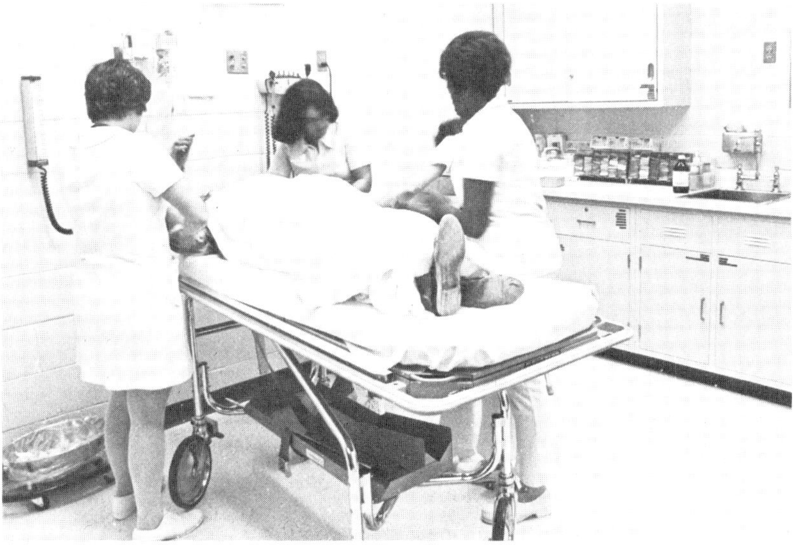

Reinhold Radke photo

***HACKETTSTOWN EMERGENCY ROOM** — The building of the Hackettstown Community Hospital enabled the Washington squad to save time and distance on calls east of Washington.*

16

The Emergency Rooms

Victims of illnesses and accidents who need more treatment than emergency-squad personnel can give them at the scene must be speedily transported to emergency medical facilities. The emergency rooms must be prepared to receive these patients at all times and have the physicians, nurses and equipment that are required to treat them properly.

For 37 years the emergency room of the Warren Hospital was the facility to which the Washington Emergency Squad delivered patients from the scenes of most of its calls.

When the Hackettstown Community Hospital opened in 1973, a second excellent emergency room became available. It is now the nearest hospital for many of the calls which originate east of Washington, and it saves the squad a considerable number of miles.

Washington is the largest Warren County municipality without a hospital, and for several years Dr. John E. Hampton, with the help of local citizens, attempted to create a family health center with diagnostic and emergency facilities. At first the efforts met with little success, but the Warren Hospital offered to build a local health center at a cost of $450,000 if one third of that figure could be raised in the area to be served. A fund drive was successfully conducted, and the $150,000 was raised. The hospital constructed the building and leased it to the Washington Clinic. Opened in 1977, the new facility was named Warren Hills Family Health Center. Its purposes were to provide diagnostic and family health services close at hand, to attract more physicians to the area, to provide 24-hour medical service in case of emergency, and to make available an emergency room. It has succeeded in all of these areas.

The Washington Emergency Squad saves many miles of transportation and much time by using the emergency room of the health

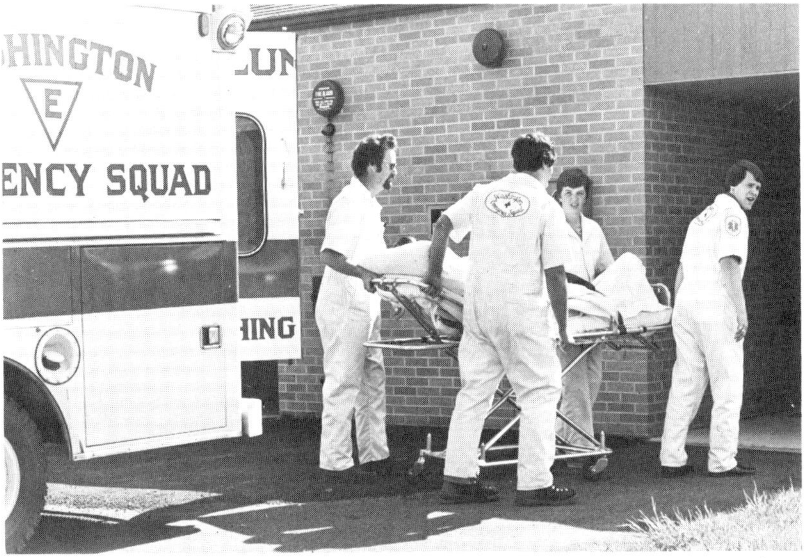

Minassian photo

EMERGENCY ENTRANCE — *Washington squad members carry patient into Warren Hills Family Health Center emergency entrance.*

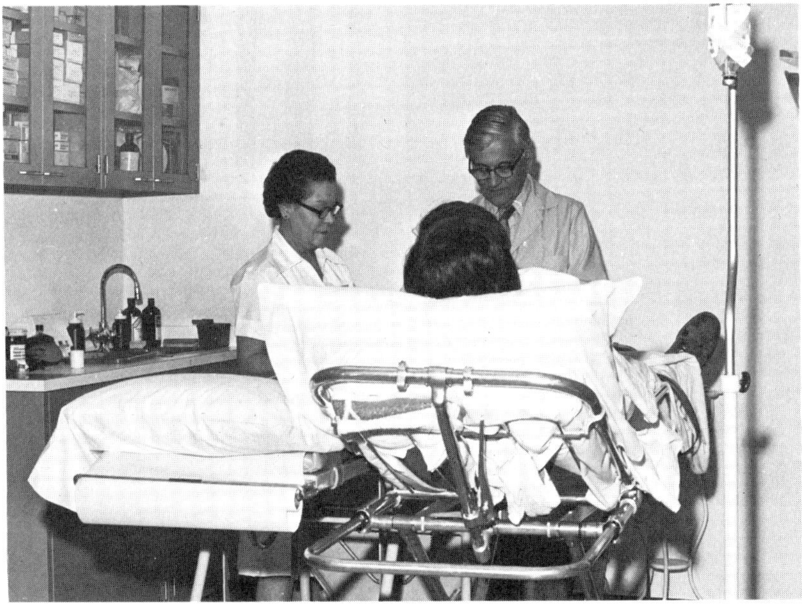

Minassian photo

HEALTH CENTER EMERGENCY ROOM — *Patient receiving treatment by nurse Muriel Brook and Dr. John Hampton.*

Minassian photo

***WARREN HILLS FAMILY HEALTH CENTER** — This facility provides many services not formerly available in Washington.*

center for the treatment of patients who do not need to be hospitalized. If the need for hospitalization is likely, patients are transported directly to the hospitals in Phillipsburg or Hackettstown.

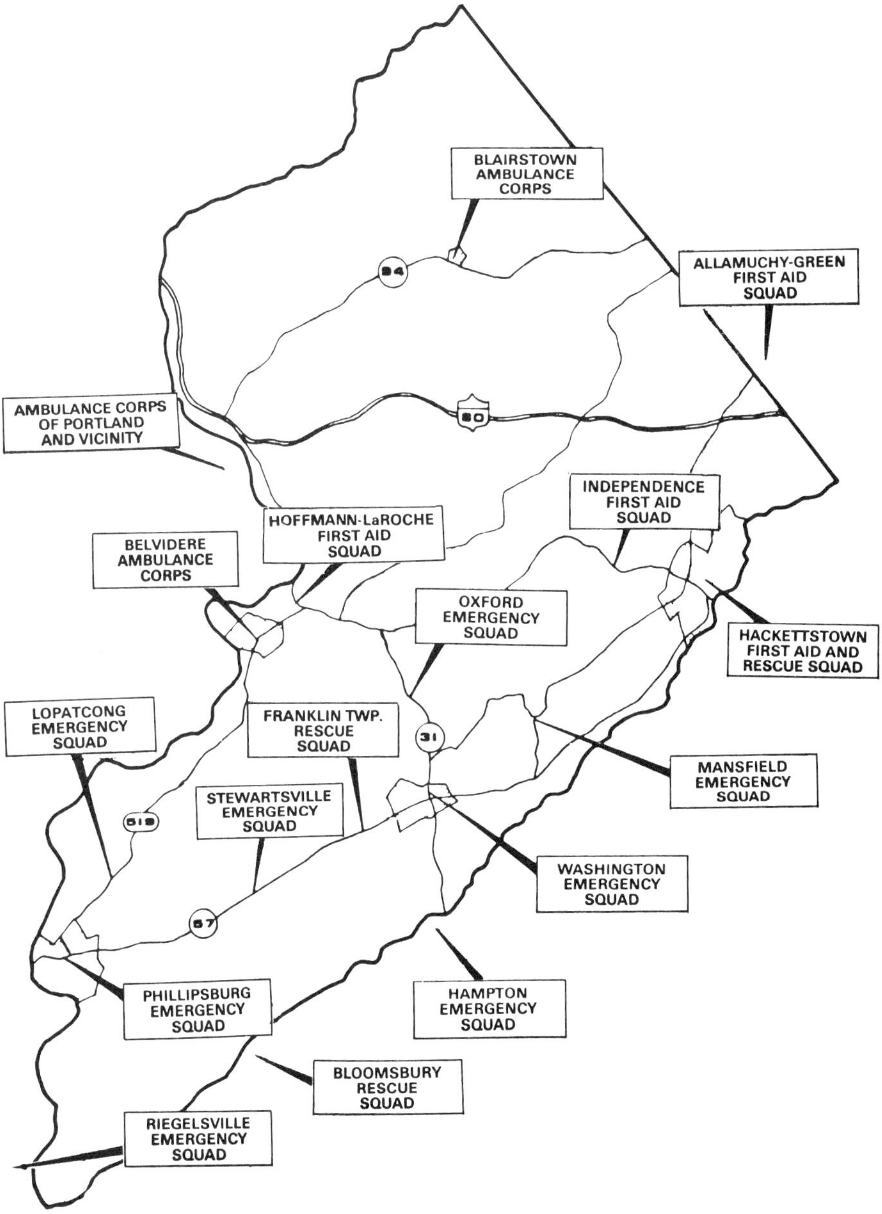

Emil Ising drawing

EMERGENCY AND AMBULANCE SQUADS SERVING WARREN COUNTY *— Thirteen squads are located within the county, and four more are located just outside its borders.*

17

Volunteer Rescue Organizations Serving Warren County

When Vernon C. "Bab" Oakes founded the Washington Emergency Squad in 1936, he set in motion the development of a comprehensive countywide rescue service. Fifty years have passed, and there are now 17 squads of fabulous volunteers serving Warren County residents and visitors. Thirteen of these squads are located within the county, and four more are located just beyond its borders as shown on the accompanying map. These squads have a total of some 400 members, operate more than 50 ambulances and other rescue vehicles, and respond to more than 8,000 calls each year.

The squads do not serve rigidly defined areas—they respond to any location to which they are summoned—but a person seeking aid usually calls the squad nearest the scene of the emergency, and this is the reason four out-of-county squads answer calls in Warren County.

The Hampton Emergency Squad is often seen at work north of the Musconetcong River bridge on Highway 31, and the Bloomsbury Rescue Squad serves the nearby portions of Franklin Township and Greenwich Township. Both are Hunterdon County Squads.

The Riegelsville Emergency Squad responds to many calls across the bridge in Pohatcong Township, and the Ambulance Corps of Portland and Vicinity serves Knowlton Township and Pahaquarry Township and occasionally the western areas of Blairstown Township and Hope Township. Both of these squads are based in Pennsylvania.

The following pages record the histories of these organizations. Squads have many similarities, and for this reason a history of any one of them is somewhat a history of all. But the names of the people and the circumstances that sparked the formation of the various groups are unique to each, and these differences are noted here. One basic similarity, of course, is the existence and availability of fabulous volunteers who possess a compelling desire to help others.

The vehicles pictured are those in service in 1985. The photographs of the squad members were taken at regular meetings held during the year

Reinhold Radke photo

PHILLIPSBURG PERSONNEL — *Front row, from left: Nancy Young, treasurer; Daniel Taylor, financial secretary; Kenneth C. Sickels, secretary; John Amendt, president; Ronald Titus, captain; Dennis Rousset, lieutenant and Stanley Garrison, lieutenant. Second row: Thomas Lucykanish, James Bianchi, Judith Garrison, Lila Lewis, Dorothy Everly, Kathleen Marino, Cindy Lewis, Louann Horn, Jeanne Titus, Diane Hess, junior; Donald Hess, Carl Baxter and Joseph Vas. Back row: Keith Trimmer, Donald Varga, junior; Angelo Tarsi, Jr., William Strausser, junior; Lloyd Gene Strausser; Richard Miers, Russell Bonano, Jr., Eugene Boyle II; Frederick Everly, Jr., and Ronald Mich. Members not present when picture was taken: Thomas Andrews, John Beatty II, junior; Rolanda Beck, Jeffrey T. Charles, Charles Young, Jr., Amy Kerbs, junior; Lester Lattig, Edward Moretti, Francis Murray, Robin Ruch, L. Gene Strausser and William Vine, Jr., junior.*

this book was in preparation. The names of members who were absent from the meetings at which the photos were taken are listed in the captions following the names of those who were present.

Phillipsburg Emergency Squad

The idea of an emergency squad for Phillipsburg was born in an automobile between Washington and Phillipsburg on an evening in 1936. The four men in the automobile were Ira Snyder, Alfred Bates, Lewis Silverthorn and Charles Shappell, Sr., who was to serve as squad captain for twenty-seven years. The group was returning from a demonstration put on by the Washington Fire Department First Aid and Rescue Squad at the Washington Borough Hall. The event had been arranged by Vernon "Bab" Oakes, captain of that squad and a former fire chief. The Phillipsburg men were impressed with what they saw, and the Phillipsburg Emergency Squad was planned on their trip home. Harvey Mowder, of Washington, was the first instructor.

The Phillipsburg squad was never a part of the fire or police department, but its original membership was drawn from those departments. Included were two firemen from each of the six fire companies and two policemen. Later the membership was increased to 16 and still later to 35.

Reinhold Radke photo

***PHILLIPSBURG VEHICLES** — From left: 1981 Ford ambulance, 1982 Ford ambulance, 1984 Chevrolet ambulance and 1971 Ford emergency truck. Not shown: 1964 GMC ambulance.*

Reinhold Radke photo

WATER-RESCUE DRILL — *Phillipsburg squadmen, from left: Charles Lilly, William Gradwell and Norman Amendt in one of squad's 14-foot outboard boats.*

In its early days the firehouse of the Lincoln Engine Company was its headquarters.

The membership was again increased in 1979, this time to 50. At the end of that year, eight of the additional openings were filled—four of them by the squad's first women members. A junior membership was instituted in 1974.

The original 1936 Dodge truck is still in service and is popular in parades. It is the oldest emergency vehicle in the area.

The squad owns two buildings on opposite sides of Prospect Street. One was built with volunteer workers on purchased land and includes sleeping quarters on the second floor. The second building was an existing one and was purchased later.

In 1985 the squad has 24 active members, 44 honorary-active members, and six junior members.

This squad responds to more calls than any other in the county. Captain Ronald Titus reports 1,895 calls were handled in 1984. Groups of volunteers sleep at headquarters in order to answer night calls more quickly.

Richard W. York photo

***OLDEST VEHICLE** — This 1937 GMC is the Phillipsburg Emergency Squad's first truck. It is the oldest emergency vehicle in service in Warren County and is popular in parades. It is still used to deliver equipment on loan to patients.*

Carl Baxter photo

LOPATCONG PERSONNEL — *Front row, from left: Russell Stewart, treasurer; Arlyne Schnell, recording secretary; Martha Case, vice-president; Ruth Stewart, president; Bruce C. Shive, captain; Robert Morgan, lieutenant and Sherry Flad, corresponding secretary. Second row: W. Howard Lawrence, instructor; Kurt Schnell, William Taggart, Linda Taggart, Suzanne Shive, junior; Rhonda Schnell and Dave Vasquez. Back row: Teddy Ryan, Steve Brickman, Mary Natisin, foreman; William Wintermute, Jann Foti and Konrad Mellert.*

Lopatcong Emergency Squad

The Lopatcong Emergency Squad has roots that go back to the very early days of emergency service in Warren County. In 1936 the Delaware Park Chemical Engine Company No. 1 created a five-member ambulance squad. The original members, all volunteer firemen, were Jess Miers, William Hackman, Edward Rodenbough, Howard Zink and J. Clifford Miller. They were trained by Red Cross instructors Matthew Amey and Howard "Bucky" Lawrence, who is still an active member and instructor.

Service began with a 1929 Henney ambulance which was purchased from a hospital in East Stroudsburg, Pennsylvania, by the fire company for $25. This vehicle had running water fed from a tank in the ceiling, an outstanding feature in those days.

The squad became a separate entity from the fire company in 1946 with Clifford Clymer as the first captain of the independent organization.

The Lopatcong Emergency Squad was the pioneer Warren County rescue organization in the enrollment of female members. The first four active women members were enrolled in 1955. They were Grace Pickel, Kay Scarlett, June Streepy and Shirley Willever. Before the end of that year 12 more women had become active members. They were Helen

Reinhold Radke photo

***LOPATCONG VEHICLES** — 1981 Ford ambulance, 1976 Chevrolet ambulance and 1981 GMC emergency truck.*

Brunner, Adele Clymer, Marie Clymer, Fern Fulmer, Lois Kupcha, Catherine Michalowski, Stella Mount, Naomi Peters, Blanche Ritz, Gloria Schmeltzly, Eleanor Thatcher and Jessie Wolf.

The squad's first member to complete the five-point training program was a woman, Ruth Stewart, who became certified in 1965. Clifford Clymer was the squad captain when it first accepted the women members, and all of them were trained by "Bucky" Lawrence.

A squad building was erected on the Belvidere highway in 1969 on land donated by Miss Kathryn E. Koch.

Today the squad has 26 active members and one junior member. A squad auxiliary, organized in 1971, is open to all who wish to help the squad and has 25 members.

Captain Bruce C. Shive reports that 720 calls were answered during 1984.

Reinhold Radke photo

***LOPATCONG SQUAD ON CALL** — Accident scene at intersection of Routes 57 and 519 by Morrie's Acres restaurant.*

Stewartsville Emergency Squad

The Stewartsville Emergency Squad was created in 1946 as part of the volunteer fire department. It became a separate organization in 1959.

Edward Gary, Fred Gary, Abraham Painter, Earl Seiple and Alden Smith, all deceased, and Donald Cole, Paul Miers and John Snover organized the squad and became charter members.

In 1959 the squad constructed its building on Main Street. The land had been donated by Mr. and Mrs. Richard Rinehart. The original building housed the vehicles and equipment. In 1972 an addition was constructed which provided a banquet hall with a capacity of 250 people. The squad raised its own funds for both building projects.

The squad's 1985 roster includes 21 active members, three junior members, a 14-member auxiliary, and two life members.

Captain Robert Hoyd reports that 204 calls were answered in 1984.

Minassian photo

***STEWARTSVILLE VEHICLES** — From left: 1970 International captain's car, 1978 Ford ambulance and 1983 Ford emergency truck.*

Minassian photo

STEWARTSVILLE PERSONNEL — *Front row, from left: Pat Karabinus, Deborah Smith, recording secretary; Tammy Hackman, junior; Terry Wolfinger, training officer; Barbara Berezansky, treasurer; Sharon Trimble and Kris Fischer, corresponding secretary. Back row: Peter Fischer, chaplain; Scott Derringer, junior; William Timble, Joseph Smith, assistant foreman; Robert Hoyd, captain; John Snover, life member; Steve Fillebrown, foreman; Bruce Wolfinger, assistant captain; Andrew Karabmus, president and William Hoser. Not present when picture was taken: Ralph Amendt, social; Shelby Hall, vice-president; Kathleen Lenert, Emanual Lutzi, life; Jack Roan, Troy Rush, junior; Jeff Solomon, social; Robert Volk and Randy Widdoss.*

Belvidere Ambulance Corps

On a summer afternoon in 1945, Matthew Hains, a popular young Belvidere merchant, was pushing his stalled car. The front door hit a power pole and he became pinned between the door and the body of the car. The victim died while a local physician, Dr. Herman Baldauf, and numerous bystanders waited helplessly for an out-of-town ambulance which arrived more than an hour later. This incident caused the organization of a volunteer ambulance corps that year.

An ambulance fund committee included David Hosier, chairman; Homer Hicks, treasurer; and Thomas Ritter, secretary. Before the end of the year $7,678.85 was raised. The Bclvidere Ambulance Corps began service when its first ambulance was delivered in 1947. Homer Hicks was its first captain.

Originally the ambulance was housed in the town garage. In 1945 construction of a corps building was started on land on Paul Street which was sold by the town to the corps for one dollar. The building, built with volunteer labor, was completed in 1947. A building-fund committee including David Hosier, Frederick Green and Lloyd Stout raised $2,300

MOTORCYCLE ACCIDENT *— Belvidere Ambulance Corps on call.*

Minassian photo

BELVIDERE PERSONNEL — *Front row, from left: Richard Bocchino, Monica Mackey, Elaine Beers, Susan Ott, second liteutenant and treasurer; Michael Ruggiero, secretary and W. Francis Hicks, assistant treasurer. Back row: Eric Rudd, assistant captain; John Rose, Carol Williams, Steve Serna, Tracy Marsh, captain and Dale Rodenbaugh, sergeant. Not present when picture was taken: Darren Albanese, Sharon Bauder, first lieutenant and vice-president; Terry Cole, Henry Dinger, Clifford Griffin, Thomas Paul, Joan Prudenti, Richard Seidler and Raymond Smickle, president.*

Minassian photo

***BELVIDERE VEHICLES** — From left: 1983 Ford ambulance, 1980 Ford ambulance, 1976 Chevrolet ambulance, 1970 Ford emergency truck and 14-foot rescue boat.*

for materials. Much material was donated. In 1962 the town sold an additional tract of land to the corps for one dollar, and an addition was built to the structure.

In 1985 the corps has 20 active members and one cadet. Several members are specially trained in diving and water rescue, and a fourteen-foot outboard boat and a seventeen-foot outboard boat are available for water rescue work.

Captain Tracy Marsh reports the corps responded to 605 calls in 1984.

Hackettstown First Aid and Rescue Squad

The Hackettstown First Aid and Rescue Squad, Inc., was created through the efforts of Robert Hayford, Allen Heath, Anthony Frontera and Anthony Meeker. Service began in 1951.

Members of this squad were instrumental in the recognition of the urgent need for a hospital in Hackettstown. Two of its members, Claude Kraft and Irvin Kraft, served on the original hospital board of trustees. The original trustees personally contributed funds and purchased the land on which the Hackettstown Community Hospital now stands.

A squad bulding was built in 1961. It contains five bays, meeting room, senior office, junior office, supply room and kitchen. Built on land purchased previously by the squad, much of the construction work was done by volunteers.

The squad now has 19 members and an two-member youth squad.

Chief Robert Biamonte reports that the squad responded to 891 calls

Niper Studio photo

HACKETTSTOWN PERSONNEL — *Front row, from left: Robert Biamonte, chief; James Caldwell, Jr., foreman; Bonnie Chudley, assistant foreman; Anthony Mutz, president; Geri Amato, secretary and George Astacio, treasurer. Back row: Al McCrea, Anthony Sasso, assistant chief; Thomas Gibbs, Fred Ficarra, Kevin Ficarra, vice-president; Edward Aton, Trisha Herbert, Alanzo Carpenter and Robert Stivala. Not present when picture was taken: Steven Darst, John Davis, Kornell Davis and David Smith.*

Niper Studio photo

HACKETTSTOWN VEHICLES — *1972 Ford emergency truck, 1961 four-wheel-drive International truck, 1975 Ford van, 1978 Chevrolet ambulance, 1976 Cadillac ambulance, 1975 Cadillac ambulance and 1977 Chevrolet chief's car. Not shown: 1951 GMC emergency truck, first vehicle owned by squad.*

Niper Studio photo

BUS ACCIDENT — *The Hackettstown squad was assisted by several squads and fire departments at scene of bus accident on Highway 57, Mansfield Township, in 1983. Chartered bus was homeward bound with visitors of the Blue Army Shrine near Washington. Extrication required more than an hour.*

in 1984. Creation of newer squads in Allamuchy, Independence and Mansfield Townships has assisted the Hackettstown squad by holding down its number of calls for the past few years.

Blairstown Ambulance Corps

In 1952 a Blairstown resident had a serious fall and there was a two-hour delay in receiving first aid and ambulance service. This incident caused concerned citizens to organize the Blairstown Ambulance Corps, Inc. The Blairstown Rotary Club financed the first ambulance, converted from a 1949 Packard hearse. The first call was answered in June of 1952. The Rotary Club has continued its financial support through the years.

The first new ambulance purchased by the corps was a 1955 Cadillac. After twelve years of service this vehicle was donated to the Clinton First Aid and Rescue Squad to start its service. The Clinton Squad later donated the vehicle to the Oxford Emergency Squad.

Calls were handled through the telephones of members until Miss Ruth Maring became the full-time dispatcher in 1955. A Plectron call system was installed in 1968 with radio dispatch from Miss Maring's residence. She served for 28 years. The Blairstown Police Department

***JAWS OF LIFE DEMONSTRATION** — Blairstown squad members demonstrate equipment. With Jaws of Life squad members can extricate trapped passengers from vehicles with ease.*

Niper Studio photo

BLAIRSTOWN PERSONNEL — *Front row, from left: Len Sandberg, Jr. and Bill Phillips. Second row: Theseia Wiesing, historian; Norris Anderson, Steve Seidel, captain; Ian H. Lothian, president; Sue Lothian, secretary; Ray Konkle, treasurer; Joseph Meile, trustee and Robert Sandberg, trustee. Third row: Debbie Jones, assistant secretary; Barbara Corby, Cindy Dugan, John Kolc, Jenny Olinsky, Richard Matricsiano, Terry Warnkin, Victor Stoffles, exempt and Barbara Wiesing. Back row: Alfred Kise, Paul McNamara, Donald Kegel, Richard Johnson, Jr., sergeant; Richard Rick, Jerry Labar, steward and Lew Miller. Not present when picture was taken: Robert Feldman, Robert Goetze, Alyson Hamilton, Charles Hamilton, first lieutenant; Bart Hull, Robert Labar, Terry Labar, Lorrie Lothian, cadet; William Meshach, trustee; Sonny Shipps, second lieutenant and John Sipley, vice-president.*

Niper Studio photo

BLAIRSTOWN VEHICLES — *From left: 1973 International emergency truck, 1960 International four-wheel-drive truck, 1974 GMC ambulance, 1979 Ford ambulance and 1980 Ford ambulance. When this photo was taken the 1974 vehicle was about to be replaced with a new 1985 Ford modular ambulance.*

now dispatches the squad.

The corps purchased land for a building from Alfred White with the stipulation that it would be used only for ambulance corps purposes. Construction began in 1953. The building was enlarged in 1963. Much donated material and labor went into the construction.

The corps now has 38 active members and two cadets. A nine-member diving team is maintained for water rescues.

Corps president Ian H. Lothian reports 562 calls were answered during 1984. The corps captain is Stephen Seidel.

Bloomsbury Rescue Squad

In the late 1940's and early 1950's the Phillipsburg Emergency squad was responding to an increasing number of calls to accidents on Jugtown Mountain and to other emergencies in the area of Bloomsbury. The squad made it known that a new rescue organization was needed to cover that territory. The need was also brought to the attention of Bloomsbury residents when a five-year-old boy drowned in the Musconetcong River. The Phillipsburg squad answered the call, but this tragedy made it clear that Phillipsburg was too far away to be the base from which timely emergency aid could be obtained.

The Bloomsbury Rescue Squad was a dream in 1952 that became a reality in January 1953. It was organized by members of Bloomsbury Hose Company No. 1 and included members from both the fire company

Royal Photographics photo

***BLOOMSBURY VEHICLES** — From left: 1981 Ford ambulance, 1981 GMC emergency truck and 1976 Chevrolet ambulance.*

Royal Photographics photo

BLOOMSBURY PERSONNEL — *Front row, from left: Rhea Race, dispatcher; Virginia Cooke, assistant captain and treasurer; Charles Kebles, president; Robin Anderson, first lieutenant and junior squad advisor and Barbara Sliva, secretary. Back row: Matthew Zeeman, David Peterson, captain; Lance Huff, Jr., Robert Weissman, John J. Curtiss, Sergeant and James Anderson, second lieutenant. Not present when picture was taken: Alan Baguskis, Renee Creveling, Neil Frankenfield, Richard Gerhardt, Sr., Christopher Heinrich, Richard Koppe, Becky Laubach, John Lenehan, Edward Pacenti, Jr., Edward Pacenti, Sr., Sharon Procita, Grace Race, Dorothy Smith, Frank Smith, Ronald Unkert, Mary Ann Wyant and Victor Zeeman.*

Free Press photos

WATER RESCUE — *Bloomsbury Rescue Squad members were among rescuers from several squads attempting to recover the body of driver of truck that went over a bank and into the Musconetcong River.*

and its auxiliary, but it was a separate organization from the fire company. Firemen members were Charles Brandt, Chris Heinrich, Harold Lutz, Roy McFarlane, Edward Pacenti and John Wieller. Members from the firemen's auxiliary were Dora Cooke, Virginia Korbobo, Grace Race and Dorothy Smith.

The first vehicle was a used LaSalle ambulance. The vehicle was garaged at the home of Brandt, the first captain of the squad, but it was later moved to the home of Heinrich because Brandt's driveway was difficult to negotiate in icy weather. A short time later the firemen built an addition to the firehouse on East Street which provided a bay for the ambulance. Most of the materials were donated by the J. C. Pickel lumberyard, and the labor was done by the firemen and their friends. A few years later the municipality built a larger addition to the firehouse on Brunswick Avenue which provided additional bays for fire and emergency vehicles. The firemen contributed much labor to this second addition.

By 1979 the squad had outgrown the firehouse quarters and moved to its present headquarters in a building owned by Koh-I-Noor Rapidograph, Inc., on Main Street. The company leases the area to the squad for one dollar per year.

The squad has 29 members and a nine-member junior squad.

Captain David Peterson reports 314 calls were answered during the year 1984.

The Ambulance Corps of Portland and Vicinity

Sidney Effross, a son of the founder of Effross' Department Store in Portland, served as a public school teacher in that community from 1939 to 1942 when he enlisted in the Army and became a staff sergeant in the 7th Infantry Division Headquarters. He is a charter member of the Lions Club in Portland. When he left the Army in 1945, he did not return to Portland to resume his teaching career,[1] but he continued his Lions Club membership there and has a 100% attendance record covering 39 years to this day. He became the Lions district governor and made official visits to the clubs in the six counties which comprised his district. In 1954 one of these trips took him to the municipality of Schuylkill Haven, where the club members proudly showed him their rescue squad—a project of their club. Impressed with that community-service effort, he returned to Portland with the conviction that a squad was needed there. The

[1]In 1946 Effross became a teacher in the Blairstown public schools and in 1951 he became superintendent of schools in that community. In 1961 he accepted a similar position in the Borough of Washington school system. Now retired, he and his wife, Esther, reside in Washington.

Royal Photographics photo

PORTLAND PERSONNEL — *Front row, from left: George Abt, second lieutenant; Richard Weaver, chief of divers; Clifford Stanmetz and Dale Smolenyak. Second row: Louis Wheeler, president; Phyllis Moser, assistant captain and secretary and Helen VanDusen, chaplain. Back row: Kandi Stanton, Bridget Miller, first lieutenant and vice-president; Sue Albert, Joseph Hurd, Edward VanDusen, William VanDusen and Darryl Moser, captain. Not present when picture was taken: Wendell Kulp, sergeant; James Potter, Claire Sorensen, Linda Meshach and Ian Loudan.*

members of the Portland club were impressed and were receptive to the idea.

A fund drive was started in 1954 with a goal of $6,500. The Lions Club contributed $2,000 as a starter, the Portland Community Board of Trade contributed $1,000, and the Woman's Club followed with a $500 contribution. Other businesses and individuals gave their support, and the goal was reached in a short time. A used Cadillac ambulance and other necessary equipment were purchased.

The Ambulance Corps of Portland and Vicinity was chartered in January 1955 with Effross as its first president, and by July of that year was ready to respond to calls. Forty members were divided into duty crews to provide around-the-clock service. At first each crew was on duty for a week, but today the crews serve on a nightly basis.

A corps member who has compiled an enviable record of service is Lou Wheeler. He became an active member in 1956 and has served in almost every office including a 15-year stint as captain. He has served as president of the board of directors and was the first-aid instructor for 20 years. He is the corps' representative to the New Jersey State First Aid Council.

Located only four miles south of the Delaware Water Gap National Recreation Area, this squad is frequently called upon to perform water rescues. An aluminum rescue boat was purchased in 1965 and was replaced in 1984 with a six-man rubber raft. Powered with a 35-horsepower jet-prop motor, this raft can skim a water surface of three inches, a valuable ability in times of low water. Also because of its location, this squad is involved in many mountain rescues and searches.

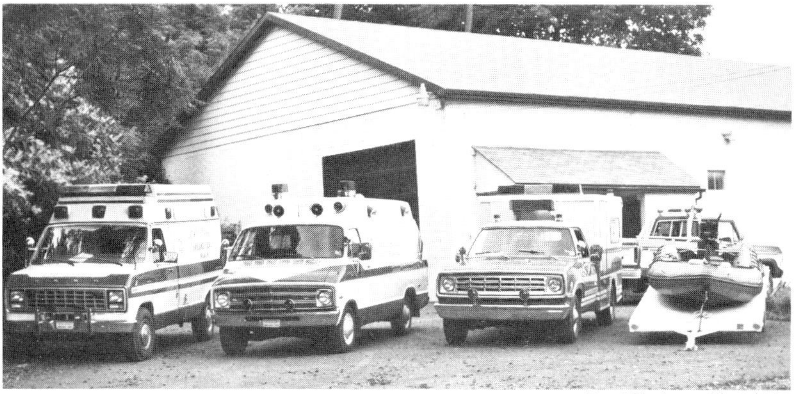

Royal Photographics photo

***PORTLAND VEHICLES** — From left: 1982 Ford ambulance, 1973 Dodge ambulance, 1974 Dodge ambulance and six-man rubber raft.*

Royal Photographics photo

***WATER RESCUE TEAM** — Members of the Portland Ambulance Water Rescue team with six-man rubber raft. From left: George Abt, Clifford Stanmetz, Dale Smolenyak and Richard Weaver, chief of divers.*

The first headquarters of the corps was an old garage across from Riverview Cemetery. Later a move was made to the old firehouse after the fire company occupied new quarters. In 1978 a garage and warehouse in the rear of the Effross' Department Store was purchased and remodeled to provide modern facilities with meeting room, officers' room, kitchen, classrooms and a four-bay garage area.

In 1985 the squad has 19 active members and an auxiliary of ten members. All of the squad's EMT's are MAST trained, two of them are certified advanced-first-aid instructors, and three are C.P.R. instructors headed by Captain Darryl Moser, whose tenure goes back to 1975. In 1985 the squad became certified by the Pennsylvania Department of Emergency Services.

Captain Moser reports 623 calls were answered during 1984.

Hampton Emergency Squad

In 1955 the membership of the Hampton Fire Company decided to create an emergency squad. Fireman Gilbert Riddle was selected to organize it. It was required that members be firemen, and 12 members of the company were chosen to be charter members of the squad. The squad became operative in 1956 and used an ambulance purchased for it by the

Royal Photographics photo

HAMPTON PERSONNEL — *Front row, from left: Penny Housman, Ernest Born, Dee Alexander, Timothy Schreck, Jeannine Paraskevas and Donna Ronco, treasurer. Back row: Richard Tampier, second lieutenant; Susan Born, Joseph Kiceina, president; Jeffrey Tampier, director of equipment; Ronald O'Rourke, John DeRemer, Roger Zimmerman, vice-president; Timothy Ganley, David Stetson, Jane Hoffman, Joseph Lusardi, first lieutenant and David Tampier, captain. Not present when picture was taken: Peter Campbell, Peachie Cole, Galen Fishburn, Anna Ganley, Pricilla Jacobson, secretary; Janet Miller, Mary Suessmann and Robert Suessmann.*

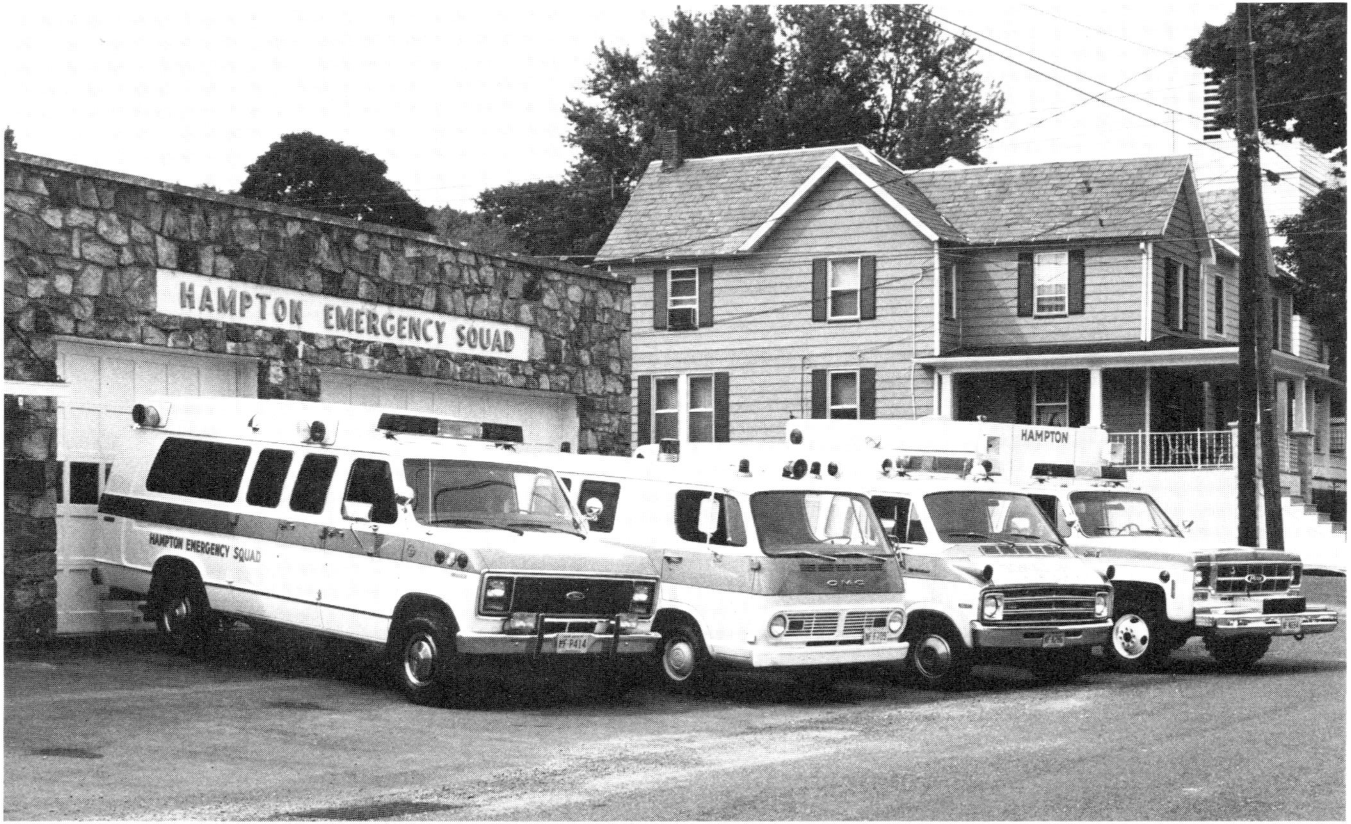

Royal Photographics photo

HAMPTON VEHICLES—*From left: 1982 Ford ambulance, 1967 GMC support truck, 1974 Dodge ambulance and 1978 GMC emergency truck.*

fire company.

As the squad expanded, it quickly outgrew the space allotted to it in the firehouse. In 1961 a committee was appointed to seek a suitable location for a new building. The problem was solved in 1963 when the Hampton borough council offered to give the squad part of a property it had purchased at the corner of Wells Avenue and South Street. A building committee was appointed, and it was decided that as much of the work as possible would be done by the squad members. The project was completed in 1966. An additional bay for emergency vehicles was added in 1979, and the fall of 1985 saw the start of construction of a second-story addition to include an office, meeting room and storage space.

In 1982 the building was rededicated in recognition of the exceptional service to the squad and the community by old-time squadmen Charles Tampier and William "Cook" Deemer. The present squad membership roll includes the names of three sons of Charles Tampier: Richard, Jeffrey and David. Richard is a former captain and David is the present captain.

In addition to the building projects, the highlights of the squad's

Royal Photographics photo

***PRIZE WINNER** — Joseph Lusarde, Captain David Tampier and Richard Tampier with trophy for best over-all squad won by the Hampton Emergency Squad at the Washington Emergency Squad's 50th-year parade in September 1985.*

Royal Photographics photo

RIEGELSVILLE PERSONNEL — *Front row, from left: Terry Evans, Robert O'Donnell, Alan Griffin and Ingvald Martinson, Jr., chief engineer. Second row: Troy Brailo, chief; Corie Martinson, Donald VanHorn and Donald King. Third row: Lois Altemose, Debra Xander, treasurer; Jane Cox, Bonnie Cutchineal and Carole Gressler, president. Back row: Thomas Werge, Lou Bell and David Kramer. Not present when picture was taken: Jeffrey Xander, James Altemose, Kelly Applegate, secretary; John Cox, trustee; Steve Cox, cadet; David Gerstenberg, Kenneth Gressler, Terri Hirthler, Kenneth Johnson, trustee; Lee Lilley, Donald Pursell, Nancy Shannon, vice-president; Kimberly Xander, Keith Williams, Lisa Rimmer, cadet and Richard Clinchy IV, cadet.*

history include purchase of a GMC van as a crash truck at a cost of $2,400 in 1962, installation of radio-communication equipment in 1963, amendment of the bylaws to permit membership of women in 1964, becoming independent of the fire company in 1976, purchase of the present crash truck for $29,000 in 1978, establishment of the squad auxiliary in 1978, purchase of a Braun ambulance to replace a 1968 Cadillac in 1982, and the first MedEvac drill in Hunterdon County in 1983.

When the squad became independent of the fire company, the corporate name, Hampton Fire Company Emergency Squad, was retained in honor of the founders.

The squad has 25 active members and 30 members in its auxiliary.

Captain David Tampier reports 318 calls were answered during 1984.

Riegelsville Emergency Squad

In 1956 a 15-year-old boy sustained severe injuries when he was struck by a car while riding his bicycle in Riegelsville, Pennsylvania. Witnesses called the Easton Hospital and requested its ambulance to transport the injured boy. The ambulance arrived in one hour and 45 minutes. A local man, David W. Utley, decided that Riegelsville needed a rescue squad and set out to organize one. He succeeded in establishing the Riegelsville Emergency Squad. It was incorporated in 1958 and answered its first calls that year. Utley was the first captain and occupied that position for 10 years.

The squad began its operation with a single ambulance, a new GMC. When the need for a second vehicle became evident, the Bound Brook

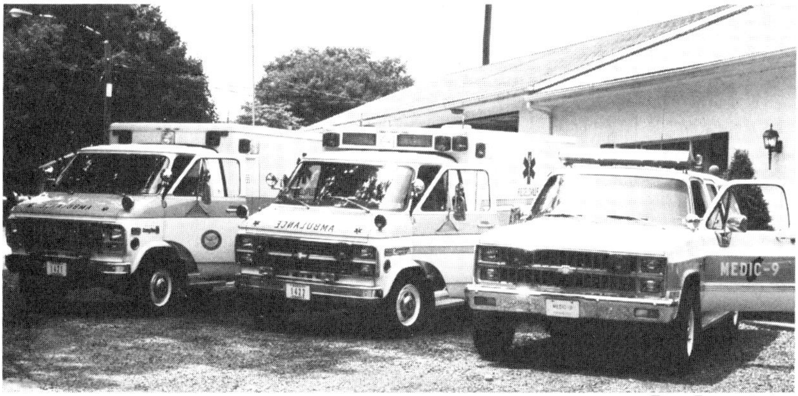

Terry Evans photo

***RIEGELSVILLE VEHICLES** — From left: 1981 Chevrolet ambulance, 1984 Chevrolet ambulance and the 1982 Chevrolet service vehicle of Medic-9.*

Emergency Squad sold its 1941 Packard to the Riegelsville squad for one dollar. Before the end of its third year, the Riegelsville squad was operating three vehicles.

The first ambulance was housed at Bartman Brothers Garage for the winter of 1985. The squad then moved to Delaware Oaks where an old barn was used. The American Legion post leased land to the squad for a dollar per year and later the squad purchased the land.

The first section of the present building was constructed by Henry Heuer with the help of community residents in 1960. An addition con-

Royal Photographics photo

***TRIPOD** — This dog was discovered by Riegelsville Emergency Squad member Ingvald Martinson, Jr., after it had been caught in a trap. One leg was badly mangled. Martinson and other squad members took the dog to a veterinarian and the leg was amputated. The squad members nursed the animal back to health and it became the mascot of the squad after receiving the appropriate name "Tripod."*

taining a kitchen, a radio room, and a training and meeting room was added 10 years later.

The second captain was David Xander who set up the squad's communication system. Dr. Gerald Nadeau served as medical director from the squad's beginning until his death in 1985.

The squad has 29 active members, three cadet members, and an auxiliary of 15 members. Two members are paramedics, two are registered nurses, nine are MAST-certified EMT's, and 20 are advanced-first-aid first responders. The Riegelsville Fire Company provides auto extrications and water rescues.

In 1982 the squad began running with the Medic-9 paramedic unit of Northampton County. Medic-9 consists of 6 paramedics, and approximately 30 drivers and attendants. It covers 115 square miles of Northampton County plus the area outside of that county covered by the Riegelsville squad. Medic-9 is a nonprofit organization funded solely by the affiliated squads. It was organized in 1982 to provide advanced life support for the area, and it responds with the Riegelsville Emergency Squad on all such calls.

Chief Troy R. Brailo reports the Riegelsville Emergency Squad answered 350 calls in 1984.

Franklin Township Rescue Squad

The Broadway Rescue Squad, as it was then named, got its start in 1963 when Morris "Moot" Adams bought a 1946 Cadillac ambulance from the fire department of Raritan Township in Hunterdon County

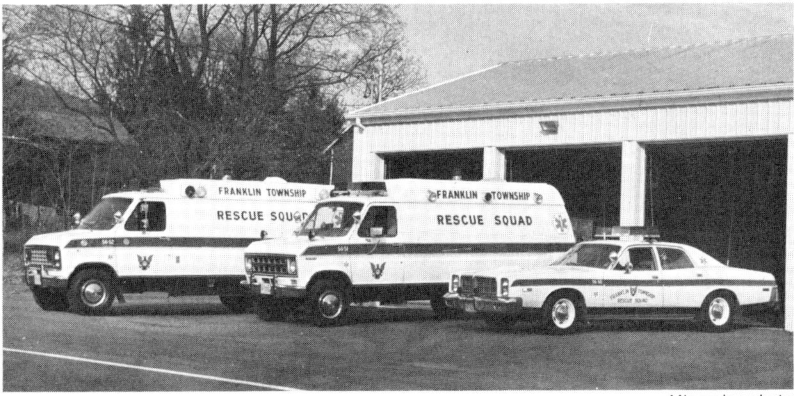

Minassian photo

***FRANKLIN VEHICLES** — From left: 1980 Ford ambulance, 1978 Ford ambulance and 1978 Dodge captain's car.*

Minassian photo

***FRANKLIN PERSONNEL** — Front row, from left: Charlotte Matheis, sergeant; Charlotte Metz, Denise Adams, recording secretary; Debbie Whitmore, sergeant; Frances Serfass, vice-president; Bonnie Skeens, corresponding secretary and Barbara Skeens. Back row: John Amy, Elmer Wyckoff, trustee; Nicholas Colucci, trustee; April Colucci, lieutenant; Randy Widdoss, president; Harvey Adams, captain and treasurer; Brian Cowie, trustee; Louise Adams and Arthur Blazier. Not present when picture was taken: Paul Sigler, Michele Stocker, Michael Vine, Gregg Warne, Wendell Whitmore, assistant captain and Wendy Wyckoff, sergeant.*

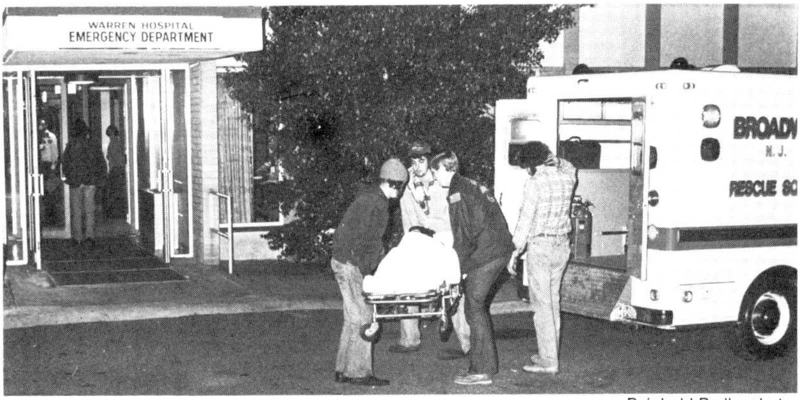

Reinhold Radke photo

***TRANSPORTING PATIENT** — Franklin (then Broadway) squad members in action at entrance to Warren Hospital emergency room.*

after a search for a suitable vehicle. He paid for it with $100 out of his own pocket. The ambulance was bare bones—completely lacking equipment—and in poor condition, but it was restorable. The restoration received a big boost with the donation of new tires by a Goodyear tire dealer in Easton.

Others instrumental in the organizing of the squad were Frank Nemeth, George Shotwell, and Harvey and Richard Adams,[1] both sons of "Moot." The new squad was also aided by members of the Washington Emergency Squad during its formative period.

"Moot" Adams was the first president, and his name is now memorialized by The Morris "Moot" Adams Society, consisting of financial supporters of the squad.

Nemeth served as the first captain, followed in order by Richard Adams and Harvey Adams. Harvey is the present captain and has held the position for 16 of his 20 years of membership.

On January 1, 1980, the name of the organization was changed to Franklin Township Rescue Squad.

The squad originally occupied part of the building owned by the volunteer fire company in Broadway where its meetings were held and its vehicles garaged. In 1980 a fund drive was started to raise funds for the construction of a new building on Broadway-Asbury Road. The land had been donated to the squad by the Township of Franklin. The project

---

[1] Richard Adams moved to Washington in 1970 and joined the borough fire department. He also joined the Washington Emergency Squad as an auxiliary member. He became a regular member in 1974 when a vacancy occurred in Washington Truck Company No. 2. He was elected to honorary squad membership in 1976.

Royal Photographics photo

HOFFMAN LaROCHE PERSONNEL — *Front row, from left: John Paulus, John Sipley, assistant captain; Donald Reed and Kenneth Johnson. Second row: Patricia Shumaker, second lieutenant; Daniel Andrews, Robert Helfrich, first lieutenant and Joan Prudenti. Back row: Charles Rosoche, Thomas Newport, Jr., Alfred Miller, David Alleger, captain; Eric Simmons, Michael Black and Barbara Cleaves. Not present when picture was taken: Joseph Barcik, Roger Learn, Henry Rebinski, Gerald Gitler, George Reeder, Jr., Austin Mosley, James Carey and Thomas Newport, Sr.*

succeeded, and on January 1, 1983, the squad occupied its new home.

An active membership of 22, a cadet squad of 10, and 10 social members comprise the 1985 roster.

Captain Adams reports the squad responded to 210 calls during 1984.

Hoffmann-LaRoche First Aid Squad

One of the smaller and less-known emergency units operating in Warren County is the Hoffmann-LaRoche, Inc., First Aid Squad which serves the plant's 800 workers. The need to create emergency services for the company was seen by James Sederis, of Allamuchy Township, who was the first general manager when the industry was established in White Township along the Delaware River just off Route 46 in 1968. The following year the squad was in service.

The squad members are all volunteers, but they are paid to attend all-day monthly drills and training sessions. The unit maintains daytime duty crews much the same as other volunteer units throughout the region. If there is an emergency, employees are instructed to call security. If the squad is needed, the members are summoned by a paging system.

The squad responds to the same types of calls as other rescue units, except that it is unlikely to encounter automobile accidents. It belongs to the region's mutual-aid system and at times responds to calls outside the plant's jurisdiction, as when it assisted the town of Belvidere in recent floods. It participates in area mutual-aid drills. If it is short-handed at one of its own calls, it calls the Belvidere Ambulance Corps for assistance. It has an ambulance, and three fire trucks are maintained at the plant.

David L. Alleger, 30, who served in the Washington Emergency Squad for five years before moving to the Belvidere area, is captain of the 23-member unit of which he has been a member since 1978. A native of Doylestown, Pennsylvania, he is a safety specialist with a major concern in industrial hygiene. He is also a member of the plant's fire brigade and has served as captain of the first-aid unit since 1983.

"Our members have taken the EMT course of the New Jersey Department of Transportation and are five-point certified. The squad is a member of the New Jersey State First Aid Council," Alleger says. He points out that one of the most difficult aspects of sustaining a small rescue unit is maintaining interest and enthusiasm. "That is because we have only a few calls each year, so we try to make our drills as interesting as possible," he says.

Despite this handicap the squad maintains a high degree of efficiency and specialization. Eight members have taken heavy-rescue training at the Hammonton Rescue School at Hammonton, New Jersey. Several

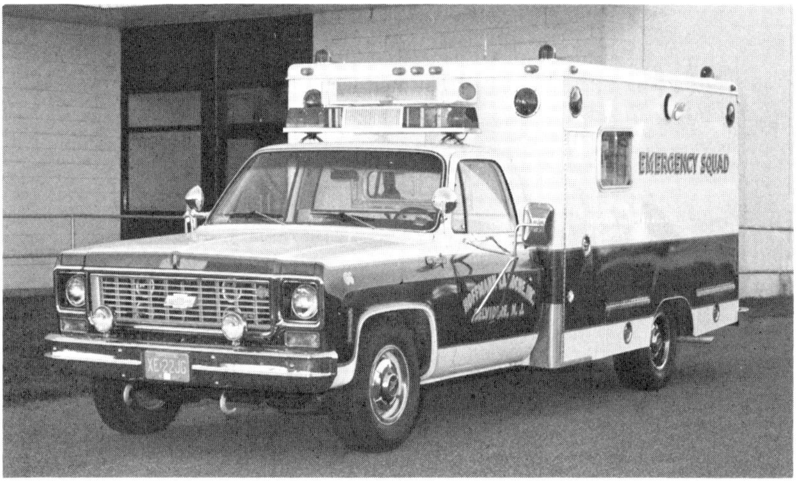

Royal Photographics photo

***HOFFMAN-LaROCHE AMBULANCE** — This squad has one vehicle, a 1973 Chevrolet ambulance.*

other members are attending the Dover, Delaware, State Fire School where they are receiving special training in confined-space rescue involving emergency situations in elevator shafts and other limited-space areas. areas.

Alleger reports that the squad responds to an average of only 10 calls per year, a record resulting from the concern for safety on the part of Hoffmann-LaRoche management. All employees are continually reminded about safety and are encouraged to attend regular courses on safety in order to keep accidents to a minimum. This program has resulted in the plant's excellent safety record.

Oxford Emergency Squad

Three members were instrumental in the formation of the Oxford Emergency Squad, Inc. They were Daniel Collins, who is its present captain, John Henderson and Harvey Hissim.

The Washington Emergency Squad aided in the creation of the organization which became active in 1971. Especially remembered by older members are the efforts of Washington squadmen Anthony Damelio and John Hoffmaster in their behalf.

The Clinton First Aid and Rescue Squad donated its 1955 Cadillac ambulance to the new group, and that was the first vehicle to be placed in service.

Royal Photographics photo

OXFORD PERSONNEL — *Front row, from left: William Collins, Daniel Collins, captain and president and Brian Brands. Back row: Kathy Specht, Katherine Mikolon, secretary; Joseph Bush, Joseph Henderson, assistant captain and vice-president; Anthony Snook, Florence Hydash and Sheila Kelson. Not present when picture was taken: Jean Docker, Robert Itterly, Raymond Kurela, Susan Kurela and Suzanne Kelley.*

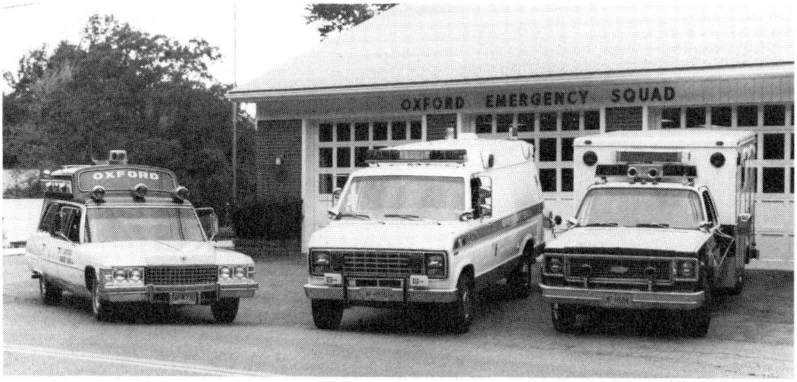

Minassian photo

***OXFORD VEHICLES:** From left: 1975 Cadillac ambulance, 1979 Ford ambulance and 1974 Chevrolet emergency truck. When this photo was taken the 1975 Cadillac was about to be replaced with a 1982 Ford modular ambulance, purchased from the Washington Emergency Squad.*

This squad has its own 24-hour volunteer dispatching service, provided by Edward and Shirley Mulligan for the past 13 years.

Vehicles were originally kept in an old garage, the use of which was donated by Mr. and Mrs. William Ruther. Later the Ruthers' sons, George and James, donated land for a new building. The building, constructed in 1972, contains three bays. Much of the labor and material for the building was donated, and it was necessary to borrow only $13,000 for its construction. That debt has been retired through fund-raising efforts of squad members.

Fifteen active members serve in 1985. This was one of the first squads in Warren County to create a junior squad, but there are no junior members this year.

The Oxford squad has relieved the heavy load of calls of the Washington and Belvidere squads.

Captain Collins reports the squad answered 225 calls during 1984.

Allamuchy-Green First Aid Squad

The Allamuchy-Green First Aid Squad, Inc., was created by residents of Allamuchy Township in Warren County and Green Township in Sussex County in March 1971.

The need for the squad was evident. Two residents, Raymond ''Mike'' Freeborn and Milton Loss, had been members of the Long Valley, Morris County, squad. They were instrumental in the creation of the new organization. The Long Valley squad donated its old Cadillac ambulance

Niper Studio photo

ALLAMUCHY-GREEN PERSONNEL — *Front row, from left: Mary Ellen Ramella, recording secretary; Robert Smith, president and Louis Caruso, captain. Second row: Ralph Bailey, Lorraine Weingast, quartermaster and corresponding secretary; Terry Saita, vice-president and Louis Casella, first lieutenant. Back row: Robert Meier, Arleigh Freeborn and Lloyd Grove. Not present when picture was taken. William Colville, William Cramer, Raymond Gormley, Leandra Gormley, Colleen Magai, Peter Niven, Denise Scairpon, Robert Vandergroef and Ann Duffy.*

Niper Studio photo

***ALLAMUCHY-GREEN VEHICLES** — From left: 1974 GMC emergency truck, 1985 Ford ambulance and 1983 Ford ambulance.*

which was placed in service as the first vehicle.

A new squad building on Maple Lane was completed in 1980. The land was purchased. Many members worked on the construction, and much material was donated. The building was estimated to cost $97,000, but donation of services and materials reduced the cost to $60,000. The building includes three bays, a meeting room, and a kitchen.

The squad lists 19 members in 1985. The Allamuchy-Green First Aid

***DISASTER DRILL** — Members of Allamuchy-Green First Aid Squad participate in drill at Tranquility.*

Squad Auxiliary was formed in 1972 and presently has a membership roll of 15.

A total of 290 responses to calls during 1984 is reported by squad captain Louis R. Caruso.

Independence First Aid Squad

In 1971 Mayor Samuel Vaia saw the need for a first-aid squad in Independence Township because of the number of calls being made to the squads of neighboring municipalities, particularly Hackettstown, and the additional need that would surely be generated by the future growth of the area. He turned to Pat Curtin to do the organizing because Curtin had served in the Wharton First Aid Squad and the Palisades Park Volunteer Ambulance Corps. Curtin was assisted by Robert Bonnell, a charter member of the squad, who now resides in Florida. The assignment was carried out, and the Independence First Aid Squad responded to its first call on July 16, 1972. Members of the Hackettstown First Aid and Rescue Squad assisted in training the personnel of the new organization. The Hackettstown squad also donated a used rescue truck which became the second vehicle of the Independence group.

A building containing three bays, a meeting room and a kitchen was built on Highway 46 with much of the work donated by squad members and other citizens. The structure was dedicated in 1976. The land had previously been purchased by the squad.

The auxiliary furnished the kitchen in the squad building and pur-

Niper Studio photo

***INDEPENDENCE VEHICLES** — From left: 1973 Chevrolet ambulance, 1984 GMC four-wheel-drive ambulance and 1980 Ford ambulance.*

Niper Studio photo

INDEPENDENCE PERSONNEL *— Front row, from left: Patricia Douglas Jarvis, second lieutenant; Mieke Cunningham, captain; Ruth Hardiman, president; Bonnie Lou Dailey, treasurer and Carole Durna, corresponding secretary. Second row: Shirley Miller, Ottlie Campbell and Jane Billows. Back row: Howard Leh, Paul Snyder, Marvin Gerrol and Peter Matsko. Not present when picture was taken: Floyd Beam; Dennis Brunck, George Brunck, Patt Ortner Clapp, recording secretary; Jospeh Durna, first lieutenant; Alice Eherts, Linda Fabian, Clara Hoffman, Mark* chased Jaws of Life extrication equipment for the squad.

The 1985 membership roll contains the names of 25 active members and an active auxiliary membership of 22.

Captain Mieke Cunningham reports 473 calls were answered during 1984.

Mansfield Emergency Squad

The Mansfield Emergency Squad is the newest rescue organization in Warren County. The Hackettstown First Aid and Rescue Squad, the Washington Emergency Squad, and the Independence First Aid Squad had been answering an increasing number of calls in Mansfield Township over the past several years. The fast growth of that township and the increasing number of calls caused the Hackettstown squad to suggest to the Mansfield Township Committee that another rescue organization be created.

In 1978 Charles Sickles, a member of the township committee, called an informal meeting at the Tri-County firehouse. The meeting was attended by several firemen, including Jeffrey Woronowicz, and a few citizens who were not members of the fire companies. The result was a proposal to the township committee that a rescue organization be formed and that the township provide a building to house the necessary vehicles and equipment. The estimated cost of the building was $20,000 and the answer was no. The negative answer stalled the project, and the

Niper Studio photo

***MANSFIELD VEHICLES** — From left: 1983 Ford ambulance and 1980 Ford ambulance.*

Richard W. York photo

ORGANIZING MANSFIELD SQUAD: *Attending meeting in summer of 1979 are, from left: Richard Burkhardt, treasurer; Marilyn Braun, Rosanne Cacciarelli, secretary; Jeffrey Woronowicz, president and John Musarra. Not present when picture was taken: JoAnn Krayniewski, Eileen Musarra and Bruce O'Reilly.*

township increased its donations to the outside squads.

The idea remained in the mind of Woronowicz, however, and he and some other citizens made a presentation to the township committee on April 11, 1979, asking support in the formation of a rescue squad, but not financial aid.

Mansfield Emergency Medical Services was incorporated in June with Woronowicz as president, Bruce O'Reilly as vice-president, Rosanne Cacciarelli as secretary, Richard Burkhardt as treasurer and members Marilyn Braun, Jo Ann Krayniewski, Eileen Musarra and John Musarra.

The first annual officers' installation dinner was held in January, 1980, at the Butler Park firehouse. Bruce O'Reilly succeeded Jeffrey Woronowicz as squad president and John Musarra was installed as vice-president, succeeding O'Reilly. Other officers continued in positions held in 1979. Robert Trawin was the squad captain.

By October the new squad had 20 members and was seeking more. Some of these members held state certification as emergency medical technicians. The remaining members were scheduled to begin the EMT course at the Warren County Vocational School and Technical Institute

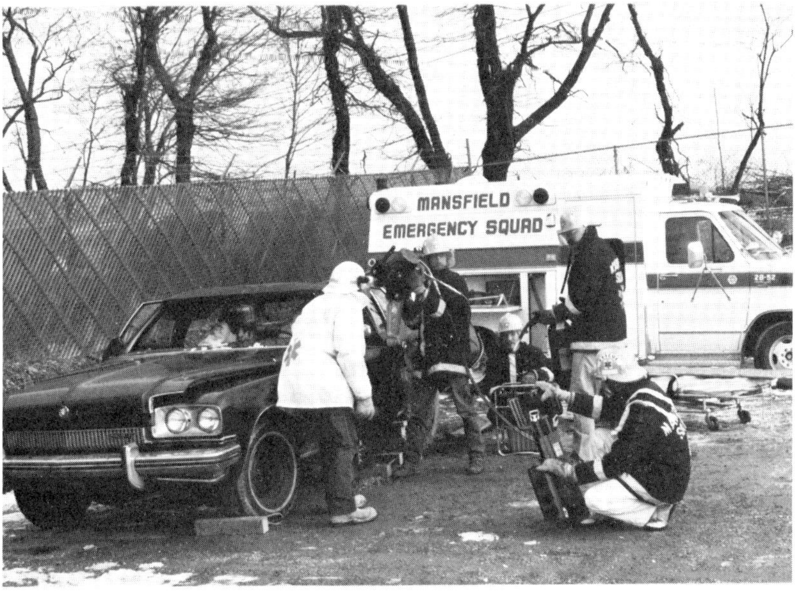

RESCUE DRILL — *Mansfield squad members practice use of Jaws of Life extrication equipment.*

Niper Studio photo

MANSFIELD PERSONNEL — *Front row, from left: Anna Humphreys, junior; Teresa Dowd, Laurie Nichols and Deborah Kreps. Second row: Robert Mayberry, Harry Appleby, Jr., chief of juniors; Robert Silvent, treasurer; Richard Alpaugh, chief; Bruce O'Reilly, assistant chief; Mark Fornier, first lieutenant; Jeffrey Marchione, second lieutenant; John Rebinski and Eugene Echevarria. Back row: Robert Hughes, Matthew Hamlen, junior; Marc Hamlen, Jeffrey Woronowicz, Bruce Sargeant, Heide Humphreys, vice-president; Michael Humphreys, Scott Churchill, John Hague and Fred Goerlitz, junior. Not present when picture was taken: Gary Bonfonte, Christopher Fournier, Jacob Garabed, Christopher Hoy, Kelvin Marshall, Edith Mayberry, Eunice Rice, secretary; Matthew Rice, Robert Sisco, Ronald Sisco, junior and Ronald Stecker, junior.*

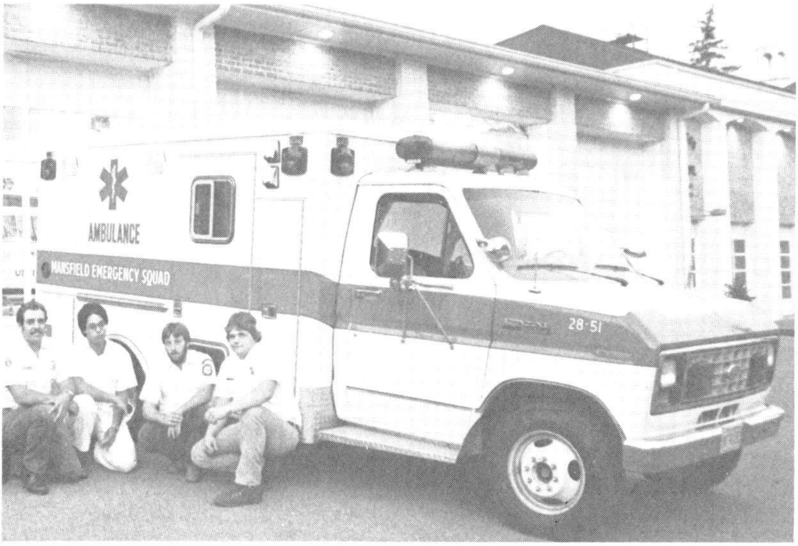

Reinhold Radke photo

***STAND BY FOR WASHINGTON** — Mutual-aid crew of the Mansfield Emergency Squad spends an evening at the Vernon Oakes Building to permit members of the Washington Emergency Squad to enjoy an uninterrupted stay at their 50th-year dinner dance in the Washington Armory.*

or five-point training to be given through the Lebanon Township First Aid Squad.

The new organization received a boost in September when the Lebanon squad presented it with a 1970 Cadillac ambulance for one dollar at a dedication ceremony in the Butler Park firehouse. A 1965 Cadillac ambulance had been received as a donation from the Oxford Emergency Squad in January. The vehicles were temporarily garaged in the Butler Park firehouse.

Squad meetings are now held in the Mansfield Township Municipal Building, a part of which is assigned to the organization. One ambulance is kept in the municipal garage at Port Murray and the other at the New Jersey game farm at Rockport.

The squad has 33 members and a junior squad of 10 members. A unique feature of this squad is its 10-member rescue team, several of whom hold certification from the Northampton Rescue School. The members of this unit spend many hours in addition to their regular squad duties on the study and practice of rescue techniques. This advanced and specialized training is over and above the required standard training set forth by the New Jersey State First Aid Council. It includes work with

MANSFIELD RESCUE TEAM *— Mansfield squad members lower mannequin from silo during demonstration.*

***ROCK-LEDGE RESCUE** — A member of Mansfield's 10-member rescue team demonstrates removal of victim from ledge.*

Jaws of Life for auto rescue, training with self-contained breathing apparatus for rescue work in toxic atmospheres, special work for ice rescue, search and rescue for lost persons, and work with ropes and special rigging for rescues in places such as rock ledges, towers and silos.

Chief Richard Alpaugh reports the Mansfield squad responded to 335 calls in 1984.

A car screeches through an intersection, its driver hitting the brakes in that moment of horror when he realizes that he's missed a red light.

The other driver never has a chance. The sounds of crunching metal and breaking glass fill the air, followed by the quiet, frightening moment when the victims assess the severity of their injuries.

Then a welcome sound shatters the stillness the way one hurtling vehicle shatters another.

A rescue squad siren.

Help is on the way.

Residents throughout The Express' circulation area have come to expect the quick and skillful help of volunteer rescue squads in all kinds of emergency situations — almost to the point of taking them for granted.

But the ambulance loaded with medical equipment and trained first-aid personnel doesn't appear by magic. Manpower, money and training are needed to keep the wheels rolling.

In a series of articles beginning today, The Express explores these key elements of volunteer rescue service.

Express/Sunday, January 27, 1985

18

What Does the Future Hold?

Early in 1985 The Express published a comprehensive series of feature articles about the rescue squads in its area. The articles were written by Greg Hanisek, of the staff of that Easton, Pennsylvania, newspaper.

Using officials of squads as his sources of information, Hanisek brought their problems into sharp focus. The problems are of such magnitude that some people feel the survival of the service may be in jeopardy in future years.

The final chapter of this book is an adaptation of these articles. The author and publisher are grateful to Greg Hanisek and The Express for permission to reprint this informative material.

"For our squad there's no question that manpower is the big problem," says Bruce Shive, who served eight years as captain of the Lopatcong Emergency Squad before temporarily passing the reins to Alan Cenci.

Shive is talking about manpower, the element cited by most first-aid, rescue or emergency-squad officials as either their most pressing need or one that challenges money closely for first place.

"It's a big problem in general to find any kind of volunteers," Shive says. "I think the economy is a big part of it. Wives have to work; husbands are taking two jobs. Between that and raising kids, it's tough to find time. Add that along with the (training) requirements of a first-aider today, and it becomes almost impossible."

Kevin Wallasea, captain and president of the Easton Emergency Squad, says manpower and money seem to shift from year to year as the top priority of his volunteer unit.

But Wallasea cites an aspect of the manpower problem that is raised by virtually every squad officer—filling the day shift.

"We have a pretty good mutual-aid system with neighboring squads, and we're staffed pretty well over all," he says, "but we have to rely on a few people too much as a day crew. If you rely too much on the same people, you burn them out. It becomes a vicious cycle."

"If you were here with me right now you would see it," said Eric Belshaw, president of the Suburban Rescue Squad in Palmer Township, one morning. "I'm the only one in the building."

The problem is an obvious one but a difficult one to solve. Most potential volunteers work during the day when they are unavailable for emergency service.

"The day crew is definitely the greatest problem," says John Stoneback, who recently completed a four-year stint as president of the Suburban Rescue Squad.

Historically, local squads have provided extensive non-emergency medical transportation as well as emergency service, but daytime manpower problems have made non-emergency service increasingly difficult.

"We've had to cut it back radically to maintain emergency service, especially during the day," says Ronald Titus, captain of the Phillipsburg Emergency Squad.

"We have 34 active members, but most of them are available on the second or third shift," Titus says. "The day shift is killing us. We get a few laid-off people from time to time, which helps, but it's not consistent."

Titus says his squad has taken its share of flak for cutting back non-emergency transport, such as trips to hospitals for special treatment, but he says it has been necessary in order to maintain emergency service in the face of decreasing manpower.

Mary Petrick, captain of the Washington Emergency Squad, says al-

***MARY PETRICK, CAPTAIN OF THE WASHINGTON EMERGENCY SQUAD** — "Day coverage is always a problem. When we see a chance to get people with days off, we grab them."*

though her unit is in good shape overall, day coverage in general is always a problem.

"When we see a chance to get people with some days off, we grab them," Petrick says.

Shive says, "We have to limit our daytime services and be very particular. You have to keep the squad available for emergencies, so we try to screen transportations. We pre-arrange them so we know who's where and what we have left. It's becoming a real problem, and organizations have to really rely on each other. Mutual aid is more important now than ever."

Several squad officials say the day-shift problem is complicated by the fact that most hospital appointments and nursing home admissions—prime sources of non-emergency transport—are scheduled during the day.

"Some medical facilities are quite inflexible," Stoneback says. Donald Hess, who served eight years as captain of the Phillipsburg squad, says, "Because of the daytime problem, we try to put a lot of stuff off until evening. But it's often tough to do a transportation then because hospitals and nursing homes might not want to take people after hours. A lot of that sort of thing is being turned over to paid ambulance services, which can be tough for a person if it's not covered by Medicare," Hess says.

Jo-Ann Stoneback, a transport officer for the Suburban Rescue Squad, says her organization's day-shift manpower problems cause it to turn over a small number of transportation calls to Valley Transport, a paid ambulance service.

DONALD HESS, FORMER CAPTAIN OF THE PHILLIPSBURG EMERGENCY SQUAD — *"It's often tough to do transportation in the evening because hospitals and nursing homes might not want to take people after hours."*

Royal Photographics photo

"We solicit donations from people every year for volunteer service, so we only turn a call over to Valley Transport as a last resort," Mrs. Stoneback says. "We try to give service to the people because they've donated for it. We get good mutual-aid help from other squads, especially Easton, but in a few cases it's impossible on non-emergency calls."

Mrs. Stoneback says the day shift consists mainly of women who have to get their children off to school and be home for them when they return. As a result, most daytime non-emergency runs must be scheduled between 9 A.M. and 1 P.M.

"We tried to have a separate transport crew, as well as the emergency crew, but it was impossible because of manpower," she says. "We had to suspend the rule of no transports by the emergency crew."

Hess says government regulations sometimes complicate matters. "The federal government has taken over a lot of decisions from hospitals," Hess says. "For example, Warren Hospital used to have a radiation machine. When it needed a new one, the federal officials turned it down because St. Luke's Hospital (in Bethlehem, Pennsylvania) already had one. But now the need for transportation to St. Luke's has caused an added burden for squads."

Squad members say finding volunteers for any shift can be difficult, but keeping them can be even tougher. "The training is becoming more and more time-consuming," John Stoneback says. "To a degree that's contributing not so much to our problems getting people but in keeping volunteers."

"There's a lot of turnover," Titus says. "We added five new people last year, and we lost three of them once they got into it and saw the amount of time and training involved."

Shive said the amount of time a volunteer puts in varies from week to week but can be very demanding at times. "Some days there may be nothing, but other days there may be six or seven calls," he says. "There have been times when I've put in an excess of 40 hours a week, although that's intermittent. And doing a captain's job right can be very timeconsuming with reading, telephone work, meetings, training sessions and seminars, as well as actual calls."

"A captain's job today is tough," Shive says. "My going eight years is rare. I stepped down because I wanted to spend more time with my family, and I probably experienced burnout. Actually, I probably went through burnout three or four times in eight years, but the other times I worked right through it."

According to squad officers, all of the problems from burnout to curtailed transportation would be lessened if more people would consider a stint as a volunteer.

BARRY POSSINGER, PRESIDENT OF THE GENERAL AMBULANCE CORPS OF THE STROUDSBURG-EAST STROUDSBURG VICINITY *— "We have set up a drivers' corps to help attract volunteers who want to help but don't want to undertake full medical training . . . all of them have CPR (cardio-pulmonary resuscitation)."*

Royal Photographics photo

How do they go about finding them? "A lot of it is word of mouth," says Barry Bittenmaster, who has served two years as membership chairman for the Clinton First Aid and Rescue Squad. "People learn about the squad through friends. Then they come around to the building and eventually come on board."

Many squad members have inherited their interest in first aid. "I came on because my dad was on the squad," says Hess. "Now my daughter is on the junior squad. So it's into the third generation."

Friends and family may provide the heart of many rescue organizations, but squad officials always are looking for ways to attract other potential volunteers. "We'd like to attract more from the general public," Bittenmaster says, "but a lot of people seem hesitant. I don't think a lot of them realize it's a volunteer organization that anyone can join."

How do squads overcome public misconceptions? A number of attention-getting devices have been tried by local squads, including signs posted near the squad building and articles on manpower needs in local newspapers.

Barry Possinger, president of the General Ambulance Corps of the Stroudsburg-East Stroudsburg vicinity, says his unit has set up a drivers' corps to help attract volunteers who want to help but don't want to undertake full medical training. "We still encourage the drivers to get some training," Possinger says, "and all of them have CPR (cardio-pulmonary resuscitation)."

Margaret Lutz, captain of the Kingwood First Aid and Rescue Squad, says volunteers try to stir up interest in membership while running an annual door-to-door fund drive and also conducting demonstrations at high schools to attract young members.

Belshaw says his unit has undertaken recruitment at special community programs held at Palmer Mall.

Bittenmaster says the Clinton squad even tried a paid advertisement in a weekly newspaper a few months ago. "We had $200 available for advertising, so I tried it," Bittenmaster says. "To be honest, I didn't get any response from the ad, but I don't feel it was a waste. I'm sure people saw it, and maybe in the future one of those people will join."

Possinger says that despite the need for members, his squad prefers to recruit through personal contact rather than general advertising. "We like to know something about the person, and we require two sponsors," he says. "If you get someone who just wants to see a lot of accidents, he won't do you much good."

Bittenmaster says the need to seek members never ends because membership seems to run in cycles. "You always need people," he says. "It isn't an emergency for us right now, but it has been critical at times." He speaks for squads throughout Pennsylvania and New Jersey when he says: "We absolutely need people."

The emergency dispatcher answers the call and quickly sets a remarkable chain of action into motion.

While a wife sits tensely at her husband's side, wringing her hands into a tight knot as he struggles for breath, men and women throughout the community bolt from warm beds to hustle a modern ambulance and its life-saving gear to the stricken man's aid.

Only later, when the crisis has passed, will the couple have time to think how fortunate they are that volunteers willingly took the time and trouble—without any thought of pay—to write a happy ending for a potential tragedy.

The script repeats itself daily throughout the area so smoothly and consistently that many overlook the time, effort and money needed for the work to continue.

Although volunteers operate without pay, the services generate considerable cost. Ambulances, advanced life-saving equipment, insurance, fuel, utilities—they all add up to a major financial commitment.

The Easton Emergency Squad, the busiest in Northampton County with an average of 9.2 calls per day, works with an annual budget of $100,000—and costs continue to escalate. "Our expenses were $90,000 last year, and the budget has doubled over the last four years," says Kevin Wallasea, the squad's president and captain. "The ambulances really take abuse. We have four, and we have to replace one a year."

He says the squad has attempted to save some capital costs by using

RICHARD ALPAUGH, CHIEF OF THE MANSFIELD EMERGENCY SQUAD — "Our squad, whose officers are all businessmen, have augmented the traditional sources of donations, municipal contributions and fund raisers with a strategic program of loans."

two modular units which can be fitted with new chassis rather than fully replaced.

"We can re-chassis them for about $17,000, which basically cuts the cost in half," Wallasea says. "But this year we have to replace a van which will cost about $35,000."

Squad officials say some full-sized, top-of-the-line ambulances can cost more than $60,000.

Where does $100,000 for an annual operating budget come from? "We bring in $20,000 to $25,000 with our fund-raising campaign," Wallasea says. "This year the city is raising its contribution from $7,000 to $10,000. We bring in a few more thousands in general contributions from users and in memorial gifts. The rest comes from private enterprises and service clubs. Every year it's a headache coming up with money. This year we need a roof for the building, which is going to cost $8,000. People forget our overhead with utility costs and things like that."

Special equipment also can be very expensive. Richard Alpaugh, chief of the Mansfield Emergency Squad, says a Jaws-of-Life extricating device can cost anywhere from $7,000 to $12,000, depending on what optional equipment a squad purchases.

Alpaugh says his squad, whose officers are all businessmen, have augmented the traditional income sources of donations, municipal contributions and fund raisers with a strategic program of loans.

Squad officials express gratitude for the financial support they receive from their communities, but several are fearful that inflation in recent years has raced ahead of people's ability to contribute.

"P'burg always has had good support, and we're probably in better shape than some towns," says Donald Hess, former captain of the Phillipsburg Emergency Squad, "but costs keep increasing beyond the level where they're easy to support."

Wallasea says, "If you look at a graph over 20 years, contributions have basically stayed the same while our costs have gone up."

Some squads enjoy the generosity of special benefactors. The Washington Emergency Squad has been able to devote more time to first-aid work and less to fund raising because of The Vernon Oakes Society.[1]

The Easton Emergency Squad receives a $5,000 donation annually from a retired businessman who wishes to remain anonymous.

Money also may come from a variety of other sources.

Eric Belshaw, president of the Suburban Rescue Squad in Palmer Township, says his unit in recent years began charging Medicare for the expenses of eligible squad users. "We're usually in pretty good shape (financially), but billing Medicare has helped," Belshaw says. "We charge Medicare $60 for a transportation. They usually pay $48 to $50, but we don't try to go after the rest (from the squad user)."

Most squads in the area seek donations and obtain varying amounts of money from municipalities but provide services free to all users, regardless of their contributions.

However, Barry Possinger, president of the General Ambulance Corps, says a membership system is used in Monroe County. Possinger says the General Ambulance Corps, which serves the Stroudsburg-East Stroudsburg vicinity, raises most of its funds through collection of $12 annual family memberships. "That covers all emergency calls for everyone in the family," he says. "We pick everyone up, but if they're not members, we send them bills that run about $50, so it's advantageous to join. At $12 for the whole family it's a minimal expense."

Most squads in other parts of the region rely heavily on donations, which they augment with fund-raising events. "Our main source is a door-to-door fund-raising campaign," says Margaret Lutz, captain of the Kingwood First Aid and Rescue Squad. "The people are very good with that, but we also do all kinds of fund raisers. We've had raffles, dinners and a coin toss."

A number of squads, especially in rural areas, use the roadside coin toss to solicit donations from motorists. These events have generated controversy at times when questions are raised about their safety, but they often prove effective. Alpaugh concedes that some law enforcement officials question the safety of coin tosses, but he says the one his Mansfield squad sponsors proves very successful.

---

[1]Complete information about The Vernon Oakes Society is contained in Chapter 12.

Group's fund-raising effort keeps ambulances running

By GREG HANISEK
Express staff writer

WASHINGTON — Alvin Sloan, a former mayor of the borough, has done his share of public service, but he's never been a member of the Washington Emergency Squad.

That hasn't stopped him from serving as one of the squad's greatest boosters.

"When 30 people answer 1,340 rescue squad calls a year, they shouldn't have to stand out on the road and collect money," Sloan said. "I figure people like me that don't answer the calls should take care of the money."

But Sloan did more than figure.

He started the Vernon Oakes Society, a coalition of contributors named after the squad's founder. The Washington unit, one of the oldest volunteer rescue squads in the country, is beginning its 50th year.

On Sunday, the society turned over more than $20,000 in donations to the squad for 1985.

And Sloan's efforts did not go unrewarded. One of the highlights of Sunday's ceremonies was dedication of the squad's new ambulance to the former mayor and current benefactor.

"I was greatly honored, surprised and shocked," Sloan said this morning. "Everybody has to have a hobby, and this (raising money for the squad) is my hobby. This is my fun.

"In the past the squad was always well-supported, but it always seemed to be about $10,000 short," Sloan said. "The members had to do things like collect money along the roadside for the balance, and I didn't think they should have to do that.

"I figured that if 100 persons contributed $100 each, that would take care of the $10,000. To memorialize the founder and publicize the squad's stature as one of the oldest, I decided contributors would belong to the Vernon Oakes Society."

Alvin Sloan

Sloan, who has solicited almost all of the donations during the society's four years of existence, said he topped his goal the first year, when 126 persons contributed $100 each.

"We've got more than 200 this year," he said.

At Sunday afternoon's program at the squad's Vernon Oakes Building in Washington, the society turned over more than 200 checks.

Squad Captain Mary Petrick gave a preview of activities planned for the 50th anniversary year. Speakers at the program included Winnie Hartvigsen of Mantoloking, president of the New Jersey First Aid Council; state Assemblyman Garabed "Chuck" Haytaian, R-Warren-Hunterdon, who brought a congratulatory letter from Gov. Thomas Kean; state Sen. Wayne Dumont Jr., R-Warren-Sussex; state Assemblyman Richard Zimmer, R-Hunterdon-Warren; Warren County Freeholders Irene Smith and Kenneth Miller; and Washington Mayor Nancy Gianni Schmidt.

The Express, January 28, 1985

Although squad members in general speak fondly of their public support, municipal contributions sometimes become a matter for dispute.

Earlier this year the Blairstown Ambulance Corps returned a $300 check to the Knowlton Township Committee, contending that the amount didn't reflect the amount of coverage provided to the township. The committee later donated $2,000 to cover services rendered in 1984.

In Belvidere some volunteers reacted with anger when the Warren County freeholders made a $10,000 grant to a community theater group. Critics contended that while the theater was a worthwhile community endeavor, local emergency units had a more pressing need for significant contributions.

(The Warren County freeholders make an annual contribution to each emergency squad in the county. In 1984 the freeholders awarded each of the 12 squads in the county $800 for a total contribution of $9,600.)

In Northampton County four volunteer paramedic units are seeking a total of $39,177 to cover their maintenance costs. They appeared twice before council's three-member Intergovernmental Affairs Committee in October and again before the entire council in November asking for the money.

Council did not act on the request, saying it needed more discussion. Several council members expressed a fear that other emergency medical providers, such as ambulance squads, also would approach the county for money, and a committee was appointed to study the request.

Volunteer rescue squads—both in New Jersey and Pennsylvania—represent an interesting paradox. Individual members undertake rigorous training to provide a high level of community service, but the organizations themselves have been able to maintain an amazing degree of independence in an era when state regulations take bigger bites each year from the cherished ideal of home rule.

Although state government has gotten its fingers into a bewildering array of decision-making processes, volunteer rescue squads operate with surprising freedom from government regulation. "There is no state law that sets down standards for going on calls," says Roy Nickels, director of New Jersey's Office of Emergency Health Services. His counterpart in Pennsylvania, Matt Matthiesen, director of the Division of Emergency Health Services, says, "There are no state requirements for license or certification."

Does this mean that untrained volunteers are whirling around both states in ambulances, doing their best to get the ill and injured to hospitals in one piece? Absolutely not. Although state regulations have been kept to a minimum, volunteer rescue-squad members in both states undertake rigorous training—so rigorous that some squad officials believe the amount of time devoted to it discourages potential volunteers.

In New Jersey the state has delegated the power to establish training criteria to the New Jersey State First Aid Council, a grass-roots organization composed of rescue squad members. The council is a statewide organization with leaders elected by squad members through a system of districts, committees and conventions.

To qualify for service in the Garden State, a volunteer can follow one of two paths. He or she either becomes an emergency medical technician (EMT) by taking one of the EMT courses offered by the state Office of Emergency Health Services, or he or she completes the five-point training program devised by the New Jersey State First Aid Council and taught by the Red Cross.

Bruce Shive, who served eight years as captain of the Lopatcong Emergency Squad, says it takes 80 to 100 hours to complete the five-point program, which consists of training in advanced first aid, cardio-pulmonary resuscitation (CPR), emergency childbirth, light extrication and defensive driving. Shive says refresher courses required under council regulations assure that volunteers will continue training throughout their years of service.

In Pennsylvania the state sets no training requirements, but the majority of volunteer squads participate in a Division of Emergency Health Services program known as voluntary ambulance-services certification (VAS).

A. J. Heightman, executive director of the Eastern Pennsylvania Emergency Medical Services Council in Allentown, says all volunteer

BRUCE SHIVE, FORMER CAPTAIN OF THE LOPATCONG EMERGENCY SQUAD — *"It takes 80 to 100 hours to complete the five-point program, and refresher courses required under council regulations assure that volunteers will continue training throughout their years of service."*

Royal Photographics photo

services in Northampton and Monroe counties have VAS certification.

Before granting certification council officials inspect each service to make sure it meets requirements, which include one emergency medical technician on all emergency calls, possession of all state-recommended equipment, participation in a good radio-communication system, use of standardized record forms, and operation of an acceptable rescue service.

Heightman says rescue service centers on tasks such as extrication, rather than on first aid. "It would make no sense to have a well-trained ambulance service if the rescue service also wasn't good," he says. "We want to make sure that rescue is carried out in conjunction with an EMT so someone with a back injury isn't ripped out through a window."

Why would a volunteer organization undertake a rigorous certification that isn't required? "Mostly it's a matter of pride," Heightman says. "They want to be able to say they meet the highest standards of the state Department of Health."

He says other inducements include the council's ability to provide money for equipment needed to meet certification requirements and a regulation that prohibits volunteer rescue squads from affiliating with a paramedic unit if the squad lacks certification. "When a person sees the certification sticker on an ambulance, that guarantees that it meets high standards," he says.

Squad officials mention pride often when describing their training, although some point to it as a two-edged sword that frightens some potential volunteers.

"Some people say that our training requirements create a hardship," says Winnie Hartvigsen, president of the New Jersey State First Aid Council, "but at our last convention the delegates unanimously voted to increase training requirements (by adding three more subjects—triage, oxygen therapy and vital signs), so it can't be such a hardship. The people want it. You get swept up in it," Hartvigsen says. "Once you want the job, you want the training. If you have a successful CPR call, it makes up for all the hours of training."

However, some squad officials speak very frankly about the problems that ever-increasing training demands present to squad recruiters. "The training is getting more and more difficult," says Tracy Marsh, captain of the Belvidere Ambulance Corps. "People just don't have the time. We have to be honest when we recruit and explain the amount of time involved. When you have to tell them it takes 100 hours of training just to run, it scares people off.

"Our older members support us well, but when we ask them if they'd like to come back on active duty, they say they don't want to because of all the extra training they'll have to take. It's not apathy. People would do it if they could afford the time."

The opinions cover a wide spectrum. At the other end is Larry Lutz, captain of the Milford-Holland Rescue Squad, who believes training must be upgraded and provision made for paramedic units in rural areas of New Jersey.

Sometimes squads undertake special training programs of their own devising. Richard Alpaugh, chief of the Mansfield Emergency Squad, says his unit has set up a special 10-man rescue team that pursues intensive training in skills such as extrication, fire-related operation and rope rescue. "We've really been getting heavily into rope rescue," Alpaugh says. "People ask how many rock ledges someone might get stuck on in Warren County, but silos and industrial towers are the same thing. We go on a camping trip twice a year to Ricketts Glen State Park in Pennsylvania to practice."

How have rescue squads managed to escape the net of state regulations that envelop many other civic organizations and activities? In New Jersey the delegation of authority to the New Jersey State First Aid Council has created regulations parallel to the type a state agency would require. The council members then take over, carefully guarding their turf.

"We're not really a lobbying organization," Hartvigsen says, "but we have 16,000 members, and if they get irate enough about something, they can make a lot of phone calls." She says that, as an example, she personally went to Trenton when the state legislature proposed taking away volunteers' exemption from jury duty. "If one person got taken off a short-handed day crew (for jury duty), it would have created a

WINNIE HARTVIGSEN, PRESIDENT OF THE NEW JERSEY STATE FIRST AID COUNCIL — *"We're not really a lobbying organization but we have 16,000 members, and if they get irate about something, they can make a lot of phone calls."*

Richard W. York photo

hardship,'' Hartvigsen says of successful efforts to oppose the measure.

Although local Pennsylvania squads all meet voluntary certification requirements, there is nothing that compels a squad in Pennsylvania to require any type of training of its members.

Heightman says, ''I can't guarantee you that if you were in an accident somewhere between here and Pittsburgh that a trained person would attend to you. It could be some guy in a station wagon with a red light on top.''

He says that situation could change if a bill now under consideration is passed by the General Assembly. The bill includes a provision to license all ambulance services in the state, including volunteer units.

Heightman says that even though the measure would increase state control, it would have little practical effect on local volunteer units. He says licensing requirements would be less strict than the voluntary requirements all Northampton and Monroe county squads now meet.

A significant difference between emergency service in eastern Pennsylvania and that in northwestern New Jersey centers on paramedic units.

Both Northampton and Monroe counties are served by volunteer paramedic units providing advanced care at accident scenes and other emergencies.

In New Jersey paramedic units affiliated with major hospitals provide advanced emergency care for most of the state's population, but they are centered in urban areas. Neither Warren nor Hunterdon County has paramedic service.

What is a paramedic? Paramedics undergo specialized training that allows them to perform advanced procedures while in radio contact with a doctor.

Heightman says all paramedics in local Pennsylvania units must complete a state-approved certification course that is given at the Lehigh Valley Hospital Center.

He explains that paramedics are qualified to carry out ''invasive treatment'' such as establishing intravenous lines, giving emergency medication, using shock techniques in heart cases, inserting tracheal tubes, and setting up heart-monitoring devices that provide information to a doctor waiting at a hospital.

He says that under Pennsylvania regulations, paramedic units must be staffed at all times with members ready to respond within 60 seconds. He says immediate response is necessary for a small number of units to cover large areas.

Northampton County has four volunteer units plus a paid municipal unit in Bethlehem, while Monroe County has only one unit.

A number of local New Jersey squad officials express concern for a

***RICHARD TAMPIER OF THE HAMPTON EMERGENCY SQUAD, CHAIRMAN OF DISTRICT 10 AND ITS ADVANCED LIFE SUPPORT COMMITTEE** — "Our efforts center on getting state approval for rural paramedics and intermediate emergency medical technicians (EMTI) who could perform more advanced procedures than regular EMT's."*

lack of paramedic capability in their rural areas, and District 10 of the New Jersey State First Aid Council, which comprises squads in Hunterdon County, has been especially active in pushing state health officials for rural paramedic service.

"Most urban areas already have paramedics, says Larry Lutz, captain of the Milford-Holland Rescue Squad, but it's the rural areas like Warren and Hunterdon that really need it. Where most of the paramedics are, it's only a five-minute ride to the hospital. For our squad it's a 20-minute ride to Warren Hospital or Hunterdon Medical Center."

Richard Tampier of Hampton, chairman of District 10 and its Advanced Life Support Committee, says efforts center on getting state approval for rural paramedics and intermediate emergency medical technicians (EMTI) who could perform more advanced procedures than regular EMT's. (Although squads may establish their own regular first-aid training, more advanced programs must be approved by the state.)

Tampier says a bill approving EMTI's has passed the Assembly and is in Senate committee, but the paramedic bill has not been voted on by either house. He says the EMTI bill would allow volunteer squads to pursue advanced training but would not make it mandatory. He says paid paramedics would be attached to hospitals, and Hunterdon Medical Center approves the concept.

Donald Hess, who served eight years as captain of the Phillipsburg Emergency Squad, says he would like to see the state approve the use of Northampton County paramedics in neighboring New Jersey. "We'll need our own eventually," Hess says. "But for the moment it seems reasonable to use the ones that are already here."

Heightman says Pennsylvania law allows paramedics to continue treatment into New Jersey if a Pennsylvania victim is being transferred to a New Jersey hospital, but they cannot respond to an emergency originating in New Jersey.

Lutz says proponents of more advanced training also have persuaded the New Jersey State First Aid Council to certify an advanced training program known as military anti-shock trouser (MAST). A high-pressure trouser helps push blood from the extremities to vital organs. Lutz says Hunterdon already has adopted its training protocol, and other counties will be able to follow.

Volunteers of all kinds do things that most of us would rather leave for others.

The problems raised by rescue-squad leaders in both New Jersey and Pennsylvania lead to an obvious question—can the volunteer system remain strong, or will it give way increasingly to the alternative—private or municipal ambulance service?

Opinions on the state of the volunteer system are wide-ranging. Some ring with optimism. ''It goes in phases,'' says Eric Belshaw, president of the Suburban Rescue Squad in Palmer Township. ''Right now we're low on manpower, but there could be a complete turnaround in six months. I see volunteers holding up well as a system in the future.''

David Tampier, captain of the Hampton Emergency Squad, says, ''We'll continue to function. There's tradition, there's pride, and there's the desire to serve your neighbor. That has a lot to do with it. It's what keeps squads together.''

ERIC BELSHAW, PRESIDENT OF THE SUBURBAN RESCUE SQUAD IN PALMER TOWNSHIP *— "It goes in phases. Right now we're low on manpower, but there could be a complete turnaround in six months. I see volunteers holding up well as a system in the future."*

Royal Photographics photo

***DAVID TAMPIER, CAPTAIN OF THE HAMPTON EMERGENCY SQUAD** — "We'll continue to function. There's tradition, there's pride, and there's the desire to help your neighbor. That has a lot to do with it. It's what keeps squads together."*

"Things are going to get tougher, especially the way the economy is," says James Uliana, president of the Liberty Ambulance Corps of Bangor, but the system will always exist because of dedicated people with a feeling for the public. I have enough faith in people that they will always keep the volunteer ambulances running."

But exactly opposite opinions well up just as easily. "In my opinion the system already is in decay," says Tracy Marsh, captain of the Belvidere Ambulance Corps. "In New Jersey we probably have the strongest volunteer system in the nation, but we've got problems. Our squad has had to cut out non-emergency daytime service because of a manpower shortage. We've gotten a lot of harsh criticism for it, but we had no choice.

"There are too many factors involved to say when, but I feel eventually paid service will be the norm," he says. "I can't say if it will be 10 years or 30 years, but volunteers just aren't getting the support they did in the postwar period."

Marsh says a lack of manpower compounds itself, leading to burnout of active squad members and creating a kind of vicious cycle. "Lack of manpower leads to burnout because it puts too much burden on too few," he says. "Recruitment is not keeping up with burnout, and training is getting more and more difficult. People just don't have the time."

But opinions cover a wide range. Larry Lutz, captain of the Milford-Holland Emergency Squad, believes the capability for higher levels of training is needed to keep the volunteer system on solid ground. He supports efforts to obtain paramedic units for Warren and Hunterdon counties and to increase the number of advanced procedures squad members are allowed to learn.

Proponents of paramedic units for rural New Jersey areas say they will save lives and provide advanced on-the-scene treatment in areas where the closest hospital is sometimes 20 or more minutes away.

Paramedics provide an additional life-saving level of service for the public, but even their presence doesn't alleviate nagging manpower shortages of volunteer squads. Kevin Wallasea, president and captain of the Easton Emergency Squad, says, "The paramedics mainly provide a higher level of care to the patient more quickly, but we still need to send a full crew to the scene. (In Pennsylvania paramedics respond to accidents and begin treatment but do not transport victims.)

A veteran of a dozen years of squad calls, who wishes to remain anonymous, also cites an unthinking public as a source of problems. "I think one of the biggest factors in burnout is squads being taken advantage of," the veteran says. "We'll get a call for a cut finger and expect to see a deep laceration or maybe a partial amputation. You get there and find a one-inch cut.

"They're nonsense calls," she says. "People used to get in the car and go to the hosptial themselves for something like that. Now they're using the squads for a free taxi service. We never mind an emergency; that's what we're there for. But sometimes we get a call and find the person sitting on the porch with bags packed, waiting to go to the hospital."

Captain Marsh, of Belvidere, says public insensitivity can prove very disheartening. "I got one fund drive pamphlet back with no money in it," he says. "They just marked up the grammatical errors with red pencil. That's what we have to put up with."

Royal Photographics photo

***TRACY MARSH, CAPTAIN OF THE BELVIDERE AMBULANCE CORPS** — "I got one drive pamphlet back with no money in it. They just marked up the grammatical errors with red pencil. That's what we have to put up with."*

Elaine Berry, lieutenant and treasurer of the Williams Township Emergency Squad, points out another interesting concern—family problems that result when one member can't understand the amount of time another devotes to squad work. "There can be some real problems at times," Berry says. "It's better when both a husband and wife or a boyfriend and girlfriend are involved."

Sometimes the reasons given by the people for avoiding volunteer service prove unexpected and surprising. Marsh says a number of people have told him they don't want to join because squad members sometimes end up in court testifying to what they saw on their calls—such as in liability or drunken-driving cases. "It's bad because you get thrust into people's private affairs," he says. "It can be a problem if someone volunteers to help and then gets pulled out of work without pay to testify in court."

The manpower problem will always be a tough one. The factors cited by squad members—the economy, burnout and increasing demands on everyone's time—make the recruiter's task a difficult one.

There are no easy solutions, but Ronald Titus, captain of the Phillipsburg Emergency Squad, has some ideas. "People have been beat into the ground so long with taxes and everything that they don't want to do something for nothing," Titus says. "We need an inducement. A tax break or something like that for squad members would help, but there's probably too much political red tape. We got membership applications back during the energy crisis when squad members were allowed to jump gas lines, but now we need a new inducement."

Monetary problems should be easier to solve, squad members say,

***RONALD TITUS, CAPTAIN OF THE PHILLIPSBURG EMERGENCY SQUAD** — "We got membership applications back during the energy crisis when squad members were allowed to jump gas lines, but now we need a new inducement."*

Royal Photographics photo

***KEVIN WALLASEA, CAPTAIN AND PRESIDENT OF THE EASTON EMERGENCY SQUAD** — "If people kick in a few more bucks now, the're going to save a lot in the future."*

Royal Photographis photo

especially if the public considers the alternatives to volunteer service. "If everyone just gave one dollar per member of their houshold, we'd be in great shape," says Wallasea of the Easton squad.

Marsh says, "We try to get across to people how much it would cost (for paid emergency service) if we weren't there. If everybody just gave a little, it would be no problem at all. Paid people just aren't going to give the same kind of service as volunteers who are there because they want to be."

"If people kick in a few more bucks now, they're going to save a lot in the future," Wallasea says.

Those who fear for the future of volunteer rescue service warn of the tremendous cost that would be involved in changing to a paid service.

Although volunteers continue to provide emergency service throughout the area, one needn't look far to find municipalities that were forced to undertake paid service because they lacked volunteer manpower.

Local rescue officials agree that finding sufficient volunteers for day-shift work ranges from difficult to almost impossible. Roy Nickels, director of New Jersey's Office of Community Health Services, says the day-shift problem has become so severe that about 20 municipalities have hired paid emergency medical technicians during the past two years to handle daytime emergencies.

Several of these municipalities are in the Trenton suburbs. Ewing Township serves as an example. "Originally we had complete volunteer fire and rescue service," says Frederick Walters, Ewing's administrator. "Then we began to have problems with daylight coverage, so we decided

Action needed to save local emergency units

For years, the emergency squads have been a vital part of most communities. Volunteers from all walks of life would give their time to join the squads, take some training and be ready to go out on the ambulances whenever a call arrived. The squads themselves operated on minimal funds, mostly from their municipalities and what they could raise through various fund drives.

But today's emergency squads have problems. Fewer people are interested in becoming the kinds of volunteers the squads need. On top of that, state laws have set some rigid requirements for training that have turned away many people. Now besides knowing basic first aid, squad members must spend possibly 50 hours learning advanced first aid, must be adept at cardiopulmonary resuscitation and some even have to take an emergency medical technician's course. And that is a lot to ask from a volunteer.

There is no question the requirements have improved the quality of the emergency squad service, but in so doing they have reduced the number of people who want to become squad members.

It isn't easy being an emergency squad member. The squad units are covered around the clock. When they aren't on a call, they have to man the phones, keep the books, keep their buildings in order and even mow the lawns. Many of the calls they answer are not pleasant ones, particularly when the squads have to cover accidents or tragedies. But the squads are reliable. People count on them, whether they live in the cities or the rural areas.

Some feel the regulations have become too rigid. It should be remembered that there is another level of health care counties have and that is the paramedic units — who are called to accident scenes when their kind of expertise is needed. With that kind of support system, is it essential that squad members be forced to take all the first aid and training courses required?

It is time communities and legislators talked about this — to make sure that the rules adopted are not typical government interference, but vital to service. Emergency squads are important to our health care and financially, there is no better bargain for anyone. They must be saved.

The Express May 14, 1984

Squads need support

Will the volunteer emergency/rescue squad system that has served the people of this area so well survive? Or will it give way to paid emergency services? The answer will be largely up to the people. If they are willing to give enough to squads' fund appeals and if enough people are willing to serve, the system will be preserved.

The four-part series by Express staff writer Greg Hanisek that concludes today has dissected the squads' problems and reviewed their admirable accomplishments. The main problems include: recruiting and keeping enough men, women and youths to maintain an adequate level of service, raising the money to meet the rising costs of equipment, maintenance, overhead and buildings, and meeting rigorous personnel training standards without discouraging some potential volunteers.

If the squads are to function well in the future, they must attract young volunteers. Their service, like that of the adults, requires a willingness to devote many hours to training. Hampering the recruitment of young people in Pennsylvania is a state law that forbids those under the age of 16 from "running" with their squads on emergency cases. Elaine Berry and Elaine McElroy of the Williams Township Emergency Squad have campaigned vigorously to have this ban lifted, and state Sen. Jeanette F. Reibman, D-Northampton, says she will help.

The area's volunteer squad system dates to the 1930s, when the Phillipsburg and Washington squads went into full operation (the Easton squad was created in 1958). The service has been of inestimable value to the public, but it is one that is easily taken for granted. It shouldn't be.

Some squads in recent years have been forced to end non-emergency transportation because of personnel shortages and cost escalation. If support for squads ever declines to the point where they must be replaced by a paid personnel system, a large new dimension will be added to the cost of health-related services. We urge the public not to let that happen.

The Express, January 30, 1985

to put one paid driver on each of the three volunteer fire companies. Then that mushroomed into the first-aid service, which had the same problem,'' he says. ''We put on two paid EMT's (emergency medical technicians) for daylight, and now we have one EMT and one paramedic.''

What has this cost the township? Walters says combined salaries for the positions will be $98,952 this year, compared with about $93,000 in 1984. In addition, the township donates $15,000 to each fire company, and it gives each fire company and the rescue squad $7,500 for equipment.

Those costs, combined with the salaries and additional fringe-benefit expenses, add up to an emergency budget—excluding police—of about $200,000.

Will the day-shift hirings solve the problem for Ewing? ''It's almost like putting your finger in the dike,'' Walters says. ''The hole keeps getting bigger and bigger. There's nothing right now that's critical toward moving to fully paid service, but I can see it down the road. We hope we can carry on.''

Express photo

***GREG HANISEK** — Express writer Greg Hanisak researched the volunteer rescue squads of the area and wrote the series of four articles for that newspaper from which the foregoing chapter of this book is adapted.*

HAROLD S. SLOAN, LL.D., D.SC.

Appendix

by Dr. Harold S. Sloan, trustee emeritus of Fairleigh Dickinson University

You have read about the emergency squads in Washington and neighboring communities in northern New Jersey, where scores of young persons undergo long and rigorous training to volunteer their time and skills to saving human lives.

But this is not confined to any particular time or location. Despite current vandalism, crime, and maleficence in high places, mutual aid is a growing force in our society. It has increased more than 50 percent during the past decade in the United States.[1]

One noted authority[2] has traced its evolution in the animal kingdom from earliest times to the present day and concludes that it is an essential factor in the struggle for survival of the species.

As such, it is a part of our national heritage and an inspiring hope for America and civilization.

HAROLD S. SLOAN

Paramus, New Jersey
March 4, 1985

---

[1]John Young, *A graceful Minority*, page 6, quoting The New York Times Op-Ed page of October 10, 1980.

[2]Peter Kropotkin, *Mutual Aid*, 1902, passim, New York University Press, reprinted 1972.

town and vicinity to
such an efficient and
ful organization as your
d.

I want to extend my deep
gratitude to those men and women
who came out to help me at my
auto accident

Thank y

...ny thanks
...sh the amount of the check could be
...er, but for now that's it.
...th God's help and a little bit of luck,
... possible the next one will be larger,
...ou will not be forgotten.
God Bless each and everyone of you, and
...eep up the Good Work.

Thanks Again

Dear Capt
wishes
to th
Wash
coun
an
4

... Emergency Squad,
...want to take this time to thank
...r the time you took me to
...in Hospital at 7:30 AM Nov.
...978. It was a very smooth,
...ortable trip and you didn't
...e any pain to my injured
...e when you carried me
...m my house to the Ambulance.

YES YOU CAN COUNT ON MY SUPPORT

Here is my contribution to back up
the work of our fabulous volunteers,
the Washington Emergency Squad

Amen!

Name Mrs

AG
Bar
OXFO

I want to t...
much for hel...
I fell out ...
and hit my ...
Grammy's. ...
I should giv...
taken of app...
for my ride
to the hospi...

I saw your
...tains out on Route 31 and Broad
... This was a welcome sight as
...e back and forth to New York

...e Lady and Gentlemen who
...ived the Call from Dr.
...s office on Friday ...
...uary 26th, I want to expres...
... appreciation and sincere
...ks for ... quick respon...

husband,
Thursday, August 16, 1979
and kindness of the squa...
crisis is greatly apprec...
much needed service is a...
donation is enclosed.

to each and
world of th...
The check be...
in Comparis...
the Emergenc...
It's ...

The generosity of the squad, who accompanied Sister in...
...ng of their time was giving true witness of their dedi...
...n and service to humani...